Talking in Clichés

For decades, social perspectives, and even academic studies of language, have considered clichés as a hackneyed, tired, lazy, unthinking and uninspiring form of communication. Authored by two established scholars in the fields of systemic functional linguistics and discourse studies and pragmatics, this cutting-edge book comprehensively explores the perception and use of clichés in language from these complementary perspectives. It draws data from a variety of both written and spoken sources, to re-interrogate and re-imagine the nature, role and usage of clichés, identifying the innovative and creative ways in which the concepts are utilised in communication, interaction and in self-presentation. Observing a rich, complex layering of usage, the authors deconstruct the many and varied ways in which clichés operate and are interdependently constructed; from the role they play in discourse in general to their functions as argumentative strategies, as constructs of social cognition, as politeness strategies and finally as markers of identity.

Stella Bullo is Researcher in Discourse Studies at Manchester Metropolitan University. She is the author of *Evaluation in Advertising Reception* (Palgrave, 2014). Her work on health discourse has been featured in *The Conversation* and the *New York Times* and on the BBC World Service.

Derek Bousfield is Head of Department and Reader in Pragmatics and Communication at Manchester Metropolitan University. Prominent publications include *Impoliteness in Interaction* (John Benjamins, 2008) and *Impoliteness in Language* (co-edited with Locher, De Gruyter, 2008).

Talking in Clichés
The Use of Stock Phrases in Discourse and Communication

Stella Bullo
Manchester Metropolitan University

Derek Bousfield
Manchester Metropolitan University

CAMBRIDGE
UNIVERSITY PRESS

University Printing House, Cambridge CB2 8BS, United Kingdom

One Liberty Plaza, 20th Floor, New York, NY 10006, USA

477 Williamstown Road, Port Melbourne, VIC 3207, Australia

314–321, 3rd Floor, Plot 3, Splendor Forum, Jasola District Centre, New Delhi – 110025, India

103 Penang Road, #05–06/07, Visioncrest Commercial, Singapore 238467

Cambridge University Press is part of the University of Cambridge.

It furthers the University's mission by disseminating knowledge in the pursuit of education, learning, and research at the highest international levels of excellence.

www.cambridge.org
Information on this title: www.cambridge.org/9781108471633
DOI: 10.1017/9781108559010

First published 2023

A catalogue record for this publication is available from the British Library.

Library of Congress Cataloging-in-Publication Data
Names: Bullo, Stella, 1975– author. | Bousfield, Derek, author.
Title: Talking in clichés : the use of stock phrases in discourse and communication / Stella Bullo, Manchester Metropolitan University ; Derek Bousfield, Manchester Metropolitan University.
Description: Cambridge ; New York : Cambridge University Press, 2023. | Includes bibliographical references and index.
Identifiers: LCCN 2022022846 | ISBN 9781108471633 (hardback) | ISBN 9781108559010 (ebook)
Subjects: LCSH: Clichés. | Discourse analysis.
Classification: LCC P301.5.C45 B85 2023 | DDC 428–dc23/eng/20220524
LC record available at https://lccn.loc.gov/2022022846

ISBN 978-1-108-47163-3 Hardback
ISBN 978-1-108-45813-9 Paperback

Contents

Figures

Tables

Acknowledgements

We would like to acknowledge a number of people who made this work possible.

The data for Chapters 4 and 6 were collected by Michaela Lunan who worked as a research associate supported by the Manchester Metropolitan University Strategic Opportunities Fund. We are grateful to Manchester Metropolitan University graduates Jack McKelvey and Thomas Smith for their help with data collection and analysis for Chapter 3, to linguistics PhD candidate Halima Benzdira for her work on Chapter 2 and to Tessa Grimshaw for her help with Chapter 6.

Special thanks to our colleague Lexi Webster for her help with the corpus linguistics aspects of the monograph, proofing, feedback, suggestions and fruitful discussions throughout the development of the book, and particularly for her unparalleled support and encouragement. We are also grateful to Mariana Pascual for her useful feedback and suggestions. Any remaining infelicities are our own. We are grateful to Andrew Winnard and Isabel Collins from Cambridge University Press for their support, patience and understanding.

We would also like to thank our spouses Stephen Parkin and Dawn Bousfield for their patience, support and encouragement.

Stella Bullo would also like to express her gratitude to her family and friends for help with childcare, and dedicates her contribution to this book to her friendly and beloved town of Berrotarán, Argentina, where most of the book was written during the pandemic.

Permissions

The authors and the publisher are grateful to the following companies who kindly granted copyright permissions free of charge for the reproduction of the adverts in Chapter 4: Slater Heelis (Figure 4.1), a South Manchester-based law firm (www.slaterheelis.co.uk/) and the London Sock Company, a London-based high-end sock manufacturing company (www.londonsockcompany.com/).

Abbreviations

CDA	Critical Discourse Analysis
CDS	Critical Discourse Studies
CMT	Conceptual Metaphor Theory
CoP	Community/ies of Practice
MIP	Metaphor Identification Procedure
RTV	Reality Television
SCR	Socio-cognitive Representations
SFL	Systemic Functional Linguistics
SM-CDS	Social Media Critical Discourse Studies
TEU	Treaty on European Union
USAS	UCREL Semantic Analysis System

CHAPTER ONE

On Clichés

1.1 Introduction

This book addresses the highly debated notion of clichés, exploring their role in discourse. Clichés are a subject that has been a matter of discussion and debate within both academic and public discourses for some time. The term 'cliché' is often used to refer to any phenomenon that is perceived as commonplace and even undesirable on account of its commonality. When it comes to the linguistic form, the *Collins English Dictionary* defines a cliché as 'a word or expression that has lost much of its force through over-exposure' (Hanks, 1996: 297). Fowler (1965) notes that clichés are common in many domains of social life; however, their original meaning of application and semantic value may, in time, be lost and only retain a more emotive meaning. Along these lines, Kirkpatrick poses that 'a cliché came to describe an expression that was repeated so often that it lost its freshness and became hackneyed' (1996: 16). Anderson-Gough et al. (1998) similarly identify clichés as 'the taken for granted and unreflexive use of language through the use of commonplace or rather "hackneyed" phrases'. (p. 566). It is therefore easy to see why such language is, at times, considered undesirable or negative by lay users of languages, as well as by experts engaging in discussion about their usage.

Indeed, the debate about the use of clichés historically takes a negative view of the phenomena. From as early 1885, *Punch* magazine published cartoons by Joseph Priestman Atkinson that mocked clichéd expressions in contemporary popular literature (Punch, 1900). This debate is still current in realms outside academia, in media and corporate as well as private domains. BBC News (2008) published '20 of your most hated clichés' featuring the votes of the audience who volunteered to participate in a survey. Among them we find the seemingly infamous *at the end of the day*, *24/7*, *literally*, *to be fair*, *110 per cent*, *let's face it*, *touch base*, *moving forward*, *I'm not being funny but*, *by end of play today*, among others. Similarly, in 2015 the *Mail Online* published a list of football clichés that 'make us cringe', (a cliché in itself), which also features the all-pervasive *at the end of the day* cliché at the top of the list (Baker, 2015, online).

Very interestingly clichés have a complex relationship with business and corporate registers and communities of practice (CoPs) (Lave and Wenger, 1991; see also Chapters 5 and 6). On the one hand, some clichés, considered 'dead' forms of figurative language, tend to be efficient forms of communication. They carry known, conventionalised (at least within specific contexts or CoPs) and, hence, unmistakable meanings between interlocutors. The efficiency of language and communication is a public relations asset in most internal business and corporate settings (see Chapters 4 and 5), and clichés often signal and enact not only efficiency of communication, but arguably also identity, membership and belonging and, to use another cliché, *being on board* with the current prevailing project, the 'direction of travel', and therefore a specific corporate culture and broader CoP.

On the other hand, it must be pointed out that, in the same domains of corporate communication, the issue of clichés as a poor form of language has also been a matter of debate. Marketing agencies, for example, are now urging businesses to stop using clichés (at least in their outward facing discourse) if they want their brand to stand out from their competitors. Agencies have labelled clichés 'an all too common enemy' (Webb, 2013: 216) precisely because of the air of negativity surrounding the use of unthinking, hackneyed and heavily conventionalised language. This apparently overwhelmingly negative outlook on clichés is also evidenced in websites suggesting alternatives to the use of clichés in CVs and job interviews (Boyce, 2015) and even in social or dating situations (Smith, 2015).

The debate has also reached organisational life. Anderson-Gough et al. (1998) studied clichés as constituting the social practice of organisational life and found that, as well as forming a core set of heavily conventionalised communication resources in set business practices, 'clichés may also demonstrate resistance in that their use can be reflexive, ironic or conflictual' (p. 566). Anecdotally, and in support of Anderson-Gough et al.'s findings, a senior manager told the authors of this book that he consciously makes an effort to avoid using clichés in business situations in order to gain credibility. Another colleague also told us that he purposively uses clichés ironically as 'a tool for surviving the boredom of meetings'. Along these lines, there are now games that people play to mock clichés and pass the time in perceived fruitless or low-value situations, such as in the case of cliché bingo where people create a cliché grid and cross them out, or tally their use on the grid as they are said in the course

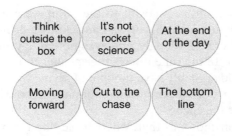

Figure 1.1 Corporate cliché bingo. Source: Adapted from www.slideserve.com/markmccrindle/conference-cliches-mccrindle-research-meeting-bingo-game [Last accessed 14 December 2021].

of a work meeting.[1] Certain internet memes have also surfaced that identify media discourse-specific, or media discourse-sensitive, grids of clichés ostensibly as a way of allowing people to play a game, but actually operating as negative metacommentary on the prevalence of the (over)reliance on clichés in certain discourse types and the perceived inherent ideological bias their use indicates. Figure 1.1 is an example of a classic 'corporate cliché bingo', modified due to copyright issues.

These anecdotes and observations of real-world practices support Anderson-Gough et al.'s (1998) findings. They also tell us that (a) clichés are so embedded in our language system that sometimes we need to 'think before we speak' if our aim is to avoid using them; and (b) people may choose to use clichés, or deliberatively avoid using them, for specific interactional or strategic reasons.

The poor reputation of clichés is so influential that, occasionally, people feel compelled to use the disclaimer 'I know it's a cliché, but … ' preceding their use. The first named author of this book overheard two people on the bus talking about the hindering and disruptive circumstances that a particularly challenging situation had caused in one of the passenger's lives. When asked how they coped, the speaker said 'I know it's a cliché but *one day at a time*'. There are two interesting points arising here: firstly, the disclaimer seems to operate as an attempt to simultaneously legitimise the use of the cliché and excuse the speaker to the listener for using it; the speaker is thus making the listener aware that the cliché is used, therefore providing an element of vindication for its

---

[1] Cliché bingo is also colloquially known as 'bullshit bingo'. The term 'bullshit', a negative epithet denoting that an item or piece of information is of zero or negative value, further signals negativity surrounding the perception of the use of clichés.

use. Secondly, and more relevant to the point we are trying to make, despite the disclaimer, which works as an acknowledgement of poor language, the speaker still willingly, and even potentially embarrassingly so, chooses to use it. In the time it took the speaker to issue the disclaimer, the speaker could arguably have thought of saying what they intended to say in a literal or even more unconventionally figurative way. Yet they still chose to use the cliché.

This discussion shows us that, whether we like them or not, whether we are aware of them or not, clichés are part of our everyday language use and further they fulfil a variety of functions in and surrounding discourse which suggests that, as Partridge (1978) points out, their 'ubiquity is remarkable' (p. 2). It is such ubiquity that constitutes an interesting starting point for our enquiry, especially given how clichés are used in specific settings for specific extra-linguistic purposes, as we explore in detail in Chapters 5 and 6.

1.2 Scope of This Book

Much of the literature on clichés, either in academic or other domains, attempts to categorise them (Kirkpatrick, 1996), explain their origin (Rogers, 1991), discuss their social standing or even provide alternatives for their use, as in the examples quoted in Section 1.1. Some scholarly work (e.g. Down and Warren, 2008) suggests that clichés can act as fillers in conversation without the need to be informative or purposive. Our informal observation and experimentation shows, however, that a close examination of clichés in the context in which the communicative event takes place can shed light onto a variety of functions that clichés perform in relation to discourse. By this we mean that the study of clichés, as with other formulaic language devices, needs to be seen in relation to the various elements of the communicative event such as the role, aims, identity of both addresser and addressee, in relation to the CoP and to the wider discoursal context in which communication takes place, be that institutional, political and so on. (Semino, 2008).

In previous work (Bullo, 2019), it has been argued that clichés constitute conventionalised linguistic structures with pre-existing meanings which function as 'valuable conduits for communicating pre-existing understanding in new ways' (Down and Warren, 2007: 8). As such they operate from the cognitive 'comfort zone', which allows them to evoke vivid imagery from a safe distance (Oswick et al., 2002: 294). By this we mean that, whilst they evoke powerful visual imagery, they offer a comfortable standpoint of commitment to the propositional content of the utterance. In this book, we elaborate on the notion of meanings and attempt to arrive at a working definition of clichés that considers the discursive functions that they fulfil. We focus on four main functions that we identify clichés as fulfilling and that constitute the scope of this book: (1) to argue, (2) to persuade, (3) to create and maintain relationships and/or (4) to create or restate identities. We introduce these functions by illustrating with examples from observation and informal experiments we have conducted by way of raising hypotheses.

One important function of clichés is that they help strengthen an argument and justify the potentially 'frowned upon' consequences of an action derived from the logical conclusion inferred from the cliché. Take, for example, *life's too short* By using this cliché, the speaker draws on conventional inferable premises about the length of life and approaching mortality that warrant prompt action, lack of action or even dismissal of the issue at stake as lacking in importance *in the grand scheme of things* and therefore justifies a potentially socially unacceptable practice. These devices, which link the argument to a claim based on inferable and socially shared premises, are known plurally as topoi or 'topos' in singular form (Kienpointner, 1992). Take, for example, *it is what it is*. By using the 'topos of reality' the speaker is resorting to a tautological argumentation scheme in order to derive a logical conclusion justifying a particular type of action, or even lack of action, or a particular type of emotional response, or advocation of emotional restraint, all of which are based on the premise that 'reality is as it is', and cannot be changed or questioned (see the discussion in Wodak and Idema, 2004: 21).

When used in advertising or corporate discourse, clichés can help 'establish a strong and stable set of associations in the minds and memories of consumers' (Moore, 2003: 335) by drawing on particular sets of pre-existing frameworks of thoughts, or sociocognitive representations (SCRs) (Koller, 2008a; Bullo, 2014). Take the infamous *the real world* cliché, which is very common in university and schools advertising, for example 'preparing students for *the real world*'. From a cognitive linguistics perspective, the *real world* cliché contains information and schematic models of professional life and employment drawn upon by institutions' promotional discourse promising appropriate preparation for the current market demands whilst also economising on the detail of how the preparation is done and what the preparation is for exactly. The cliché works as a tool of efficiency and consequently allows for this economy of information due to the entailments contained in the cognitive model drawn upon. Such entailments are socially shared and accepted precisely because they call to the familiar, the 'known', and are hence comforting. At the same time, the cliché serves as a bridge between the professional world and the traditionally perceived theoretical, if not sometimes considered idealistic, academic world. Similarly, cognitive models drawn upon by clichés in advertising are used to build credibility and reassure people of the quality of an entity, product, or agent as in *you are in good hands* by virtue of the qualities contained within the cognitive model, such as safety and trust, which are borne out as metonymical to the aforementioned functions of comfort and familiarity.

In a study of clichés used to convey an evaluative position in an institutional setting, Bullo (2019) concluded that clichés were not always or even regularly used and perceived negatively (as might be imagined from the observations made earlier) but rather they were used positively, in order to mitigate a negative assessment of people's performance. Take the infamous *think outside the box* cliché, for example, where normal thinking is metaphorically seen as contained 'within' the box in joint THINKING IS CONTAINED, INNOVATION IS BOUNDLESS[2] conceptual metaphors (Lakoff and Johnson, 1980), which represents a practice of working and thinking as mundane and unimaginative if artificially constrained. In more detail, the cliché seems to suggest that innovative ideas are found in an alternative space to the enclosed surroundings of a box. The box is seen as artificially restraining imagination and hence innovation. It is only by stepping out of the conventional boundaries of the box that innovative ideas are allowed to expand to their natural limit. Imagine a manager telling her or his colleagues to redesign a new project or change a plan of action by asking them to *think outside the box* rather than telling them that their current ideas or plan are 'not good enough'. The use of such standard, conventional language as clichés in this way is a face-saving and politeness marker, one that, by the very nature of its commonplace use in communities of (business) practice, is safe, comforting, familiar and hence supportive as its use at the interactional level avoids the face threat of direct criticism inherent in 'not good enough'. Furthermore, they also constitute a sign of trust and approval in the employees' capability for improvement of the task, therefore fulfilling a positive face-enhancing function (Brown and Levinson, 1987). Finally, the imagery conveyed by the constraining box also allows the boss to safely mitigate the imposition of ordering employees to

---

[2] Traditionally within cognitive linguistics, conceptual metaphors are CAPITALISED to distinguish them from linguistic metaphors. We will follow this practice in this book.

redo the job, thus acting as a negative face-oriented politeness strategy (Brown and Levinson, 1987). In this way, by virtue of the imagery they convey, clichés can be seen as fulfilling not only an interactional function, but also an interpersonal function by negotiating relationships without the potential face-threatening effects of the literal expression. We discuss this aspect in more detail in Chapter 5, where we elaborate on the argument that clichés help mitigate a negative evaluation whilst softening the positive face threat posed by criticising the employees' inability to perform effectively.

Finally, clichés can be used as 'discursive self-builders' (Kupferberg and Green, 2005: 28) allowing narrators to present specific self-narratives in relation to the unfolding story and its sociocultural dimensions. In a study of entrepreneurial discourse, Down and Warren (2008) found that entrepreneurs use certain clichés to establish, maintain and convey the sense of an entrepreneurial identity (p. 6). A couple of years ago, one of the contestants on the BBC's version of the television show, *The Apprentice* was criticised by one of the members of the panel for using too many business-related clichés but not performing to the expected standard that his language suggested or indeed promised. The contestant was clearly using clichés as a tool for projecting a desired identity for himself, an identity that he associated with the use of such language. Similarly, we asked a number of university students why they use certain clichés, for example *literally*, when, as linguists-in-training, they know very well that its use is mostly figurative. A few of them claimed that the reason for using such clichés was 'just because the people I hang out with use them and they catch on'. We also encountered those who rejected them and (claimed to) avoid using them because they want to sound credible or educated. An example of this is the anecdotal observation of the senior manager discussed in Section 1.1 who, in his case, avoids using clichés as a way of constructing the identity he wishes to project for himself in his organisational setting. In both other examples in this section, clichés, or their deliberate avoidance, also constitute tools for constructing a certain type of identity. Of course, the question remains how effectively he or the students described actually avoid using clichés, given that they are heavily conventionalised and thus may be difficult lexical tokens to self-monitor constantly.

The examples discussed in this section point to the fact that the seemingly straightforward definition of clichés with which this chapter was introduced falls short of illustrating their wider scope and the reasons for their usage. That is exactly the problem we encounter when we try to attempt a definition of clichés by either trying to spell out what they are, or their constitution, instead of asking what functions they perform in the particular context of occurrence at interactional and discoursal levels. Our examples earlier in this section, rather, support Partridge's view on the ubiquity of clichés and point to the need to build an enquiry about clichés based on the function(s) that they fulfil in specific contexts and for particular reasons and purposes. Therefore, this book aims to account for the different functions clichés fulfil in language use, which we call discourse (e.g. van Dijk, 1997b), and explore them from a range of available discourse analytic approaches that can provide an explanation of the different functions that clichés fulfil.

As well as problematising clichés as a formulaic language strategy in discourse, fulfilling specific strategic functions, this book offers a variety of sources of data covering a wide spectrum of usage that ranges from online platforms and media text producers to institutional usage of language and personal narratives. This will ensure that different CoPs in which clichés are used are represented: from the elusive reception data in discourse analysis and the established corporate communication discourse analysis, to people interacting in a work environment and people talking about themselves. Therefore this book draws from a variety of sources of data, and offers a variety of discourse-based approaches to the analysis of such data. As equally important, it explains why clichés are useful resources given their strategic potential, which may account for their widespread use despite their negative reputation.

1.3 Structure of the Book

This book is structured as follows. Chapter 2 outlines established disciplines that have addressed the study of clichés, from lexicography to formulaic language. It also addresses the issue of defining clichés based on form and the blurred boundaries between clichés, idioms and other figurative language devices. Most importantly, it positions linguistic clichés within discourse studies and conceptualises them as socio-semiotic resources and discursive strategies that fulfil a range of specific functions in different discourse types and sites.

Chapter 3 explores clichés as argumentation strategies in public responses to online articles on current political issues. Chapter 4 investigates clichés as socio-cognitive representations, or SCRs in advertising and corporate branding discourse, drawing on theories of social cognition and sociocognitive discourse analysis. Chapter 5 draws on sociopragmatic theories and explores clichés as face-saving devices in evaluative discourse in interaction from an im/politeness perspective in organisational settings. Chapter 6 investigates clichés from a face and identity perspective and explores their role in the construction of entrepreneurial identity, examining extracts from reality television (RTV) show *The Apprentice*. Finally, Chapter 7 summarises the findings and considers implications for further research and the contributions this book has made.

CHAPTER TWO

Clichés in Discourse

2.1 Approaches to Clichés

Clichés have long been studied from various perspectives within academia. Monroe (1990) explores them in terms of their role as stylistic devices in literature. In creative writing studies, Schultz (2015) approaches clichés as cognitive processes linked to habits of thoughts, while Jackendoff (1995) explores the role of clichés in idiom recognition.

Some scholars have concluded that the meaning of clichés cannot be predicted from the individual lexical items that compose the sequence (see Jordan-Barker, 2017), but rather from their functionality in the context of their usage. In so doing, clichés are partially analysable linguistically; that is, their 'symbolic components' are not entirely 'discernible within a complex expression' (Langacker, 1999: 13). Further to this, claims that they are 'multi-word units' or 'multi-word tokens' (sometimes also referred to as 'lexical chunks') abound, with arguments that clichés, for example, are 'stored as complete units in the minds of speech participants. They are easy to retrieve for the speaker and easy to decode for the hearer' (Hamawand, 2015: 115). This equates them to idioms, not only in terms of retrieval but also in relation to the (non)compositionality problematic distinction (e.g. Jackendoff, 1995). In fact, the distinction between idioms and cliches is not clear-cut. For example, expressions listed in dictionaries of idioms (e.g. Cambridge University Press, 2017) also appear in any online search for clichés and published dictionaries of clichés (e.g. Fountain, 2012; Rogers, 1991). The classic at *the end of the day* or *think outside the box* are examples of this fuzzy boundary. Various linguists (e.g. Ricks, 1980) have problematised the issue of boundaries between idioms and clichés and some have concluded that 'some clichés are idioms and some idioms are clichés, but neither group includes the other fully' (Makkai, 1972: 171). Nunberg et al. (1994: 492) discuss that clichés, like other formulaic and fixed phrases, as well as idioms, proverbs and allusions 'inhabit the ungoverned country between lay metalanguage and the theoretical terminology of linguistics'.

In adding to the understanding of clichés as non-compositional, Tretyakova (2010: 58) defines them as 'specific structural linguistic units consisting of several lexemes whose meaning cannot be deduced from the meaning of its constituents'. Furthermore researchers such as Kuiper and Scott Allan (1996) view clichés as lexicalised syntactic structures. By lexicalised the authors mean that people use clichés as a common and shared resource to communicate, and also that they might use them repetitively. Lexicalisation for Kuiper and Allan (2017) is a consequence of social factors; that is, a word or phrase becomes lexicalised when it meets a lexical need. Furthermore, they argue that lexicalised expressions are memorised by speakers and used by a community of people in a frozen form (Kuiper and Allan, 2017: 278).

Although written clichés are a scrutinised and criticised form of language, and many researchers (e.g. van Cranenburgh, 2018) advise against their use – not least as they raise questions about the author's command of originality – Rank (1984: 46), points out the advantages of using clichés on the grounds of clarity and speed. He asserts that uncommon words and expressions take a long(er) time to be understood. Similarly, other researchers (e.g. Chumbley and Balota, 1984) argue that the more a word/phrase is frequently used, the more easily it is remembered. The more that lexical words and phrases are used, however, the greater the risk of losing their semantic value (and hence, over time, becoming non-compositional and a cliché candidate).

More extensive investigations of clichés have taken places within lexicography studies where they are also considered overused fixed phrases that tend to be seen negatively as unimaginative resources. Partridge, for example, defines a cliché as 'a phrase, or short sentence, that has become so hackneyed that careful speakers and scrupulous writers shrink from it because they feel that its use is an insult to the intelligence of their audience or public' (Partridge, 1978: xii).

Within this perspective of fixedness, and negatively evaluated ubiquity, lexicographers have, at various points, explored clichés by cataloguing them in various ways. Three main taxonomies of clichés have been outlined and can be found in the seminal works of Fowler (1965), Partridge (1978) and Kirkpatrick (1996). A brief summary of each classification, as outlined by Kirkpatrick (1996), is provided here.

Fowler

The earliest categorisation of clichés by Fowler (1965: 91) distinguishes two main types. The first type refers to overused and ineffective 'ways of saying simple things', which Kirkpatrick (1996: 19) terms as 'hard-core'. An example provided by Fowler is *to suffer a sea of change*. The second type relates to expressions that have the potential to be used as clichés when they are chosen as an off-the-shelf expression considered the best way to capture and communicate an idea (Fowler, 1956), for example *a foregone conclusion*.

Kirkpatrick acknowledges that the distinction between these two suggested categories is not very clear and is open to question, and adds that 'if a writer can use *Hobson's choice* as the finest way of saying what needs to be said rather than as a cliché, why should he/she not be able to use *suffer a sea change* in the same way? Or has time destroyed some subtle distinction between them?' (Kirkpatrick, 1996: 19).

Fowler (1965: 51) further subcategorises expressions that have the potential to be considered as clichés as follows:

- battered ornaments also referred to as a *rubbish heap*,
- irrelevant allusions (e.g. *method in the madness*),
- Siamese twins [sic!] or expressions linked as pairs (e.g. *bits and pieces*),
- vogue words or expressions that become trendy after undergoing a variation from the original meaning (e.g. *the bottom line*).

Partridge

A few years later, Partridge (1978) published *A Dictionary of Clichés* where, in the introductory essay to the dictionary, a new categorisation was offered. This was more refined and consisted of four categories, as follows:

- idiom clichés: 'those idioms which have become so indiscriminately used that the original point has been blunted or even removed entirely' (e.g. *to leave the sinking ship*);
- non-idiomatic clichés: 'phrases so hackneyed as to be knock-kneed and spavined'. There are various categories of examples provided here: (i) general: *nip in the bud*; (ii) sociological, political, economic: *leave the door open*; (iii) journalism: *reliable source of information*; (iv) literary: *Pandora's box*;
- quotations from dead and foreign languages, with two subtypes: (i) tag: 'phrases apprehended without reference to an author' (e.g. *terra firma*); (ii) full-blooded quotations: *sic transit Gloria mundi*;
- quotations from literature (e.g. *fresh fields and pastures new* by John Milton) (Partridge, 1978: 2–8).

This classification, despite providing a more clear-cut distinction, does not offer a clear ontological relationship. We see that the first two categories can be understood semantically in terms of their compositional aspects; however, the latter two seem to be based more on usage and could indeed be grouped among the former. Kirpatrick (1996) critiques some aspects of this taxonomy explaining that several examples 'have passed from common use with the general decrease in familiarity with the classical languages and so have forfeited their cliché status' (p. 17). Nevertheless, we certainly see an orientation towards usage and stylistic value and, as Kirkpatrick points out, this taxonomy 'serves as a valuable jumping off point for any more modern attempt at definition and categorization' (p. 19).

Kirkpatrick

As alluded to, above, Barbara Kirkpatrick (1996: 21–24) revisited the previous categorisations and offered a much more extensive one that attempts to bridge the gaps left by previous taxonomies:

- simile cliché (e.g. *cool as a cucumber*);
- foreign clichés (e.g. 'those clichés which retain their foreign form although they have been welcomed with open arms into the English language' (p. 21) (e.g. *je ne sais quoi, terra firma*);
- proverb clichés: clichés that came into existence as proverbs or sayings (e.g. *the early bird catches the worm*);
- allusion clichés: includes parts of proverbs and sayings, references to quotations, legends and anecdotes (e.g. *a bird in the hand, the grass is always greener, forbidden fruit*);
- quotation clichés: this includes full quotations, either from literature or other sources, such as religious writings (e.g. *for this relief much thanks* (Shakespeare's Hamlet), *cover a multitude of sins* (Peter 3:8) or misquotations, e.g. *a little knowledge is a dangerous thing* (original, *a little learning is a dangerous thing* in Alexander Pope's *An Essay on Criticism*));
- doublet clichés: containing doublets with synonyms, near-synonyms and associated ideas (e.g. *bits and pieces, leaps and bounds, over and done with*);
- euphemism clichés: frequently used euphemisms used mechanically without reflection (e.g. *economical with the truth, powder one's nose*);
- idiom cliché: includes metaphor clichés (e.g. *the light at the end of the tunnel*);

- catchphrase clichés: overly used catchphrases commonly found in advertising campaigns, memorable remarks in popular films or television that gain public appeal and become clichés (e.g. *a man's gotta do what a man's gotta do*);
- vogue expressions: buzzwords that become fashionable yet ephemeral. They may arise in a technical or specialist area of language and acquire cliché status when transferred to general language and overused (e.g. *the bottom line*);
- filler clichés: used in informal speech as discourse markers (e.g. *the thing is*, *you know what I mean*);
- hackneyed phrase: Kirpatrick warns that 'this could encompass the whole of the cliché linguistic category' but she restricts it to 'those overused phrases which have lost their freshness and which cannot be neatly or justifiably slotted in elsewhere, phrases that have gained widespread popularity over a period of time and sometimes seem to have come out of nowhere' (p. 22) (e.g. *better late than never, in the cold light of day, the one that got away*);
- situational cliché: Kirkpatrick defines this as 'a kind of verbal Pavlovian response invariably given by someone when encountering a certain situation' (p. 24) (e.g. *when you've finished that you can come and do mine* – one neighbour talking to the other who is washing their own car);
- in-group cliché: restricted to the family or close group circle.

Kirkpatrick's latter taxonomy is much more extensive and comprehensive and covers a wide range of clichés used in everyday language. However, the ontological aspect of this categorisation is unexplained as is the selection of clichés used for this classification. Nor does the selection seem to be based on empirical studies. We can see that the categorisation criteria range from structure and meaning (similes clichés, idiom clichés, doublet clichés) to function in language (filler clichés), interactional aspects (situational, in-group clichés), sociocultural influences (vogue expression and catch phrases) and even stylistic usage (allusion clichés, quotation clichés and proverb clichés). Despite the theoretical and methodological gaps, we can clearly see two aspects worth exploring: firstly, the aspect of 'fixedness' or formulaicity, even in clichés that reference, say an idiom, without fully quoting it, the cliché remains fixed across contexts of use and rates of occurrence, e.g. *early bird*; secondly, what Partridge called their 'ubiquity' (1978: 2) in terms of the various functions that they can be seen to perform. Zijderveld (1979) claims that clichés lose their semantic force but, at the same time, increase their function in the particular context of usage. Ilie (2000) critiques this view, explaining that meaning and function cannot be separated and both should rather be seen as co-existing and acquiring 'varying degrees of significance in discourse' (p. 67). We explore both aspects in the following pages.

2.2 A Formulaic Language View

The study of language as fixed chunks that are governed by rules has been the domain of formulaic language studies since the mid-nineteenth century. Wray (2002: 8) claims that the introduction of different approaches to grammar, especially generative grammar by Chomsky (e.g. 1964; 2004), helped identify particular patterns of language and, therefore, allowed the recognition of formulaic language.

Over the years, there has been a growing body of research on formulaic units and sequences (e.g. Wood, 2002; 2006; Wray, 2002; 2008; 2009; Wray and Perkins, 2000). Most of it argues for the importance of formulaic language and its vital role in language acquisition and learning while trying to define and delimit the concept per se. The most cited characteristics of formulaic language are fixedness and frequency of use or reoccurrence. Indeed, fixed words (e.g. consequently, accordingly), phrases (on one hand..., on the other), and idioms (it is raining cats and dogs) among other language patterns are considered formulaic language. Accordingly, researchers (e.g. Paquot and Granger, 2012; Wray and Perkins, 2000) assume that formulaicity is very natural when it comes to language use. Therefore, while we converse, we come to use some of these known and conventionally agreed-on phrases and sayings whether we are fully aware of the process of using them or not. Moreover, Hymes (1968) asserts that our speech is a reoccurrence of particular patterns that can conventionally be linked to a speaker, a community or a whole culture. This means that formulaic language is dynamic and changes in regard to the speaker's needs; thus its functions and definitions might differ depending on different variables and contexts of use. Consequently, a vast body of research attempts to provide definitions and categories of these, which has resulted in conceptual duplications. In regard to the former point, Weinert (1995: 182) asserts that it is likely that researchers might have a common phenomenon in mind but label it differently and this results in a plethora of concepts (e.g. cliché, collocations, conventional forms, fixed expressions, idioms and the like) and how each is defined is therefore problematic. In other words, many scholars have referred to this phenomenon of language patterning but each of them have provided different terminology. Other researchers (e.g. Schmitt and Carter, 2004; Wray,

2008) argue that the variety of forms that formulaic sequences take is the reason behind the impossibility of providing a unified definition for the phenomenon. Put simply, although there is a general agreement upon what formulaic language is, the diversity of this linguistic phenomenon has made it difficult to set a cutting-edge definition. Besides, formulaic language becomes inclusive by including different linked phenomena or subcategories that are sometimes used interchangeably. For instance, Cranenburgh (2018: 34–35) explicitly defines clichés as fixed, recognised chunks of language which are conventionalised and overused shortcuts that have lost their meanings; his definition of clichés, however, is very close to the definition of idioms, as these are also defined as conventional and culturally rooted reoccurring sayings. To put it another way, there is a blurred distinction between the different subcategories of formulaic expressions. Further to this, Wray (2002: 9) rejects the use of formulaic language as a concept and tries to alternatively replace it with the more unified and inclusive term 'formulaic sequences'. In other words, Wray (2002) considers formulaic sequences an umbrella term that includes a set of either connected or unconnected words, the use of which differs depending on the situation. She also rejects any conventionalised use of these sequences or its analysis from a grammatical perspective. In the field of forensic linguistics, Larner (2019: 327) defines formulaic sequences as 'an umbrella term for sequences of words including metaphors, clichés, collocations, and routine phrases' that are 'stored holistically as single lexical items[;] they make the act of producing language less cognitively demanding' and therefore compensate for other cognitive efforts, such as deception. All in all, a definition of formulaic language, or sequences, that encompasses all aspects discussed here, is Wray's (2002: 9) as word combinations which are, 'or appear to be, prefabricated' – that is, stored holistically and retrieved as a whole 'from memory at time of use, rather than being subject to generation or analysis by the language grammar'.

   This definition concerns formulaic sequences that range from idiomatic, immutable and syntactically irregular to transparent and syntactically decomposable sequences that are retrieved as single items (Wray and Perkins, 2000: 1–2).

Categories of Formulaic Sequences

A considerable body of research, often based on corpus studies, has attempted to catalogue the forms and subcategories that formulaic sequences take in discourse. Accordingly, most research (e.g. Biber, 2009) has been interested in depicting the reoccurrence and the re-use of particular formulaic sequences. In this regard, Wray and Perkins (2000: 1), while defining formulaicity, claim that formulaic sequences can be either words/meanings that are either continuous or discontinuous. This, in turn, entails that these multi-word expressions can take various and different forms. In other words, while continuous means that the words are placed all together like *break the ice, blessing in disguise, cutting corners, fast food, quick meal, ladies and gentlemen*; discontinuous means that words can be located in different parts of discourse like *on one hand … on the other hand*. Formulaic sequences can be fixed in terms of syntax and orthography like *in other words* and *as a result*. However, these sequences might allow room for flexibility and change where language users can change nouns/pronouns and the tense such as *s/he cries/cried her/his eyes out/I cried my eyes out*; *it is my/her/his/our cup of tea*.

Wood (1998: 4) discusses that as the archetypal formulaic sequences, idioms are 'fixed and semantically opaque or metaphorical'. This is the case in expressions such as *spill the beans*. A key quality of the meaning of an idiom is that it is non-compositional and its structure is non-transformable, that is, non-productive or frozen. An example of this is *by and large*, which Wood advises 'cannot be understood by means of its constituent parts, nor can (it) be grammatically manipulated' (2020: 32).

According to Wood (2020: 32), there are five basic defining criteria of an idiom. These criteria are that they are:

- more than two words in length;
- semantically opaque, that is 'the meaning of the whole is not the sum of the meanings of the individual components', and that they have some words that are never used outside the contexts of the idioms;
- non-compositional;
- in a relationship of mutual expectancy or lexicality where component words occur in a fixed manner giving the idiom a unitary, stand-alone meaning;
- demonstrate lexico-grammatical invariability, frozenness or fixedness: the component words in an idiom are fixed and cannot be substituted by synonyms.

Grant and Bauer (2004) added a condition that an idiom is also non-figurative. This means that *spill the beans* could not be considered an idiom because its meaning could be non-literal and needs to be reinterpreted by examination of its pragmatic intention, whilst *by and large* is neither literal nor does it shows traces of figurative meaning.

In light of this, Wood (2020) discusses that some categories of formulaic sequences overlap and 'there is no consensus that all categories are similarly processed semantically or psycholinguistically' (p. 31). Therefore it is difficult to identify and classify formulaic sequences and multi-word combinations that can be formulaic. A combination of native-speaker judgement, corpus frequency, statistical measures of co-occurrence and acoustical features can give an indication for formulaicity but they cannot always be considered reliable means of identifying formulaic language.

The issue of figurativeness is important in discussing metaphorical clichés. Some researchers (e.g. Down and Warren, 2008; Le Sage, 1941) consider clichés of this nature as dead metaphors, for example, *the mouth of a river*. This refers to fixed metaphorical expression where usage has become habitual and the initial imagery is not evoked anymore. Psycholinguistic studies (e.g. Gibbs, 1993), however, have argued that dead metaphors still allow for an unconscious mental mapping that evokes the initial imagery that is now seen at a distance (as argued in Oswick et al., 2002: 294). Down and Warren (2008: 8) also suggest that such clichés sit in a comfort zone because they allow a 'weak [...] attachment' to the propositional content which allows them to function effectively in negotiating interpersonal relationships, as we will now argue in subsequent chapters (cf. Chapter 5). This was foreshadowed by Lerner (1956: 250), who observed that 'a cliché is not a half-dead metaphor, it is one that refuses to die'.

For Wray and Perkins (2000), formulaicity can be either literal and transparent like *good evening* or non-literal and opaque as in *break a leg*. These set of wordings or meanings were usually conceptually differently to create a variety of formulaic language subcategories. This variety of forms, consequently, results in a variety of conceptualisations. Indeed, if formulaic language/sequence is to be considered an umbrella term for a linguistic patterning phenomenon, thus there are several and different subcategories for it like idioms, clichés, collocations, phrasal expressions and so on; each with its own particular characteristics. To support the previous claim, Schmitt and Carter (2004: 2) assert that formulaic sequences operate in the form of idioms, proverbs and sayings and that these subcategories function as a unit even though they might have orthographically different components. Some of these subcategories (e.g. clichés and idioms) are, however, confusing and their definitions and extraction from a corpus are blurred and problematic. Like clichés and idioms, collocations also have been at the core of corpus studies discussions (e.g. Granger and Paquot, 2008). They are commonly defined as lexical combinations of two or more words like *face a problem*, *take a step ahead* that go together and which sound natural to native speakers, where some collocations (usually performed by non-natives) might not (e.g. *fast food/*rapid food*). The study of collocations, nonetheless, focuses on the co-occurrence more than on reoccurrence of linguistic patterns. Thereafter, Wray (2009: 9) asserts that it is difficult from a formulaic research point of view to envisage the relationship between collocations that are in the form of two ordinary words that can be allowed to pair with many other words (e.g. *happy event, happy birthday, happy ending*). This is, on one hand, one of the challenges that corpus linguistics has forwarded to research on formulaic language regarding collocations in particular and other subcategories in general. On the other hand, Wray (2009: 10) discusses that the focus of corpus linguistics on word associations is questionable by asserting that although frequency is usually linked to formulaicity, this does not mean that more reoccurring patterns are the most formulaic ones. To support her claim, Wray (2009) asserts that there are infrequent words or strings of words that predominate in the expression of particular ideas or situations. Consequently, matters of frequency should not be at the core of formulaic research but further attention should be paid to the different functions they provide for interlocutors, the latter being a key aspect of this book.

Functions of Formulaic Sequences

Schmitt and Carter (2004: 9) question the definitions of formulaic sequences solely based on the description of their forms and meaning and argue that definitions of these language patterns should be made in relation to the conditions of use and on their functions as well. To investigate the effect of using formulaic language in communication, Wray (2002) claims that we should look for its popularity in terms of usage and what forms it has along with the functions these forms convey and how they are affecting our production and perception of language.

Researchers like Schmitt and Carter (2004: 10) acknowledge the functions of formulaic sequences in maintaining communication and discourse structure as well as in transferring meaning in a precise and concise manner. In the same vein, other researchers also assert that formulaic sequences manipulate language use in interaction (e.g. Wray, 2002; Wray and Perkins, 2000). Thus, formulaic sequences are usually used to assist communication in the sense that they help speakers to start, carry and end different conversations by the use of openers, discourse conjunctions, and so on. Accordingly, Wray and Perkins (2000: 13–22) discuss four functions the formulaic sequences perform but with a focus on their role in organising the content of a text, performing rhetorical functions and aiding cohesive relationships. These are: introducing a topic, comparing, expressing a cause, summarising and concluding.

Formulaic sequences also work to engage the reader in the argumentation process (e.g. *from this point, it is now crystal clear*). Schmitt and Carter (2004) discuss a number of broader purposes such as expressing a message of an idea (*early bird*), realising social functions (*just looking*, when declining an offer to assistance at a shop), expressing solidarity (*sure*, i.e. agreement), transacting information (*cleared for take-off*, i.e. confirming permission) and signalling discourse organisation (*on the one/other hand*). In other words, formulaicity is used to achieve speakers' wants (Wray, 2009: 8) thereby fulfilling pragmatic functions in interaction.

Formulaic sequences can also be used creatively with speakers' being playful when using conventionalised utterances (Wray, 2009). This means that clichés could be seen to be given meaning depending on the context in which they are used, the interlocutors using them and the purposes for using them. For example, they can be used creatively as subversive strategies in certain contexts, for example as argumentative strategies in political discourse (see Chapter 3). However, this can become problematic as the more the speakers use formulaic language to achieve communicative and interactional goals, the more they risk the hearer not decoding their intention successfully as this will require less effort on the part of the speaker and more processing effort for the hearer (Wray, 2009).

Further to this, Boers (2014) discusses that metaphorical idioms fulfil important functions in discourse such as conveying evaluative positioning (e.g. Martin and White, 2005) or signalling topic changes (O'Keeffe et al., 2007), in other words, fulfilling interpersonal and textual functions, respectively (cf. Section 2.4). Boers concludes that formulaic expressions 'are not just a colourful but dispensable way of conveying a message that could also be conveyed by literal means' (2014: 193).

These arguments therefore point to the need to explore the functions that clichés, as formulaic sequences, fulfil in discourse. In the following sections we elaborate on both aspects: that is what we mean by 'function' and 'discourse' in this book. We also address the issue of usage, not only in relation to genre but also to CoPs.

2.3 A Discourse View

In this work, we are interested in the functional aspects of clichés. By function, we echo and expand Schmitt and Carter (2004) views and pose that the function of clichés goes beyond the local level of discourse. We add that in exploring the function of clichés we should argue for an understanding of clichés as socio-semiotic resources that allow speakers to use language to fulfil a number of social functions.

Before exploring the socio-semiotic aspects of clichés, though, we need to address the notion of discourse. The word 'discourse' refers to 'a unit of language larger than a sentence and which is firmly rooted in a specific context [...] [T]here are different types of discourse under this heading, such as academic discourse, legal discourse, and media discourse, for example. Each discourse type possesses its own characteristic linguistic features' (Martin and Ringham, 1999: 51). For our purposes, however, we adhere to a more complex view of discourse.

Following contemporary (critical) discourse analysis, we view discourse, that is, language use in speech, writing and even visual communication, 'as a form of social practice' (e.g. Fairclough and Wodak, 1997: 258), that is, as a social phenomenon. This definition poses that social reality is constructed and made real through discourse, and social interactions are understood by reference to discourses that give them meaning (Phillips and Hardy, 2002: 3).

Van Dijk (2007) discusses that discourse is an interdisciplinary notion, the dimension of study of which extends to disciplines such as semiotics, pragmatics, sociolinguistics and cognitive linguistics as well as to areas such as cultural studies, etc. In this book, we find van Dijk's (2009: 65–66) definition of discourse of particular relevance:

discourse is a multidimensional social phenomenon. It is at the same time a linguistic (verbal, grammatical) object (meaningful sequences or words or sentences), an action (such as an assertion or a threat), a form of social interaction (like a conversation), a social practice (such as a lecture), a mental representation (a meaning, a mental model, an opinion, knowledge), an interactional or communicative event or activity (like a parliamentary debate), a cultural product (like a telenovela) or even an economic commodity that is being sold and bought (like a novel). In other words, a more or less complete 'definition' of the notion of discourse would involve many dimensions.

This definition helps account for the interdisciplinary nature of the data and diversity of methods we use in this book to outline uses and functions of clichés without losing sight of the core principle of discourse studies; that is, the systematic and explicit analysis of the various structures and strategies of different levels and aspects of text and talk (van Dijk, 2007). Despite conceptualising discourse as a broad phenomenon, we remain consistent with contemporary approaches to (critical) discourse studies in that we are concerned with exploring a number of dimensions of clichés in discourse, as follows: (a) as the properties of 'naturally occurring' language used by real language users (instead of the study of abstract language systems and invented examples); (b) with a focus on larger units than isolated words and sentences, and hence, new basic units of analysis: texts, discourses, conversations, speech acts, or communicative events; (c) as the extension of linguistics beyond sentence grammar towards a study of action and interaction; (d) with focus on dynamic (socio)-cognitive or interactional moves and strategies; (e) as the study of the functions of (social, cultural, situative and cognitive) contexts of language use; and (f) analysis of a vast number of phenomena of text grammar and language use – macrostructures, speech acts, interactions, politeness, argumentation, mental models, and many other aspects of text and discourse (Reisigl and Wodak, 2009: 2).

This socially bound view indicates that analytical approaches to discourse can be characterised by reference to the semiotic environment in which discourses operate – what is known as the three parameters of context proposed by systemic functional linguistics (SFL) (e.g. Halliday, 1978), that is, field, tenor and mode, discussed in Section 2.4.

Matthiessen (2012: 444) offers a useful outline of different approaches to discourse viewed in terms of those three contextual parameters. According to him, approaches concerned with systems of power and dominance (e.g. CDS), inclusion (e.g. positive discourse analysis) and solidarity (e.g. socio-pragmatics) are positioned within the contextual parameter of tenor. Similarly, approaches concerned with socio-semiotic processes, such as recreating, construing, etc. (e.g. narrative analysis, media discourse analysis) correspond to the contextual parameter of field.

In an attempt to draw connections between SFL and Critical Discourse Analysis (CDA), Matthiessen (2012: 446) advises that CDA, as a socially oriented discourse analysis discipline, strives to bridge micro-patterns of text-level analyses to the macro-patterns of the culture or society where the discourses being investigated operate. Indeed, Fairclough (e.g. 1992: 71–73) has addressed this endeavour in his 'social theory of discourse' where he proposed a well-known three-dimensional framework involving various levels of analysis that combine the close textual and linguistic analysis tradition with the 'macrosociological tradition of analysing social practice in relation to social structure', as well as 'the interpretivist tradition of seeing social practice as something which people actively produce and make sense of on the basis of shared commonsense procedures'.

2.4 A Socio-semiotic View

Having established our view on discourse, we need to go back to the socio-semiotic nature we claim clichés to have. For this, we draw on Halliday's (e.g. 1978) theory of language from a social-functional perspective in which he claims that language is a part of society and the social system. As such, it is regarded as a system where interlocutors make choices while conversing to reach a goal and/or convey linguistic functions that are socially motivated/shaped. Halliday (1978: 4) considers language as repetitive and routinised. In his description of this process of conveying meaning using formal rules, Halliday (1978) argues that meaning is coded lexicogrammatically in forms and then recoded in sounds. For Halliday there is no distinction between meaning coded in grammatical structures and those coded as lexical items. By considering the role of language in the understanding and construction of reality, Halliday (1978) poses that reality is realised through words, forms and structures and argues that if reality is a social construct, then it is (more often) expressed through meanings and therefore through language. Accordingly, the interpretation of language should always adhere to the sociocultural context, an information system where language is one of the semiotic systems that encodes meaning; thereafter, context and language have reciprocal effects on each other (Halliday, 1978). Language as 'social semiotic' encompasses language as 'a social fact', and by social fact he refers to the role the sociocultural context plays in shaping language and how it is, in turn, shaped by it.

He outlines the elements that are essential to understanding a socio-semiotic theory of language: text, situation, register, code, the linguistic system and social structures (Halliday, 1978: 108–114). Texts 'actualise meaning potential'; that is, the range of options that characterise a situation to represent 'what is meant'. The 'semantic variety of which a text may be regarded as an instance of' is the register, whilst the code refers to the 'semiotic organisation governing the text' by reference to the 'semantic style of the culture' (Halliday, 2014: 264–268). Drawing on Wegener (1885), Malinowski (1923) and Firth (1957), Halliday observed that the situation 'is the environment in which the text comes to life' (Halliday, 2014: 265). As a theoretical sociolinguistic construct, the situation type is interpreted as the social context or 'semiotic structure'. Halliday poses that there are three dimensions to the 'semiotic structure' of a situation. These are (a) field, which refers to what the text is about, the nature of ongoing the social activity or action that includes the subject matter, as one particular manifestation of field; (b) tenor, which refers to the interpersonal relationships between participants and their social roles and relationships, including levels of formality; and (c) mode, referring to the role played by various semiotic systems in the context, that is the channel of communication (Matthiessen, 2012: 443). These parameters of context constitute the 'conceptual framework for representing the social context as the semiotic environment in which people exchange meanings' (Halliday, 2014: 266).

Halliday's view of language falls under the realm of its functions as part of the linguistic system, which is an essential element to his socio-semiotic theory of language. The linguistic system, and the semantic system within it, is of 'primary concern in a sociolinguistic context' given its components 'are the modes of meaning that are present in every use of language in every social event' (Halliday, 2014: 268). These components are known as the *ideational, interpersonal* and *textual* functional constituents of the semantic system, which are interrelated and co-exist simultaneously to produce a text. Each component is functional in that it contributes a type of meaning to the text and is realised as integrated structures of lexico-grammatical features. Halliday explains that:

> The ideational function represents the speaker's meaning potential as an observer [...] [T]his is the component through which the language encodes the cultural experience, and the speaker encodes its own individual experience as a member of the culture. It expresses the phenomenon of the environment: the things [...] of the world and of our own consciousness, including the phenomenon of language itself, and also the 'metaphenomena', the things that are already encoded as facts. (Halliday, 2014: 268)

In other words, this function is language as reflection; it is also defined as the content of language, which is composed of choices, which users select depending on their goal. The ideational function of language might be composed of two other processes: experiential and logical, which are almost inseparable (see Halliday, 1978: 128). The type and nature of activity determines the experiential choices. In other words, the collection of choices made (objects, persons and events) is controlled by the ongoing social actions of individuals to express their realities or experiences. Therefore, the ideational function is concerned with people's expression of experiences and, thus, their realities.

The second metafunction of language posed by Halliday is the interpersonal. Halliday (1978) claims that the mastery of language has the potential to engage the individual into personal relationships and to enable him/her to explore his/her environment. Put differently, language provides its user with the ability to express his/her own role in a particular situation and any other role/roles that s/he would assign to his/ her hearer and construe and maintain interpersonal relationships. An important aspect of language that falls within the interpersonal metafunctions, and is of particular relevance to this book, is the enactment of attitudinal stance.

This aspect is exemplarily accounted for in Martin and White's (2005) appraisal system, which focuses on the way the text creates, negotiates and maintains relationships between interactants through lexical choices in expressing attitude. We will deal with this approach in detail in Chapter 5.

Finally, the textual metafunction, according to Halliday (1978), is intrinsic to language and relates to the ability of language to associate with particular context. Halliday regards the text as language in operation; through text we demonstrate the ideational and interpersonal functions as the text embodies the semantic system, that is, the textual function enables the other two. In his work, Halliday (1978) exemplifies how the textual functionality of language is determined by the text mode (oral/written) and its genre. Certain choices in the selection and positioning of clichés, to create certain effects such as parallelism, as well as repetition or recurrence, intertextual references, and the like may all contribute to create cohesive relations.

2.5 Clichés as Socio-semiotic Resources in Discourse

In this book, we argue that clichés are socio-semiotic resources of language in that people use them in different contexts for a variety of purposes. Considering Halliday's (1978: 4) claim that linguistic structures should be interpreted in relation to their functions by referring to the social processes in which they occur, we argue that clichés serve a function in their sociocultural context and in so doing they convey meaning, therefore becoming socio-semiotic resources. We see clichés as ideational and interpersonal resources (albeit also unavoidably having a textual role, which is beyond the remit of this book) that functions in various levels in discourse.

First, at the immediate situational level of context, we pose that they may be seen to function as ideational, in that they help construe aspects of reality by virtue of the fixed meaning attached to them and so they can carry unchallenged knowledge assumptions. Anderson-Gough et al. (1998: 566), in a study of cliché use in organisational discourse, argue that clichés are tools used by formal power practices (e.g. culture management programmes) manifested in mottoes and slogans, and as such, they serve to reproduce assumptions and construct 'the tacit social "realities" of organisational life'. Therefore, clichés work as rhetorical devices that function as 'a vehicle for organisational sense making and an area for organisational and managerial control' that legitimise power relations and naturalise practices (Anderson-Gough et al., 1998: 566). Similarly, clichés that take the form of metaphors work in a similar way. Semino (2008: 30) explains that 'metaphor enables us to think and talk about (experiences) in a concrete (often more simplistic) way'; that is, abstract ideas and processes can be constructed by means of linguistics choices to reflect on experiences and thus realities. Semino (2008) argues that through reoccurrence and repetition within a particular discourse, some metaphors represent aspects of reality as 'common sense' or 'natural' (p. 33). Additionally, Semino (2008) claims that the use of metaphors can reflect on private and subjective experiences such as the expression of chronic pain in health discourse (Bullo, 2018).

Further to this, we pose that clichés fulfil an interpersonal function in that language users employ them to sustain interaction and to control others and thus attain their interactional goals. We draw on Wray and Perkins (2000: 13), who suggest that formulaicity provides the individual with the ability to manipulate his/her world and express his/ her individual and group identity. Likewise, following Nattinger and DeCarrico (1992), we assert that clichés as formulaic sequences provide conversational functions such as social interactions and discourse devices. We pose that cliché choices can have various purposes, depending on the speakers' desired outcomes. For example, they can be used for creating social bonding in a number of ways. Rank (1984) claims that the use of cliché helps to create a sort of connection between those sharing the same discourse practice. The nature and predictability of clichés enables the interlocutors to overcome anxiety, as they have meaning known to most or all members of the culture, thus strengthening social belonging (Filley, 1975). Zijderveld poses that clichés 'enable us to interact mechanically [...] without reflection' (1979: 58), which allows for smooth interactions. According to Baider (2013), clichés also convey an implicit cultural belonging and 'exemplify the typical way of expressing oneself as a native speaker' (p. 1167). Furthermore, Baider suggests that when used appropriately by speakers of other languages, they can facilitate acceptance in the target linguistic community (2013). Ilie (2000: 66) argues that clichés fulfil the function of controlling and persuading an audience and public reactions in certain discourse sites, such as political discourse. Clichés are also seen to facilitate and enable action in complex situations from a 'safer' standpoint (Shapin, 2001: 740). For example, they can help communication by facilitating turn taking (Van Lancker-Sidtis and Rallon, 2004). Finally, they can also be used as politeness devices to save or maintain face or to negotiate certain identities, as we discuss extensively in Chapters 5 and 6.

Second, and as we demonstrate in each subsequent chapter, we pose that clichés are used for specific goals by reference to broader discourses and processes that we analyse from various discourse analytical perspectives. For example, we analyse how they fulfil various social functions such as expressing solidarity. By reference to socio-pragmatic theories. We are not concerned with a problem-oriented approach to clichés in discourse but we do pose that a study of the functions that clichés fulfil in discourse needs to be carried out by reference to multidimensional and interdisciplinary approaches. We do not propose the need for a micro/macro level distinction in the CDA sense. However, we find that accounting for the functions of clichés is best achieved by a similar approach to Matthiessen's correspondences between discourse analytical approaches and contextual parameters of discourse. We do not claim to integrate approaches but rather *co-deploy* tools from various approaches that aid the description and explanation of how clichés function in discourse by reference to two pathways of exploration. That is, we describe how clichés as formulaic expressions work as and/or around choices of language (e.g. appraisal choices in Chapter 5), fulfilling metafunctions (e.g. interpersonal, that is to construe and maintain interpersonal relationships corresponding to the contextual parameter of tenor), as described earlier. Further to this, by co-deploying tools from what Matthiessen (2012: 444) refers to as 'special-purpose approaches' to discourse, we explain how they work as multidimensional phenomena (i.e. they use a naturally occurring language, used in action and interaction, and so on.) as discussed earlier by Reisigl and Wodak (2009: 2). We refer to the account of the former as a first-level description whilst the latter, by virtue of the explanation of the function of clichés as social phenomena (i.e. politeness) offered, is seen as a second-level description. The first level accounts for the contextual function whilst the second level accounts for the social function of clichés in the broader context of study.

2.6 Clichés, Genre and Communities of Practice

Another aspect to mention is that clichés are intrinsically linked to genres and CoPs. A large body of work in linguistics has dealt with the notion of genre. Within SFL, Martin (1985: 25) defines genre as a 'staged, goal-oriented, purposeful activity in which speakers engage as members of our culture'. In metaphor studies, Semino (2008: 29) uses the term 'genre' and 'text type' interchangeably to refer to how language reoccurs and becomes conventional in specific activities, including different text/genre types like newspapers, novels, advertisement and so on. In CDA, Fairclough (1992, 2003) uses the term 'genre' to refer to the set of 'conventions associated with [...] a socially ratified activity type' (p. 126). A view generally shared is that different genres have specific types of composition and structure and they all must comply to specific conventions to be recognisable as belonging to a certain type of text (Peterson, 2017). According to Peterson (2017: 59), clichés can be conventionalised in different genres. For example, the expression *silver bullet* is mostly seen in (scientific) journalism, meaning to find a solution or to fix something. In the field of literature, van Cranenburgh (2018) conducted a corpus study of literary texts and found that clichés recurred more in romantic and suspense novels than in non-fiction. Another genre where clichés operate is narratives. Down and Warren (2008) investigate the role of clichés in narratives of identity construction of entrepreneurs (Down and Warren, 2008; cf. Chapter 6) and argue that clichés are narrative resources that introduce new experiences to people's narratives. Other scholars (e.g. Dann, 2001) have investigated the use of clichés in promotional marketing advertisements. Boorstin (1987) argues that the language of tourism and clichés are similar and reoccurring, especially when it comes to images. For example, the frequent use of iconic photographs in tourist destinations, such as the Eiffel Tower, Tower Bridge, the Statue of Liberty, Uluru, Christ the Redeemer and the Colosseum, have led to such images to be considered clichés.

This difference in use has been explained by the need to understand the function of clichés in different genres and in relation to different audiences and producers. Peterson (2017: 58) argues that specific genres are intended for specific readers/listeners and the appropriate use of clichés as a convention is dependent on the type of audience and how they will react to it. The familiarity of the producers and audience with clichés is a sign of familiarity with the genres in which they occur whilst any unfamiliarity reflects lack of experience in a particular genre (Peterson, 2017).

It is worth pointing out that in this study we do not set out to investigate whether different clichés feature in different texts across different genres, as the nature of the study is not designed for such purposes.

Rather, we acknowledge that the genres of texts studied in this book (e.g. within participatory social media, promotional and marketing material and RTV genres) were chosen based on the findings of the research in this section. We do not aim to compare and contrast so as to add to the existing body of literature in this area but rather use these genres (as text types within discourse sites) due to the accessibility to data they provide, which will facilitate the exploration of the functions that clichés are found to perform, as per our aims.

Further to this, given their rootedness within specific sociocultural contexts, clichés are grounded in a community with embedded regulatory functions and even nonverbal cues that accompany them. Wray and Grace (2007) propose that language forms stretch and retract in response to the behaviour of a community of speakers, – particularly how they interact with outsiders. They argue that formulaic language marks insider status, protecting the identity of linguistic groups.

The term 'community' has various implications and definitions. For the purposes of this study, we find the concept of CoP (community of practice) the most relevant. This notion was first coined by Lave and Wenger (1991) in relation to learning processes within a new framework. For Wenger (1998), CoPs engage in an ongoing joint enterprise where participants share and negotiate ways of doing things, behaving and making use of language (such as vocabulary and discourse). People become members through ongoing shared practices and build a shared repertoire of resources for negotiating meaning (Ostermann, 2015: 1–2), which allows them to collaborate in presenting themselves as a group to the world. This is linked to the notion of genre familiarity, as discussed, albeit at a more social level. Eckert (2006) also discusses that CoPs engage participants in shared sense-making practices, whether consensual or conflictual, about the shared endeavour, participation and their orientation to other groups and world views in general. In engaging in shared experience over time, meanings become conventionalised leading to a commitment to shared understanding and 'ultimately with the development of a style, including a linguistic style, that embodies these interpretations' (Eckert, 2006: 683). According to Eckert (2006), an important aspect of CoP is the participants' identity construction, as we explore in Chapter 6.

All in all, both concepts – in shaping members' orientation towards, and engagement in, discourse – can be seen to offer interpersonal and ideational dimensions. We find these relevant to our study and discuss them in the following chapters.

2.7 What Counts as a Cliché in This Book

For our definition of clichés, we draw on formulaic language studies (e.g. Wray, 2002), SFL (e.g. Halliday, 1978) and discourse studies (e.g. Reisigl and Wodak, 2009; van Dijk, 2009).

We conceptualise and classify clichés as chunks of language that present the following characteristics:

- conventionalised prefabricated, multi-word expressions stored and retrieved from memory as a whole item
- take the form of various features of language such as (although not limited to)
    - cognitive linguistic devices (e.g. metaphor and metonymy)
    - textual resources (e.g. intertextual references)
    - rhetorical devices (tautologies and antithesis)
    - lexico-grammatical resources (e.g. neologisms; mental/psychological or action processes).

Further to this, clichés

- evoke shared values and knowledge within a CoP or genre
- fulfil interpersonal and/or ideational meanings
- perform a number of functions in discourse (as per our discussion in Section 2.5).

We explain the various sites from where clichés were collected and the analytical methods employed in each chapter. However, what remains consistent across all chapters is our definition of clichés. Once clichés are considered as such, that is, they fulfil all five characteristics, we cross-reference them with published dictionaries of clichés (e.g. Rogers, 1991; Fountain, 2012) in order to ensure that the clichés used in this study are available to all speakers of British English and not a specific CoP.

In the next four chapters, we analyse four different corpora of clichés, as introduced in Chapter 1.

CHAPTER THREE

Clichés as Argumentative Strategies

3.1 Clichés as Topoi

In this chapter, we investigate clichés as argumentative tools used to achieve certain strategic aims in discourse.

Argumentative strategies have been extensively developed and applied to the study of political discourse. They are a key theoretical and analytical concept within the Discourse Historical Approach (DHA) (e.g. Reisigl and Wodak, 2009), which attempts to describe the use of language and other semiotic practices in power and domination (Reisigl and Wodak 2009). Drawing on linguistic models and argumentation theory, this approach has developed a series of analytical strategies for the identification of ideological positioning.

A key concept within this approach, which is of relevance to this work, is that of *topoi*. Kienpointner (1992) defined topoi as conventionalised inferable premises within argumentation. They are the content-related warrants that can be seen as 'conclusion rules' which connect an argument with the conclusion and justify the transition from said argument to a claim (Kienpointner, 1992: 194).

According to Kienpointner (2011), topoi are essentially formulas that enable the search and location of certain arguments within a discourse. Rubinelli (2009) argues that these argumentation techniques are frequently used in political discourse in order to help the author or speaker to gain the upper hand in a discussion or speech. Wodak (2015), warns that the use of topoi can often be 'fallacious and manipulative' (2015: 52) as they predominantly work by appealing to existing knowledge, regardless of whether that existing knowledge is fallacious or not.

A list of the topoi and their meaning and definitions is presented in Table 3.1. Wodak, however, acknowledges that this is not a full list, and that different contexts may have different topoi (Wodak, 2015: 51–53).

Three aspects of this definition are relevant to our proposition of clichés as topoi. First, we have so far argued that clichés are expressions that are part of ordinary language use, in other words, they are conventionalised. Secondly, we have argued that clichés are normally

Table 3.1 List of topoi

Topos	Meaning
Topos of authority	If something/someone with authority says it is true, then it must be true
Topos of burden	If a country/institution is burdened by a specific problem, then you should work to diminish that problem
Topos of certainty	If an argument has certainty, then it should be listened to more
Topos of common sense	If something is clearly beneficial, it should be done
Topos of desperation	If an argument seems desperate, then it should be ignored
Topos of elitism	If something is beneficial to the elites, it should be opposed
Topos of history	If something was successful/unsuccessful in the past, it should/should not be replicated now
Topos of immaturity	If someone is behaving immaturely then they should be ignored
Topos of numbers	If the numbers prove/disprove a certain argument, then that argument should be implemented/ignored
Topos of people	If the people favour/oppose an action, that action should be implemented/opposed
Topos of reality	If something is true, then it cannot be disputed
Topos of responsibility	If someone holds a position or idea, they should take responsibility for the effects that the position/idea has
Topos of strength	If something makes you appear stronger/weaker then it should/shouldn't be done
Topos of threat	If you are faced by specific threats, you should do something to reduce the threat
Topos of uncertainty	If an argument is uncertain, it should be listened to less
Topos of urgency	If something needs to be done, then it should be done quickly
Topos of usefulness	If an action/person will be useful, then that action/person should be supported
Topos of uselessness	If an action/person will not be useful, then that action/person should not be supported

multi-word expressions that are used in a fixed way; that is, they are formulas. Finally, as is further argued in Chapter 4, clichés work as underlying frameworks of thought or information that is accessible to a community of speakers, in other words, they carry existing knowledge. These three aspects are parallel to the characteristics of topoi discussed here and that make clichés ideal candidates in argumentation, as these features facilitate the construal of experiential meanings in discourse, independent of how 'fallacious or not' they could be deemed. Take for example this comment to a news article from *The Guardian* titled 'Nine days from Brexit Day, does anybody have a clue about what's happening', which was published on 20 March 2019 during Brexit negotiations (Appendix 1). This opinion piece is critical of the negotiations and the perceived lack of action by the then prime minister, Theresa May. This extract is one of the many comments in response to the piece.

it's easy to see what is happening. The liars have lied, the lies were believed, the lies are now just washing away the people who embraced them and those that rejected them. It's *not rocket science*. (*Guardian*)

The comment features the cliché *it's not rocket science*. If we analyse content-related argument schemes featuring this expression against the background of a list of topoi, we can argue that it draws on the topoi of common sense and uselessness. In so doing, the expression warrants that a task is not complex to the standards of a perceived extremely difficult one, and therefore the people not performing or carrying out such tasks efficiently are incompetent and thus should not be supported. The comment containing the cliché could then be seen to legitimise the anti-Brexit position by claiming it as common sense and that the people not carrying out such action or task are inefficient. In so doing, it also others those who have advocated for Brexit by arguing that they lack intelligence.

In the context of political discourse, topoi are usually used as part of wider strategic and intentional discursive practices that are deployed and explored in (usually political) arguments and which aim to achieve a specific goal in discourse. Of concern to this study are three strategies: othering, legitimisation and authenticity. Othering refers to the idea of creating an 'us' versus 'them' narrative, where group(s) are often demonised or dehumanised owing to a multitude of different identity markers, such as race, religion or political ideology (Dervin 2015; Wodak, 2015). Othering is achieved by means of interpersonal resources, such as pronouns, positioning perceived opponents as dis-aligned with the speaker's views. Legitimisation is used, obviously, to add legitimacy and accreditation to potentially controversial policies and ideologies (Wodak, 2015), and is often achieved through the use of argumentation devices – topoi – that reflect a certain worldview (Reyes, 2011), thereby fulfilling an ideational function. Similar to legitimation, authenticity is created in order to seem more in touch with and representative of the electorate (Ekström et al, 2018). Other strategies relate to justification of certain policies and ideologies by making them seem more mainstream and less extreme (van Dijk 1992; Wodak 2015), denial as a form of blame avoidance – often used as a way of refuting accusations of racism but also potentially in order to refute other claims/accusations (van Dijk, 1992), scandalisation by means of provocative and inflammatory language when making an argument (Wodak, 2015) and singularisation as a way of constructing a sense of superiority and uniqueness (Wodak 2015).

For our purposes, the use of clichés in the reception of political news is one example of argumentation where clichés are used as argumentation techniques vis-a-vis discourse strategies in the construction of an argument. As this analysis shows, each cliché identified in the data encompasses both an argumentation technique and a strategy, which combine to form the political argument. Take the infamous expression 'Brexit means Brexit'. This cliché works intertextually as an extension of the commonly known tautological cliché *it is what it is*. That is, 'Brexit is Brexit' is 'full of snatches […] of other texts […] explicitly demarcated or merged in' that have been assimilated or even ironically echoed by the current take (Fairclough, 1992: 84). By using the expression in her argumentation to assert her intention of making Brexit happen, the then British prime minister used the novel cliché as a topos of authority, that is, the authority provided by the referendum, which legitimised the implementation of Brexit.

All in all, we pose that by using topoi that clichés draw from in news' reception, users are able to achieve certain strategic aims in discourse, which allows them to construe a certain aspect of reality in a particular way.

3.2 Argumentation in News Reception and Audience Participation

The exploration of audiences' response to media is the realm of reception research. This tradition has been concerned with exploring audiences' use and interpretation of media as a reflection of sociocultural contexts and as a process of giving meaning to cultural practices, urging audiences to resist and subvert the hegemonic meanings offered by the mass media (McQuail, 1997). Influenced by theorists such as Hall (1980), Barthes (e.g. 1977) and Eco (e.g. 1979), reception research has focused on the active role of the reader in constructing meanings from media texts. Research in linguistics introduced the notion of 'hybridity', posing that a variety of interpretations allows for a variety of discourses to be brought into the sense-making process. In this way a new hybrid text that results from the interpreted texts, along with the discourses that are brought to it in the sense-making process, is created (Chouliaraki and Fairclough, 1999).

With the development of social media, new participatory opportunities have arisen for media users (Bruns, 2008), which has meant a redefinition of the public space whereby passive recipients of media content, who were hitherto referred to as 'audiences' or 'readers', have now become active participants or even co-creators of such content (Almgren and Olsson, 2015). In such transformations, the discursive power of the 'participatory web is fluid, changeable, and non-static' (KhosraviNik, 2017: 582) allowing for new forms of co-existence between producers and consumers of texts (Almgren and Olsson, 2015). This new form of 'participatory communication' is considered to have the potential to 'lead to a fully decentralised and democratised access to discursive power' (KhosraviNik, 2017: 582) allowing 'open and democratic exchanges around many controversial topics' (Sharma et al, 2017: 19).

Within discourse studies, there is a growing body of work in what has become known as Social Media Critical Discourse Studies (SM-CDS) (e.g. Unger et al., 2016), a school of thought that focuses on how what happens in media 'may shape and influence social and political sphere of our life worlds' (KhosraviNik, 2017: 586). SM-CDS postulates the existence of intertextual and interdiscursive chains between discursive practice in online and offline sites and advises that the interpretation of media content should take place in relation to the wider sociopolitical, historical, cultural, etc. processes of the society in which the discourse under investigation is embedded. Therefore, 'the form, processes, and projected meanings of the content itself and their calculated impacts in society' should be maintained (KhosraviNik, 2017: 587).

In terms of argumentative practices in audience reception and/or participation, Tindale (2015) rejects the exclusive attribution of meaning to a single actor involved in argumentation and the normativity of correct versus incorrect interpretation by reference to prior shared fixed meanings in communicative practice. Tindale poses that meanings rely on collaborative work 'of individuals engaged in the shared practices of interpretation' (2015: 125). Therefore, opinions are situated 'within an interactive and collective context of epistemic co-production' (Olmos, 2018: 152) or 'dependence' that is not solely reliant on 'transmission' of media content anymore but on active co-construction by various actors engaged in argumentative practice.

When engaging in argumentative discourse in a shared mediated and institutionalised context, actors do not just assume the responsibility of

justifying their claims but also license others to 'undertake a corresponding commitment' (Tindale, 2015: 128)

This active involvement of the participating audience requires an
understanding, conceptualisation and examination of the 'rhetorical
audience' and how rhetorical communication works (Kjeldsen, 2016). It
is in this context of dialogic reception that shared meanings embedded
in linguistic structures, such as clichés within a linguistic community, are
of particular significance not only in allowing the construal of ideational
meanings, given the premises they afford, as discussed, but also interpersonally in facilitating rhetorical effects.

3.3 Data and Methods

News Comments as Social Media and the Brexit Context

Following from KhosraviNik (2017: 582), we consider news comments
platforms as social media communication in which users can 'have
access to see and respond to institutionally (e.g. [...] newspaper articles)
generated content/texts' and 'perform interpersonal communication'
in participating whilst also licensing others to engage correspondingly
(Tindale, 2015). Further to this, news comment features, given their participatory potential, allow users the opportunity to negotiate the meanings of media content (e.g. Hall, 1980) in order to 'enact membership in
particular social groups' (Jones et al., 2015: 2) or align themselves with
particular ideological standpoints. As such they are a useful platform for
the enactment of ideational and interpersonal meanings in discourse.

In this chapter, we align ourselves partially with CDS in that we
explore news comments as providing convenient access to bottom-up
discourses (Unger et al., 2016) but we do not explore such discourses
critically in depth at the level of ideology and power (e.g. Reisigl and
Wodak 2009). We therefore do not place this chapter within political
discourse analysis (e.g. Chilton, 2004) as we do not explore the 'text and
talk of politicians within overtly political contexts' (van Dijk, 1997c: 11)
nor are we 'concerned with understanding the nature and function of
political discourse and with critiquing the role discourse plays in producing, maintaining, abusing, and resisting power in contemporary society'
(Dunmire, 2012: 736). Rather we focus on explaining how clichés operate at text and discourse practice level (Fairclough, e.g. 1992) to allow
social media users to construe ideational meanings in the argumentation
process. In this way, we explore the 'concrete, situated actions people
perform with particular mediational means' (Jones, et al, 2015: 2).

In terms of the context of study, it is important to clarify that we do not intend to contextualise this chapter within the Brexit context, nor do we take a position on this, but rather we use it as a sort of 'convenience stimuli'. By this we mean that, as it was a highly debated and polemised topic of discussion at the time of collecting data for this study, we considered Brexit-related news an appropriate debate-inducing stimulus to explore the use of clichés, given that our purpose was to explore the function of clichés as argumentative devices. We therefore do not intend to contribute to the body of literature on language use in the Brexit campaign as having an impact on the result (for literature relating to this, see Koller, 2019).

Data Description

The data consisted of responses to the reporting of news on the revoking of Article 50 between 20 March and 1 April 2019.

On 29 March 2017, the United Kingdom (UK) invoked Article 50 of the Treaty on European Union (TEU) by which it gave formal notice to the European Council of its intention to withdraw from the European Union to start withdrawal negotiations. In compliance with the TEU regulations, the UK would leave the EU on 29 March 2019, initially.

In the subsequent two years, differing views regarding the Brexit negotiations, and the Brexit process overall, led to the 'Remainer' side of the debate issuing a public petition – submitted to the UK Government and Parliament 'Petitions' website – calling on the UK government to revoke Article 50 of the TEU and to remain a member state of the European Union. The petition ran between February and August 2019.

The data for this chapter was collected during the period of the petition running. It consisted of responses to media articles reporting on the petition.

Three online news sites were selected: *The Guardian* (20 March 2019), the *Daily Mail* (31 March 2019) and *BBC News* (1 April 2019). These dates were randomly selected within the period of the Article 50 revoking discussions.

The purpose of the selection was to use a combination of broadsheet and tabloid media sites with varied political orientations to ensure coverage, inclusion and variety. However, we selected a sample of media sites that are not necessarily comparable, that is, *The Guardian* is considered a broadsheet with a left-wing orientation, the *Daily Mail* is a tabloid with a right-wing inclination and the BBC is allegedly neutral. This selection was made randomly within the inclusion criteria (i.e. all major print/online media) as our purpose was not to consider the use

Table 3.2 Data set			
Source	Date	Comments n	Clichés n
The Guardian	20 March 2019	1,033	58
The Mail	31 March 2019	2,204	102
BBC News	1 April 2019	1,924	109

of clichés in relation to the political orientation or to the readership demographic characteristics, though the latter aspect will be briefly addressed in the discussion of this chapter. Rather, our aim was, as stated, to explore *how* clichés are used as argumentative devices and discursive strategies. We chose the reception of a political issue as we speculated that this was likely to generate more discussion and thereby use of argumentative strategies considering the heated debates that Brexit generated.

We carried out a manual collection of online responses across all three media sites. A total of 5,161 comments were selected for analysis, as shown in Table 3.2.

A total of 269 clichés were identified out of 5,161 comments. Clichés were considered as such following the definition outlined in Chapter 2. That is, stretches of language that (a) are multi-word, conventionalised expressions, (b) take the form of various features of language as outlined in Section 2.7, (c) evoke shared values and knowledge within a community, (d) construe ideational and/or interpersonal meanings and (e) perform discursive functions outlined in Section 2.5. In this case, they function as argumentative devices, as discussed in Section 3.1.

The identifiable comments were anonymised prior to analysis.

Analytical Tools

When analysing clichés as topoi in the comments, we draw on a list of content-specific topoi devised by Wodak (2015: 51–53) that are relevant to the political context of the cliché, as introduced in Section 3.1. For analysis of the data, we identified the comments containing clichés, which were then selected for analysis. Co-text and context were considered when discarding comments not containing clichés. For example, if a cliché was made in response to a comment, the former was left as context. The following steps were taken for the identification and classification of topoi and the strategy they are seen to fulfil:

Table 3.3 Example: fact of the matter

Cliché	Contextual analysis and interpretation	Topos of	Purpose
Fact of the matter is Leave voters already had their say in the referendum	The Revoke Article 50 petition is irrelevant as in reality people already voted to leave in the referendum	Reality: 'If something is true, then it cannot be disputed'	delegitimise the petition

a. Firstly, the cliché that was present in the data was identified (e.g. *fact of the matter*).
b. This was followed by a brief contextual discussion of the political argument being made.
c. Based on the analysis, we allocated a topos to the cliché.
d. We interpreted the cliché in its context in terms of what its purpose in the discussion was (e.g. legitimation, etc.).

Table 3.3 illustrates the process we have just described.

The use of the cliché indicates the topos of reality at use, as it is asserting the leave vote as something that is true and therefore cannot be disputed. The use of the cliché thereby indicates legitimation of Brexit despite being a contentious issue (as evidenced through the existence of the petition) and de-legitimation of the Remain argument and of the validity of the petition.

A selection of comments has been included in Appendix 1 of this book. We selected and organised comments by topoi (alphabetically) so that there is a selection of clichés illustrating the topos they were allocated as embodied in each media platform in which the comments appear. They are all accompanied by a contextual analysis and interpretation as illustrated earlier. Where comments often feature two or more clichés, the comment is listed by the topos that corresponds to the first cliché category in the extract. In cases where the cliché is relevant in a dialogue, that is, responding directly to another comment, we have left both. We have also provided examples where the same cliché is used for opposite arguments. The number of comments illustrating the topoi we interpreted to embody included in the appendix is representative of their frequency in the corpus. So, for example, there are more examples of the topos of reality than common sense. This is because there are more instances of the former in the corpus.

3.4 Findings

The analysis of clichés as data reveals certain argumentation techniques
that are more prominent than others. Table 3.4 shows the most prevalent
categories of topoi as argument techniques that clichés were allocated to
in the analysis.

Table 3.4 Most frequent topoi in the corpus

Clichés as topoi	Frequency in data	Example
reality	34	There are far more non-EU immigrants coming into this country today. Look up the figures *Wake up get real!*
Authority/definition	30	PLEASE REMEMBER THAT LEAVE WON. LEAVE NOW WITHOUT A DEAL. *LEAVE MEANS LEAVE* (emphasis in original)
Threat	28	The alternative is far worse that leaving the EU without a deal, so *careful what you wish for*
Uselessness	28	She chose a mostly Remain cabinet and made out she had changed her spots. *COMPLETE STITCH UP* (emphasis in original)
Strength	19	Your side lost, we are leaving, *suck it up*
Urgency	18	The government said quite clearly that they would obey the result of the referendum! thats called democracy so *get on with it*
Elitism	15	don't forget the *gold-plated* pension and all the after-dinner speaking
Denial	14	Fake signatures, all *a load of rubbish*!!!
Burden	14	I am *sick to death* of hearing about Brexit
Immaturity	14	Nick Boles has a *hissy fit* because he can't get his own way...
People	12	*Mickey mouse* has voted 50,000 times...

*Comments as they originally appeared in the media sites

The most frequent ones are clichés that carry the topoi of reality, authority, threat and uselessness. These are used strategically in discourse for three main purposes: *legitimation, othering* and to a lesser extent as an *authenticity* strategy.

Legitimation

One of the main functions of clichés as argumentative techniques in the corpus is to convey legitimation of either Brexit overall or aspects of it, such as the petition being reported in the news items to which the comments respond; or to delegitimise the argument of their opponents. This is achieved by means of clichés embodying four main topoi: *authority, reality, threat* and *urgency*. The former three are the most frequent in the corpus overall.

Arguments relying on the 'reality' topos are often levelled at Remain voters by Brexiteers, whose opposition to Brexit is deemed irrelevant (See 1 below). Many comments are targeted at the petition, which is considered inappropriate (See 3) or even untrue (2).

On the Remain side, arguments based on 'reality' clichés relate to the fact that large numbers of people did protest and oppose Brexit and that should be considered as well (4) or that reasons for Brexit, such as immigration from the EU, are flawed (5). We want to point out that we offer the media site where the comments appeared in brackets, next to the comment (e.g. BBC). However, it is paramount to bear in mind that we are not attributing the comments to such media sites but rather offer the name of the site where the comments appeared for contextual information.[1]

(1) You keep bleating on about the version of brexit that YOU want; there was NO definition in the EU referendum Act nor on the voting slip. If an option takes us out of EU membership it de facto delivers brexit; *whether YOU like it or not.* (Mail)

(2) *Not in a million years* this Petition was signed by the British people (laughable!!) By the way Tusk, what about the 17 million + 'leavers' that have been betrayed. Go away, you fool. (Mail)

(3) *Fact of the matter is* Leave voters already had their say in the referendum. so why would they feel the need to sign another (BBC)

(4) While a march by 1m people for another referendum, and a petition from 6m people for revoking Article 50 is not, and should not,

---

[1] Comments as they originally appeared in the media sites.

overturn the 2016 referendum result, it is *a wake up call*. It can not be ignored (BBC)

(5) There are far more non-EU immigrants coming into this country today. Look up the figures *Wake up get real!* (BBC)

Further to this, a very recurrent pattern of clichés in the comments relates to the topos of authority, by reference to the votes/election, percentage of voters (6), intertextually to the government's discourse (e.g. 'leave means leave' alluding to Theresa May's infamous 'Brexit means Brexit' catchphrase) (7), which function to legitimise Brexit and its strategy and delegitimise the petition. The Remain side often use similar clichés to delegitimise the Brexit argument by encouraging revoking Article 50 as the only way in which the UK government can control its own fate (8).

(6) Great for them, but 'Leave the E.U' has 17.4 million votes, so *mine is bigger than yours* (Mail)

(7) We live in a democracy and *leave should mean LEAVE*. (Mail) [emphasis in original]

(8) Revoke is the only remaining way to *take back control*. We need to pause, reflect and find a new way (BBC)

A third frequent type of cliché expressions in the corpus relates to the topos of threat, which is also used both as a legitimation and othering strategy. These expressions are normally used to legitimise support for Brexit as the proposed options are construed as a threat to democracy (9). A good number of clichés in this category work to legitimise opposition to Brexit based on the potential threat of it. In (10), the cliché helps construe fear of Brexit by suggesting that it is threatening to the country's prosperity. Similarly, clichés as topos of threat are used to refer to Brexit supporters (11), in this case suggesting that they are threatened by the idea of a second referendum.

(9) Without democracy we have nothing. *Don't play with fire* (BBC)

(10) Be very, very careful what you wish for, *your world could come crashing down around you* (BBC)

(11) Of the 17 million that voted leave at least 50% have changed their mind now that they see it's not the easiest deal ever. That's why Brexiters are *scared to death* of a second vote (Mail)

Another technique used to de/legitimise Brexit-related practices is the topos of urgency. In 12–15, the clichés suggest the urgency to leave by any means necessary (12), as a way of resolving problems (13) and as a way of honouring the democratic process (14), the latter aided by the numbers of topos. Similarly, urgency is used as an argument against Brexit and pro-petition by reference to history (15).

(12) No deal it is then. *Just get on with it* (Guardian)

(13) There is an opportunity here to resolve this once and for all by just leaving so just *get on with it* (BBC)

(14) If only six million people have signed this petition then this surely indicates that there are now at least 10 million people who voted remain in the referendum who would now either vote to leave, or at the very least respect democracy and want the government to just *get on with it*! (Mail)

(15) They've been discussing it for more than 40 years. They still haven't got a plan but somehow there are millions of people who take them seriously. Cancel A50. *Just get on with it*! (Guardian)

Othering

The second main function of clichés working as topoi in the corpus is to represent people from the opposite side of the debate negatively. This includes both individuals and the ideas that they promote as way of 'othering'. According to Wodak (2015) othering is a strategy in which members of a group seek to differentiate 'us' from 'them' by first establishing a positive 'us' and then showing how 'they' are different, through the attribution of negative traits. For example, we can see this with the labelling of 'remoaners' where Brexit voters attempted to portray Remain voters in a negative manner. Similarly, remain voters also try to portray Brexiteers in a negative light through the use of expressions such as 'brextremists', which is used to portray people in favour of Brexit as extreme and threatening.

Three main trends of clichés as argumentation techniques in the data set are those that rely on the topos of elitism, the topos of uselessness and the topos of people.

Clichés as the topos of elitism, for example (16, 17) are used to construct separation with supporters of the opposite party by portraying them as elitists, suggesting that they believe they are morally/intellectually superior due to their stance on leave/remain. These types are normally used to attack individuals/groups based on their social status (18).

(16) Who do BREXITERS *think they are?* (BBC)

(17) Who do REMAINERS *think they are?* (BBC)

(18) the tory voters must be choking on their tea and crumpets (BBC)

The topos of uselessness is also used for the purpose of othering. As such, clichés are used by both sides of the debate to deem inefficient various aspects of the Brexit processes – be it individual politicians, voters (19), groups and/or political strategies. The example in (20) is aimed at those who have signed the revoke Article 50 petition as opting for an easy way out of the situation.

(19) You're clearly not the *sharpest tool in the box*! (Guardian)
(20) Click bait is so easy! To click on a campaign takes no effort at all. *Lazy gits*! (Mail)

Similarly, clichés as topos of immaturity are frequently incorporated in the data to attack other individuals and groups, mostly Remain voters, arguing that they behave immaturely in refusing to accept the result (21).

(21) Stop *chucking your toys out your pram*. Guess what... If there's another vote then your precious 17.4m who voted leave can STILL VOTE LEAVE! (Mail)
(22) Nick Boles sums up remainer temperament perfectly. If you don't get your own way, *stamp your feet* and refuse to co-operate *like a spoilt child*.
(23) it isn't a petition to revoke Article 50; it's a petition organised by *Remoaners* to revoke the legal result of a legitimate referendum because they didn't like the result for which the majority voted.

Finally, the topos of threat is also strategically used to create separation from either side of the debate in expressions that represent the other side of the debate as extremist, threatening and dangerous (24). These expressions, whilst coined for use in this context only, also fulfil the characteristics of clichés that we outlined, hence we decided to include them in this discussion, as is the case of (23). Interestingly, in the case of the topos of threat, these expressions work by virtue of intertextual chains to political discourses of immigration and even racism.

(24) The ONLY reason Brextremists don't want a 2nd ref is because they KNOW they will LOSE! (BBC)
(25) It's high time *wrexiteers* faced the facts that they are a minority group now... (Mail)
(26) G o o g l e e u t r u t h s......d a v i d n o a k e s......have a good read......... surely a lot of u *remaniacs* can read this and understand !!!!!! (Mail)

Authenticity

The strategy of *authenticity* is also found in the data, to a lesser extent but still showing some prominence. This is perhaps due to each side of the debate wanting to be recognised as the authentic representation of the people with the ability to portray one's side as authentic and truly representative of the majority view being important in winning the overall argument. Therefore, clichés as topoi of people and denial are used to convey authenticity on both sides of the debate, with specific, coined expressions consistently used across all platforms.

The topos of people is mostly illustrated by the expression *the will of the people*, which is used by both sides of the debate equally. In (27) the leave vote is represented as an authentic demonstration of the preference of the majority of the population whilst in (28) it is used to support the authenticity of the petition for revoking Article 50. As a way of portraying a different side of the story, the topos of denial is commonly used to deny the authenticity of the petition against the referendum (29).

(27) If you want to live in a democracy that refuses to honour the *will of the people*, move to Syria or Zimbabwe under Mugabe. Minimize the damage. Leave now and stop this madness (BBC)
(28) The *will of the people* is to remain within the EU (BBC)
(29) Fake signatures, *fake news* (Mail)

3.5 Discussion

This analysis demonstrates the use of clichés as different kinds of argumentation techniques in the data to construe different versions of the same reality. Two types of effects are found in the data. Firstly, comments containing clichés are seen to attempt to de/legitimate Brexit-related practices by giving seemingly 'objective' reasons for Brexit or the Article 50 petition to revoke, based on authority, reality and threat arguments contained in the clichés. Secondly, they are used to create othering between the Brexit supporters and the petition supporters by representing them as an out-group, antagonistic and wrong by means of clichés carrying topoi of elistism, immaturity and threat. In so doing users position themselves ideologically, in agreement or disagreement, with both the news item being reported, the Brexit processes and with other users' comments, thereby operating within an intertextual and dialogic space.

If we look at how othering is achieved, we see a predominance of clichés that work as topoi of elitism, immaturity and uselessness, all of them antagonistic in their nature. These clichés are used as argumentation devices that aim to attribute negative qualities to certain individuals and groups constructing othering. For example, the topos of elitism looks to represent people in a negative light by portraying users who disagree with their views as elitist. The topos of immaturity perpetuates the notion than an individual or group does not have the maturity levels required to understand or deal with the concept of Brexit. Meanwhile, the topos of uselessness creates the idea that certain people do not have the intelligence or ability to comprehend Brexit, which in turn nullifies their view on the matter.

Contrariwise, legitimation is achieved by means of clichés operating as topoi of reality, authority and urgency, all of which appear to be less aggressive and seemingly logical or reasoned with the aim of attributing validity to the argument at hand. Each of these argumentation techniques allows authors to build the argument around why something *should* be done, as opposed to why it *should not*. For example, in the case of the topos of reality, the general argument being made is that the UK should accept the result of the referendum and try and make the best out of Brexit, regardless of whether people agree with it or not. With the topos of authority, many examples refer to the importance of upholding the democratic vote as the reason as to why Brexit should go ahead. The topos of urgency relates to the idea of uncertainty and supports the argument that a decision on Brexit needs to be made quickly either way so as to allow the country to return to a sense of normalcy. Each of these argumentation techniques reflects the nature of legitimation, which, in contrast to othering, appears to be less confrontational and is more centred around a positive rhetoric.

Interestingly, though, by means of clichés embodied in the topos of threat both othering and legitimation are also achieved. This demonstrates a level of versatility that is not present in any of the other argumentation techniques and highlights the contrast between the two. When it comes to legitimation, clichés embodying the topos of threat are used to highlight the potential dangers of a certain decision, such as leaving the EU, and attempts to use that danger as a way of reasoning with people and persuading them to oppose it (*be careful what you wish for*). On the other hand, clichés alluding to the topos of threat to create othering are used in a much more personal way, in an attempt to punish a certain individual or group and create a negative image of them (e.g. Brexit voters as extreme and dangerous, i.e. *dark side*). Because of its versatility and capacity to be used to implement each of the main two discourse strategies, the analysis of clichés as topos of threat offer us a good insight into the difference between legitimation and othering. They allows us to see how similar types of clichés that employ similar argumentation techniques can be implemented in different ways in order to implement a certain strategy, thereby pointing at the ubiquity of clichés in construing meanings. This then gives us an even greater understanding of the different effects the use of clichés can have in discourse.

The data also shows that legitimation and othering (in that order) are the most common across all three publications consistently. However, patterns of clichés as argumentative techniques vary per publication. In the data sourced from the BBC, the most prominent clichés alluded to the topos of reality and the topos of people as argumentation techniques. In *The Guardian* data, most are the topos of uselessness and the topos of threat. The topos of denial and the topos of authority are most prominent in the *Daily Mail* data set. Although these figures are telling of the prominence of clichés as argumentation techniques for the purposes of de/legitimising Brexit-related arguments or creating othering, we are not arguing that there is a relationship between the readership and the media site's political alignments or that the data is suggestive of the ideological role that these publications play in shaping the political discourse of Brexit. Firstly, the data comes from readers' comments on various Brexit-related articles, many of whom posted anonymously or under a pseudonym without demographic data. It is neither possible nor our aim to examine the political leanings of the authors in relation to the editorial stance of the publication. Secondly, even if we do assume that the readers' comments are somewhat reflective of the editorial stance of each publication, analysis of the data does not really identify any correlation between the publication's editorial stance and the patterns of use of clichés as argumentation techniques. For example, in each of the three publications we see how legitimation and othering are construed with relatively similar frequency of use. Further to this, although the specific type of argumentation technique that appears in each publication varies, many of the argumentation techniques appear quite frequently in all three publications. An example of this is clichés that work as topos of reality (e.g. 'please *get a grip* on reality'). Even in the examples where clichés working as one specific type of topos feature more prominently, such as the topos of denial in members of the public's comments made on the website of the *Daily Mail*, or the topos of uselessness in members of the public's comments on the website of *The Guardian*, we are not presuming any ideological reason as to why clichés as topoi of denial would appear more frequently in an arguably more conservative publication, whilst the topos of uselessness would appear more frequently in an allegedly more liberal publication. Therefore, we cannot really argue that editorial stance plays a significant role in the type of argumentation technique each cliché in the data employs. In fact, we have provided some examples of comments against Brexit appearing in the *Daily Mail* and pro-Brexit in *The Guardian*. However, we do acknowledge that the views of the readership may have some alignment and influence from the editorial political leanings which may have an impact on the overall discourse and strategy (i.e. legitimisation, othering) with clichés being off-the-self convenient tools chosen as argumentation devices. This is consistent with views from SM-CDS that 'discourse is independent of the medium although the magnitude, penetrability, and formal aspects of its realised forms may be heavily influenced by the medium' (KhosraviNik, 2017: 585). What we do argue is that, as suggested by the data analysed, clichés do play an important role in shaping arguments in the postings due to their ubiquity that allows for versatility of use, as demonstrated. Further to this, as shown by their use in both sides of the argument, their socially shared formulaic nature allows them to function as stereotypical arguments that work as 'common sense reasoning schemes' (Van Dijk 2000: 98) for the strategic usages outlined alone.

In the context of this chapter, we focus on how clichés work as topoi that carry ideational components from where language users choose tools for finding arguments to heighten and defend their point of view (Aristotle, 2006). We did mention an interpersonal function briefly but did not explore that aspect in the data analysis. However, it is worth pointing out a number of interpersonal aspects of clichés in comments that are afforded by the nature of online participatory conversation.

The first one has to do with the positioning of clichés appearing at the end of a comments. Consider the following examples (emphasis in originals):

(30) PLEASE REMEMBER THAT LEAVE WON.
      LEAVE NOW WITHOUT A DEAL.
      LEAVE MEANS LEAVE (BBC)

(31) The best vote we've had of the British people was the referendum and the majority who voted, voted to leave and leave we must!!
      END OF. (BBC)

(32) Oh well done to them. But until it reaches 17.4 million and one I'm not interested. *Jog on* (Mail)

Interpersonally, the use of capitals, which in some cases could be argued to be deliberate, as in the second extract, from a multimodal perspective (e.g. Kress and van Leeuwen, 2006) points to an emphatic and assertive reinforcement of the ideational meaning of the cliché-indicating confrontation. This is an important feature of online communication where capitals letters are considered 'shouting' as a way of conveying emphasis, demonstrating annoyance, insulting the interlocutor, or showing a similar expression of negative emotional state (Serafini and Clausen, 2012). But more importantly, by placing clichés at the end of the comments and formulating them as categorical assertions, the contributors seem to be signalling closure of the argument thereby contracting the dialogic space excluding dissident voices and suppressing any opposing positions. This can be explained by reference to appraisal theory's engagement resources in which the textual voice acts to overtly reject or counter a contrary position (Martin and White, 2005). When it comes to participatory communication in news comments, this system is highly relevant as it helps explain the way in which users 'self-expressly announce their personal attitudinal positions to various value positions referenced in a text' whilst simultaneously dis/aligning 'their putative addressees into a community of shared values and beliefs' (Aragbuwa, 2020: 134). Without going into the details of the framework and its various analytical categories, we suggest that the placement of the clichés at the end of the comment thereby 'act to close down or contract the space for (dialogic alternatives) [...] and [...] increase the interpersonal cost to those who would challenge the viewpoint being advanced' (White, 2003: 268). This is certainly an aspect that merits further in-depth investigation.

The analysis also demonstrates the versatility of clichés to help construe arguments and how they can commonly be used to either attack a concept or policy – such as Brexit – or attack another individual or group – such as Remain voters, or even to show both sides of the same argument. In (33), the cliché is used to assert the reality of the UK leaving the EU and therefore point out the banality of the opposition. Contrariwise, in (34), the cliché is used to argue that the reality is that Brexit voters have been misled, which legitimises opposition to Brexit.

(33) *Bottom line* is we are leaving, sorry chaps but that is what will happen, I am not one for gambling but I am risking a pound on it (A pound rather than a euro because *lets be straight* we never really joined) (Guardian)

(34) *Bottom line* is, the brexiteers have been had! We are not leaving, at least not with a no deal wto exit! The madness of May in my view was to frustrate and confuse, all with the intent to remain! (Guardian)

Both of these examples appear in the comments to the news item, separate from each other – the latter appears five entries after the first one and does not reply to it. We therefore do not consider it to be a rhetorical repetition made in response to the first comment in particular but a generic contribution in response the news item.

In other cases, the same clichés are used dialogically as a way of reversing a previously made argument and offer a counter argument, as in example (35), which responds to the headline (and article) in *The Guardian* 'Nine days from "Brexit day", does anyone have a clue what's happening?' that has a rhetoric around the incompetence to carry out Brexit.

(35) I have learned that *strong and stable means weak and incompetent* and *Brexit does not mean Brexit* (Guardian)

The comment uses clichés embodying topoi of strength and uselessness to eventually revert the topos of authority in *Brexit means Brexit* used by Theresa May and featuring in many comments in the corpus. The comment therefore works dialogically and intertextually to challenge the topos of authority and subvert arguments about an efficient Brexit strategy.

A further interesting use of clichés among comments is for deconstructing an argument, again based on the recurrent 'Brexit means Brexit' expression not only by the government officials but also – and mostly – by users' comments.

(36) *enough is enough*, well what an argument like *leave means leave, brexit means brexit* ? really do you know what you voted for ? the problems are so easy to solve ? really thats why 3 years later nobody knows so great leave without a deal fantastic like *shoot yourself in both feet* ... please *get a grip on reality*. (Mail)

In this comment (kept as it originally appeared in the media platform) the user uses the expression as a way of challenging the arguments based on the authority of the vote claimed by Brexit supporters and calling for common sense and reality in order to legitimate the petition.

Finally, a few words on context-specific expressions that we have considered clichés due to their frequent use in the corpus, the meaning they carry and the way in which they are used both ideationally and interpersonally. A number of expressions have been coined during the Brexit debate to refer to Brexit supporters such as 'brextremists', 'brexit camp' and 'wrexiteers', as well as Remain supporters, for example, 'remoaners' and 'remainacs'. These are well-documented Brexit-induced neologisms (Lalić-Krstin and Silaški, 2018) which have been introduced, as with other forms of linguistic creativity, and frequently used due to their compactness, that is, their ability to reduce lexical items whilst conveying the maximum amount of information (Benczes, 2009), evoking a much more vivid image than their full forms (e.g. 'remoaners' versus 'remainers are moaners') (Lalić-Krstin and Silaški, 2018), an aspect that is consistent with our definition of clichés in this book. According to Benczes, another principle behind this type of creativity is analogy, whereby speakers apply the principles of previously learned combinations to new word combinations. Considering 'Brexit' being a neologism in itself, it is no surprise that new words are formed and coined in relation to it. Further expressions found in the corpus and considered as clichés for analysis, mostly from the leave side, are *make Britain great again* and *fake news*, which clearly work as intertextual references to Donald Trump's arguments during his presidential campaign and in defence of his arguments of policies when in power.

According to Lalić-Krstin and Silaški (2018), Brexit is a prime example of a political event that is easily prone to the formation of new coinages given its controversial nature. These words carry extensive ideational meaning not only as a result of the controversial, politicised and highly debated and questioned operationalisation of Brexit but also due to the intertextual and interdiscursive chains that come into the morphological process. Take, for example, 'brextremists' (Brexit supporter + extremist), which carries associations with religious extremist discourses. Given the extensive usage of all such words in current political discourse, they are part of our everyday repertoire and hence tools for easily accessible socially shared knowledge that are selected, blended and coined strategically for ideological purposes. They, in turn, become naturalised ways of referring to and labelling groups (e.g. Remoaners, Brextremists) thereby facilitating the construal of 'us' versus 'them' paradigms, at an interpersonal level. Clearly this is an area that grants further research and investigation (see Buckledee, 2018 for an analysis of the language of Brexit) and it is too early to claim them as cliché given their recent development. However, we considered them important in the context of this chapter given their extensive use and the meanings they construe. These become a crucial point that needs investigating in the context of participatory media, as mediated platforms are the site par excellence for their construction, uptake, activation and propagation given the affordances of such spaces.

All in all, we see that clichés work as tools to construe arguments with the intention of legitimising certain views, actions or practices or creating separation between users who share the same view and those that do not. In the context of the participatory media genre, where opinions are co-constructed in an interactive and institutionalised space, clichés become accessible rhetorical tools for dialogic reception, negotiation and co-construction of meanings that facilitate the construal of ideational meanings and interpersonal positionings.

CHAPTER FOUR

Clichés as Social Cognition

4.1 Clichés as Socio-cognitive Representations

Rooted within the discipline of social psychology (e.g. Moscovici and Duveen, 2000), the notion of social representations refers to ways of creating and communicating reality and common sense. Moscovici (1981: 181) defines social representations as:

a set of concepts, statements and explanations originating in daily life in the course of inter-individual communications. They are the equivalent, in our society, of the myths and beliefs systems in traditional societies; they might even be said to be the contemporary version of common sense.

Social representations are inscribed within a shared framework of pre-existing thought and are attached to the systems of belief, anchored in values and traditions (Sperber, 1985). Van Dijk adds that social beliefs, such as attitudes, are thus 'constituent elements' of social representations (2001: 46) and suggests that cognitive structures have an important discourse dimension; that is, the acquisition, use and change of social representations occurs through discourse (van Dijk, 2001).

As the main proponent of sociocognitive discourse analysis, van Dijk argues that personal and social cognition is the interface which mediates discourse structures and social structures (van Dijk, 2001), therefore any study of discourse as language in action should encompass an exploration of the social, the cognitive and the discourse components and their interaction with each other.

Discourse analysts, referring to them as sociocognitive representations (SCRs) (e.g. Koller, 2008a; Bullo, 2014), have used the term to indicate underlying frameworks of thought used in certain discursive practices that fulfil ideational and interpersonal functions (e.g. Halliday, 1994, cf. Chapter 2). SCRs are instantiated by linguistic features or structures which work as anchors for cognitive models in the text and allow for analytical deconstruction. Based on this premise, Koller (2008a) argues that, in offering a shared frame of reference in communication, SCRs make available taken for granted, naturalised knowledge in hegemonic discourses, mainly instantiated through metaphorical meanings. Following from Augoustinos and Walker (1995) who also point out that, in being communicated, social representations can be seen as establishing social relationships, Bullo (2014) explores SCRs as carrying attitudinal positions manifested in evaluative language.

In terms of clichés, Bullo (2019) poses that they can be seen as SCRs in that they are socially shared within a speech community and rely on the interlocutors' reservoir of knowledge for their sense making and meaning-potential realisation. Therefore, they can be seen as pre-existing frameworks of thought embodying a stock of collective experience (Moscovici and Duveen, 2000) that are naturalised and conventionalised in discourse allowing them to carry, and construe, ideational meanings (Bullo, 2019). Further to this, by relying on such reservoirs of socially shared meanings, they allow communication in a mechanical way 'without reflection [...] routinely and in a facile manner' (Zijderveld, 1979: 58) whilst also offering a cognitive 'comfort zone' facilitating a 'weak [...] attachment' to the propositional content (Down and Warren, 2008: 8). As such, they are safe resources for negotiating interpersonal relationships thereby also fulfilling an interpersonal function (Bullo, 2019).

4.2 Brands in Advertising and Corporate Discourse

An interesting site to explore clichés as sociocognitive resources in action is corporate discourse, and brands in particular (e.g. Koller, 2008a). Brands are defined as evolving complexes embodying and carrying cultural information and expectations associated with a product purposefully developed with the aim of engaging consumers at emotional, moral and intellectual levels (Holt, 2004). As such, they are interesting sociocognitive complexes worth exploring as they are able to 'communicate and reinforce particular concepts through various texts' (Koller, 2008a: 392). Brands allow the establishment of a strong and stable set of associations in the minds and memories of consumers' (Moore, 2003: 335). Koller (2008b: 432) argues that 'brands are cognitive structures jointly held by members of a group' and therefore provide 'a shared frame of reference for communication'. As such, they can be related to SCRs. Brands carry several levels of meaning, such as 'attributes, benefits, values, culture, and personality' (Kapferer, 1997: 38), which advertisers may operationalise when advertising products or services (Kotler, 2003). Brands communicate the ideal self (Markus and Nurius, 1986);

that is, the image an organisation 'wishes to convey to its stakeholders' (Kapferer 2002: 185).

In this work, we demonstrate how clichés as cognitive structures used in advertising and corporate mission statements carry shared knowledge that allows brands to convey the 'ideal self' and encapsulated values whilst also positioning themselves interpersonally in relation to various stakeholders.

As the 'placement of announcements and messages in time or space [that] seek(s) to inform and/or persuade' (American Marketing Association, 2021: online), advertising constitutes a site par excellence where cognitive models instantiating interpersonal discursive functions can be witnessed. Kotler (2003) proposed that advertisers resort to different strategic appeals when conveying the message content of an advert. Rational appeals are built on fact, reason, information and logic (Akbari, 2015). They resort to consumers' logical and rational decisions about products or services primarily emphasising attributes such as quality, value or performance (Albers-Miller and Stafford, 1999). Contrariwise, emotional appeals aim to elicit positive emotions and elicit 'brand personality' (Akbari, 2015: 480). They try to induce feelings and create positive associations with the product or service advertised (Albers-Miller and Stafford, 1999). Emotional appeals can elicit excitement, fear, love, nostalgia, pleasure, sorrow, anger, fear, etc. (Moriarty, 1991; Verma, 2009). Such appeals rely on attitudinal dispositions that form part of the SCRs of the audience that may go on to elicit attitudes towards the brand. In fact, emotional appeals, in particular, have been proven to affect attitudes towards the brand (Aaker et al., 1986). In this way brands can be seen to 'represent the cognitive-affective concepts stakeholders maintain about a particular product' (Koller, 2008a: 391).

Cognitive models contained in clichés can also be seen to construe ideational meanings by virtue of the shared knowledge they carry in corporate mission statements. According to Swales and Rogers (1995: 225) mission statements fulfil two functions: firstly, they allow the internal communication of corporate identity for the purposes of identification and cohesion. They also allow corporations to 'both actualise and constitute their sense of a self' (Abrams 1999: 206) into an established set of social representations that enable comparisons with other companies and products (Koller, 2008b). Therefore, organisational culture and brand identity are communicated, reinforced and reproduced in mission statements (Christensen and Askegaard 2001). Further to this, mission statements try to persuade stakeholders of the value of the organisation

(Swales and Rogers, 1995: 225) by drawing on specific models to communicate a particular impression of an organisation's agents, their actions
and the relations between them (Koller, 2008b). In other words, they
fulfil ideational and interpersonal functions (cf. Chapter 2) which are
realised through language choices and facilitated by clichés owing to the
shared knowledge they carry as SCRs.

4.3 Data and Methods

Following the genres of corporate discourse discussed, two data sets
were used for this chapter which we outline here. Firstly, we introduce
the two adverts used for analysis. Following this, we outline the process
of collecting mission statements and provide a description of the data
set and its characteristics, including the main industries in which they
were found. We then outline the methods of data analysis applied to
both data sets.

Data Description

For the first data set, two adverts were selected for analysis. The adverts
were selected on the basis that they use clichés, as per our definition
in Chapter 2. Fifteen adverts in English published in print and television in the UK were collected. Some adverts used more than one cliché.
Nine of those were found through internet searches and six featured
in magazines or posters that we came across in the two-year period of
writing this book. The adverts selected for analysis belonged to the latter category. They were chosen partly for that reason, as they appeared
'naturally' in everyday life and partly because the organisations were
kind enough to respond to our request for permission to use the ads in
this book.[1]

The ads advertise UK products and services and each one illustrates a
type of advertising appeal put forward by Kotler (2003); that is, emotional
and rational. The first advert featured in a local South Manchester magazine, delivered to the population of that postcode though the letterbox. It

---

[1] It is worth mentioning that they were the only two small local businesses. All others we
approached were large organisations from whom we did not obtain any responses and, as
such, we did not use their advertisements despite the creative ways in which clichés were
used to engage the public.

Figure 4.1 'Separation is no one's cup of tea' advert (copyright by Slater Heelis https://www.slaterheelis.co.uk/)

advertises legal services for divorce proceedings and financial settlements for Manchester-based law firm Slater Heelis (Figure 4.1).[2] The second advert was a poster displayed in the London Underground. It advertises high-end socks produced by the London Socks Company (Figure 4.2).[3]

For the second data set, 250 mission statements were gathered from companies listed in the London Stock Exchange's *1,000 Companies to Inspire Britain* 2019 report. The report identifies 1,000 small to medium-size enterprises in the UK that are expanding and are seen as dynamic.[4] Mission statements were extracted from each company's website that appeared in the list alphabetically and were added to the corpus. Exclusion criteria included websites that were not working, sites without information that could be seen to resemble a mission

---

[2] We are grateful to Slater Heelis for granting us permission to use this advert free of charge. https://www.slaterheelis.co.uk/.

[3] We are grateful to the London Socks Company for granting us permission to use this advert free of charge. https://www.londonsockcompany.com/.

[4] The list can be accessed by following this link: https://www.lseg.com/resources/1000-companies-inspire/2018-report-1000-companies-uk/search-1000-companies-uk-2018.

Figure 4.2 'Sometimes it pays to think inside the box' advert (copyright by https://londonsockcompany.com)

statement and companies that were part of a group which did not have a single mission statement. The texts then were grouped according to the industry sector to which organisations belong and the total number of clichés found across all texts within each industry was recorded (Table 4.2). A corpus of 71,915 words (average 288 words per text) was created.

The mission statements were perused individually and any instance of formulaic language that could be understood as cliché, as per our definition in Chapter 2, was highlighted. Upon finding 112 different clichés, the texts were rescanned using Atlas.ti to check for iterations. A total of 442 clichés were found across 250 texts in the corpus with a mean number of 1.7 clichés per text.

Table 4.1 Frequency of clichés		
Cliché	n	Texts n
at the heart of	31	29
pride ourselves on	31	30
everything we do	26	25
at the forefront of	20	19
track record of	18	14
first class	13	11
a wealth of	12	10
go the extra mile	11	10
sets us apart	11	11
state of the art	9	9
forward-thinking	8	8
peace of mind	8	8
second to none	8	8
best in class	7	7
one stop shop	7	7
put (the customer) first	7	7
cutting edge	6	6
each and every	6	6
from strength to strength	6	6
lead the way	6	6
at the centre of	5	5
at the core of	5	4
every step of the way	5	5
is key	5	5
small enough to/big enough to	5	5
stand still	5	5

Table 4.1 shows raw frequencies of the clichés identified as used more than ten times in the corpus in descending order and the number of texts containing each cliché.

A total of eighty-five other clichés were used less than five times in the corpus. They appear 144 times overall across 141 texts with an average frequency of 0.1634 times per 10,000 words. These include, among others: *in our DNA* (n4), *fit for purpose* (n3), *day in day out* (n2), *one size fits all* (n2), *110 percent* (n1), *ahead of the game* (n1), *down to earth* (n1),

Table 4.2 Most frequent clichés per industry

Industry	Texts n	Clichés n across all texts/industry	At the heart of	Pride ourselves on	Everything we do	At the forefront of	Track record of	First class	A wealth of	Go the extra mile	Set us apart
			31	31	26	20	18	13	12	11	11
Architecture and engineering	5	6				x			x		
Automotive	4	12	x			x				x	x
Building and landscape services	24	34	x	x	x	x	x	x	x		x
Building materials	5	5		x					x		
Engineering and construction	30	56	x	x	x	x	x	x	x	x	
Farming and fishery	6	10	x	x	x						
Financial services	25	45	x		x		x	x	x		
Food and beverage	14	28	x	x		x		x			x
Healthcare	16	30	x	x	x	x		x		x	
Information technology	21	38	x	x	x	x	x				x
Legal and accounting	4	4					x				
Leisure	6	11	x	x	x				x	x	
Manufacturing	13	36	x	x	x	x		x		x	x

Most frequent clichés/industry

	Texts n	Clichés n across all texts/industry	At the heart of	Pride ourselves on	Everything we do	At the forefront of	Track record of	First class	A wealth of	Go the extra mile	Set us apart
Metal manufacturing and engineering	8	15	x		x						
Oil and gas support services	2	3								x	
Postal services	1	3		x				x			
Printing	2	6					x			x	
Professional services	12	18	x	x	x		x	x			x
Real estate	4	10	x	x	x			x			
Rental and Leasing	2	6	x	x	x		x				
Research	2	2		x	x						
Retail	11	17	x	x	x						
Transportation services	6	14	x	x				x		x	x
Waste management	2	3									
Wholesale	6	10	x	x		x				x	

first and foremost (n1), *in a nutshell* (n1), *in no small part* (n1), *scratch the surface* (n1), *sky is the limit* (n1), *stay ahead of the curve* (n1) and *sum of parts* (n1). Interestingly, the expressions that feature in the adverts (*not my cup of tea* and *think outside the box*) do not appear in the mission statements' corpus.

For the in-depth analysis, we selected the clichés used more than ten times in the corpus. Table 4.2 shows the most frequently used clichés in the mission statements and the industries in which they feature. Some clichés appear more than once in a single text and/or texts in the same industry.

Analytical Tools

Given the sociocognitive nature of clichés, as conceptualised in this chapter, we started the analysis by establishing a connection of word sense to mental concepts. We did so by identifying semantic macrostructures in the corpus indicating 'global meanings, topics or themes' (van Dijk, 2009: 68) that provide a framework for SCRs using corpus linguistics tools. A semantic tagging of the most frequent clichés in the mission statement corpus, as well as the ones found in the two adverts, using the vertical output style of the Semantic Analysis System (USAS) online English tagger was carried out in order to identify the semantic domains for each word. The semantic tagging is useful in that 'tags show semantic fields which group together word senses that are related by virtue of their being connected at some level of generality with the same mental concept' (Archer et al., 2002: 1). In multiple tag cases, the tag that was closest in meaning to the contextual use of the clichés was preserved and the clichés were grouped into the specific semantic domains as per the USAS '21 major discourse fields' (Archer et al., 2002). Table 4.3 shows the main discourse fields where the contextual meaning of the clichés explored fitted, the corresponding subfield and other tags that contribute to the contextual meaning of the expression, when relevant.

Once the macrostructures were identified and clichés grouped within them, we analysed the clichés by examining the features of language they contain (i.e. metaphors, verb processes, actors, and the like.) and their usage in context by reference to the co-text. In the mission statements corpus, the latter was carried out by examining three collocates to the right and to the left of the expression using AntConc. Collocates with mutual information scores greater than three were selected given their conventional significance (Church and Hanks, 1990; Webster, 2018). Once functional words (e.g. the, in) were discarded, the collocates were then organised into themes by reference to the local discourse in

Table 4.3 Clichés per discourse field

Discourse field	n	Subfield	Relevant discourse field 2	Cliché	Corpus
Numbers and measurements	60	Entirety		Everything we do	Mission statements
		Linear order	Money and commerce	First class	Mission statements
		Quantities	Movement, location, travel and transport	Go the extra mile	Mission statements
		Distance		Sets us apart	Mission statements
General and abstract terms	51	Importance		At the heart of	Mission statements
		Importance		At the forefront of	Mission statements
Emotional actions, states and processes	32	Contentment	Names and grammatical categories	Pride ourselves on	Mission statements
		Liking		Not […] cup of tea	Advertisement
Psychological actions, states and processes	19	Ability		Track record of	Mission statements
		Thought and belief	Movement, location, travel and transport	Think inside the box	Advertisement
Money and commerce	12	Money: affluence		A wealth of	Mission statements

concordance lines considering the immediate co-text (van Dijk, 1977a) and the most predominant features of language found were analysed.

The selection of parameters for analysis of the features of language for functional analysis of clichés in use considers the chapter premise that clichés evoke SCRs that allow brands to project an ideal self to the public (Koller, 2008b) and the book premise that clichés fulfil ideational and interpersonal functions in discourse. In light of this, we deployed a number of tools that allow the examination of different layers of meanings.

- Transitivity: in order to examine how clichés were used to construe the brand image or self, a close examination of grammatical choices by means of transitivity analysis was carried out. This looked at the role given to clichés in the clause and their interaction with other participants. This system allows for a thorough account of the construction of inner and outer experience by the selection of verb processes, circumstances and participants in a clause. As per Halliday and Matthiessen's (2004) transitivity system, relational process types identify or provide information about the qualities of the participant (participants token/value; carrier/attribute), material processes construe outer experience (participants actor/goal) and mental processes represent inner experience (participants senser/phenomenon). Circumstances can be important in revealing certain aspects of experience.
- Social actors: in order to explore how brands are personified and construed by clichés, we explore explicit actors by reference to van Leeuwen's (1996) social actor representation framework. We mainly focus on how actors, mainly brands and customers, are represented and grammatically endowed with agency through personalisation (by means of personal pronouns, names, and other forms of nominalisation) and collectivisation ('the team').
- Appraisal: in this chapter, we refer to the attitude system of the appraisal framework when clichés are seen to convey attitudinal positioning through evaluation. We do not however focus solely on this or analyse it in depth but rather make reference to the generic categories of appreciation (evaluation based on aesthetic grounds), judgement (evaluation based on moral/ethical grounds) and affect (evaluation based on emotional dispositions). A full outline of the attitude system of appraisal is provided in Chapter 5.
- Other features such as tense, modality markers and deictic devices are also highlighted when relevant in the examination of choices in the co-text to examine how clichés represent brands and position themselves interpersonally in relation to various stakeholders. These are defined as they are discussed in the data analysis section.
- Metaphor and metonymy: several clichés take the form of metaphorical expressions. We examine these by reference to Conceptual Metaphor Theory (CMT) (Lakoff and Johnson 1980). CMT poses that metaphors help us understand abstract concepts by borrowing structures from more concrete ones. Thus, one abstract concept (referred

to as target domain) is understood in terms of another, usually more concrete one (known as source domain) and realised through a metaphoric linguistic expression. For example, the conceptual metaphor LIFE IS A JOURNEY is linguistically manifested in expressions such as *I am at a crossroads*. We categorised clichés as metaphorical by use of the metaphor identification procedure (MIP) (Pragglejaz Group 2007), contrasting the basic and contextual meanings of every lexical component in the expression and identifying those with a clash between both meanings as metaphorical.

4.4 Findings

Clichés in Advertisements

In this section we present two adverts that use clichés. We start by introducing the adverts and their thematic macrostructure and offer a text-level description of usage. We then discuss how they fulfil an interpersonal function of persuasion by reference to the advertising appeals outlined earlier.[5] We structured the findings in relation to the themes identified by the semantic tagging based on the premise that word senses are related somehow to mental concepts, as discussed.

Preference and Emotion

The advert features two white cups on a black background (see Figure 4.1, above). The cups have 'his' and 'hers' written on them in blue and pink with an icon of a moustache and a heart in the same colours respectively. The conjunction 'or' features in between the cups. Underneath, written in yellow capital letters we find the copy 'separation is no one's cup of tea'. In the next line, in smaller case there is an offer 'to help you find the best deal' followed by information about the services provided by the company. The company logo and contact details are found at the bottom of the advert on a green background.

The semantic tagging that we found most appropriate shows this expression within the emotional actions, states and processes semantic

---

[5] Both expressions found in these adverts appear in any online search for clichés and published dictionaries of clichés (e.g. Fountain 2012; Rogers 1991) and they are also considered idioms (e.g. Cambridge University Press, 2017). We do not focus on the distinction in this book but it is worth mentioning that they are examples of the fuzzy boundaries between the two discussed in Chapter 2.

field indicating liking. We decided on this field given that the subfield 'liking' was more in line with the contextual and metaphorical meaning of the cliché and the cognitive models of unpleasantness and lack of inclination it evokes.

Grammatically, the cliché acts as a participant attribute of the carrier 'separation', as a nominalised process, in a relational clause. Experientially, the expression attributes negative emotions to the termination of relationships. The latter achieves its force by virtue of the idiomatic cliché. As a versatile expression that can be assigned to different emoters not my/her/his *cup of tea*, this expression is widely used to indicate lack of preference, inclination or interest towards people, entities or practices, working as a token of affect in the appraisal framework (cf. Chapter 5). In addition, in using the generic 'no one', the advert appeals to shared knowledge and feelings towards the practice and therefore construes solidarity with the targeted consumer.

Since tea is considered to be one of the most widely consumed beverages in the UK with peculiarities in the ways the way in which people prepare it, the cliché is highly idiomatic and culturally grounded. As such, the cup of tea is a metonymy for Britishness and the practice of tea drinking in particular.

The cliché operates within the primary metaphor FOOD IS THOUGHT, the cup of tea expression reflects the extended TEA DRINKING AS PREFERENCE metaphor. The cliché also works by means of a metonymic relationship where the cup of tea stands for the action of tea drinking in an OBJECT FOR ACTION relationship.

Visually the advert creates gender separation within a heteronormative gender discourse, assuming the heterosexuality of the consumers, by virtue of the pink and blue wording of the pronouns his and hers on the cups as semiotic markers of gender, as well as traditional gendered symbols such as the heart on the woman's cup suggesting emotion and the moustache on the man's cup symbolising, perhaps, masculinity, virility, etc. (Eyben, 2019). Both semiotic constructs stand metonymically for man and woman. The conjunction 'or' marks a contrast between the gender constructs construing opposition and, potentially, antagonism and reliant on the cultural expectations of dividing 'community property' in divorce (i.e. 'who gets what?'). All these semiotic and cognitive systems, albeit their conventionality, are used deliberately and consciously to frame the process of relationships dissolution as unpleasant, burdensome and taxing and convey the emotional appeal of the advert (Kotler, 2003) as effectively as possible whilst also appealing to a wider population and hence its social cognition.

Concurrently, the brand positions itself as empathetic towards such emotional states and as providers of solutions to relieve the consumers from such burdens. Interestingly, the discourse involved in the actual advertising of the service is factual, informative, inclusive ('civil partnerships') and more logical sounding, thereby suggesting a rational appeal (Akbari, 2015). The expression 'first-class' is used to qualify the service and evoke SCRs indicating superiority, excellence and cost (see later section for a full analysis of uses of 'first-class' in mission statements). The brand features prominently as an actor in this part of the advert by being named (Slater Heelis), personalised by means of pronouns ('our', 'we' or collectivised, 'team'), and directly addressing the specified customer ('you') as opposed to the generified, as earlier, 'no one' (van Leeuwen, 1996). These resources purposefully construe a brand–client relationship by juxtaposition of emotional vs rational appeals where the clichés are successfully exploited to evoke corresponding cognitive models for the purposes of establishing interpersonal relationships of solidarity and problem solving and construing a brand identity effectively.

Locality and Rationality

The advert features the company logo at the top of the page, followed by the copy 'sometimes it pays to think inside the box'. Underneath, on the right-hand side, we find a box of elegantly displayed socks on a stool with text about the company and the products on the left-hand side. This is signed by the company's founders.

This advert relies entirely on the consumers' knowledge of the original cliché 'think outside the box' and, potentially, negative associations towards the use of clichés. The semantic tagging positions this expression across the psychological actions, states and processes discourse field, indicating thought and belief, and the movement, location, travel and transport discourse fields. But it is the latter, by virtue of the subfields of location and direction tag, that gives the cliché, and this extended one in particular, its rhetorical force.

Both the original and this novel take on the cliché operate within the CONTAINER metaphor. The conventional metaphor 'think outside the box' is frequently employed as a way or urging others to imagine atypical, novel solutions to problems as innovative ideas are found in an alternative space in relation to the enclosed surroundings of the box.

In the case of this advert, the embodied physical metaphor plays 'an important role in creative cognition' (Gibbs, 2014: 176) and works by virtue of the reversal of the original deictic 'outside' to 'inside' in order to exploit the conventional metaphors for rhetorical purposes (Semino, 2008). This is accompanied by the time referent 'sometimes' indicating lack of frequency and the positive appraisal of the activity ('it pays') creating the co-text for the rhetorical aim of subverting SCRs associated with the original cliché and conveying a sense of exclusivity. By reversing the deictic centre, the consumer is drawn to the box as a metonymy for the product and into the box as a metaphor for uniqueness and selectness. These are framed within a monetary metaphor where the successful outcome of a deal is associated with monetary value, as indicated by the source domain 'pay'. The adverbial 'sometimes' indicating lack of frequency draws on knowledge of the recurrent use of original expression and reinforces its generic metaphorical use (i.e. original is outside) whilst hinting at exclusivity, thereby positioning the brand as a provider of an exclusive traditional, everyday product. In so doing the conventional metaphor is purposefully reversed and stretched to indicate that exceptionality and exclusivity are found in the metaphorical, and literal, container.

The rest of the text in the advert speaks directly to the consumer. Both the brand and the consumer are personalised by pronouns (i.e. 'you', 'we', 'our') creating a close relationship that offers an understanding of corporate life ('we used to be right where you are'). The text creates a location semantic space positioning both the personalised brand and the consumer in the same places ('where you are', 'the tube', 'city', 'office') using deictics indicating location ('find', 'everywhere', 'on the ankles', 'around') and the movement metaphor ('step up'). The advert appeals to a consumer that identifies with the brand ('our jobs in the city') and appeals to a sense of belonging and corporate identity ('ankles of CEOs', 'gents') by offering quality, comfort and positive feelings ('feel great'). In this way, the advert conveys a rational appeal, featuring the quality of the product and the preferences of the ideal consumer who is construed as a member of the same group, through the metaphorical sense of 'where you are', therefore building solidarity with the consumer, and the general public that will be at that location looking at the advert ('London').

Clichés in Corporate Mission Statements

As with the adverts, this section has also been structured in relation to the semantic tagging themes identified to show relatedness of words to mental concepts. As per the semantic tagging, there are five macrostructures encapsulating the main thematic areas of clichés in the organisational discourses. These macrostructures account for the 'global meaning' of SCRs and constitute the bases for the text-level description of clichés in use and convey the main values attributed to the brand: confidence, priority, expertise, difference, effort and quality.

Most clichés examined in this section, as the most frequent ones in the data set, are textually structured by conceptual metaphors, evaluative language, processes and action markers, etc. We examine their function in discourse by reference to the parameters already outlined.

Numbers and Measurements

The majority of clichés under this category instantiate numbering or measurement of some kind evoking superiority, difference or wholeness of the brand.

everything we do

This highly frequent expression is normally combined with others, e.g. *at the heart/forefront of everything we do* in the data set. Structurally it represents action and processes, and agency, of the also explicitly represented actors in the expression; that is, the brand ('we'). The semantic tagging suggests 'entirety or maximum' evoking wholeness and completeness.

In most cases, the expression works to foreground service, as the highest thematic collocate, as the main actor with a clear formula of 'clarity', 'values embodied', 'client/customer at the centre/heart', 'standards' + of 'everything we do'.

(1) We apply these standards to *everything we do*
(2) Customers are central to *everything we do*

Grammatically, the cliché works as a circumstance in material (1) and relational (2) process types.

(3) In *everything we do* we strive to find the simple answer

In (3) it works as a circumstance in a prepositional clause. Ontologically, this functions as a container metaphor ('in') where the entirety of operations (i.e. 'everything we do') is contained.

More often than not, however, the cliché works as an extension of the circumstance of another cliché:

(4) Community is *at the heart* of *everything we do*
(5) Innovation is *at the core* of *everything we do*

first-class

Textually realised and an ordinal ranking, this expression recalls everyday models of postal services, transport, and other forms of exemplary service that all serve to further reinforce the SCR indicating superiority and excellence. In itself, the ordinal item 'first' and the nominal form 'class' indicating 'affiliation', constitute positive evaluation, falling under the appreciation category, valuation subcategory, of the appraisal framework, which is concerned with entities or things (cf. Chapter 5).

In terms of usage of the expression in the texts, as shown in examples 6–8, unsurprisingly, the collocate analysis indicates that the main actors are the brand, indicated by the plural pronouns 'we', 'our' and service, expressed in lexemes such as 'treatment', 'provision', 'solution', 'attention'.

(6) We will deliver a *first-class* service ensuring that the clients arrive in a safe, well-controlled and happy environment

(7) Our trading partners enjoy a *first-class* service

(8) Our unique and rewarding approach means we have *first-class* relationships with our key delivery partners

Interestingly, this is one of the most ubiquitous clichés in how it works as participant in verb processes, with an almost equal distribution across verb process types. For example, in (6) it works as a goal in a material process ('deliver'); in (7) it is construed as a phenomenon of the mental process 'enjoy' with 'trading partners' being the senser; finally, in (8) it functions as an attribute to the carrier 'we' in a relational process, marked by 'have'.

go the extra mile

Lexically realised as the conventional metaphor BUSINESS IS A JOURNEY, mapping business operations to mileage, the cliché works by virtue of the tag indicating the aggregated effort (i.e. 'extra') that allows the quantification of mileage to frame the success narrative and anchor the brands as offering additional services that make a difference in relation to the absent actor that is the competition (van Leeuwen, 1996). The quantifier 'extra' also works as a graduating device intensifying the force of the already positive judgement of ability ('go the mile') in this case indicating an extra amount of effort put into the business operations (Martin and White, 2005, cf. Chapter 5). Below there is a typical example of the cliché as it tends to be found in the data set:

(9)   We *go the extra mile* to make sure safety is not compromised

Normally as a self-standing material process type clause, the 'extra mile' works as the key circumstance for meaning construal. In all cases but one, the actor (i.e. the brand) is personalised in the form of the first-person plural pronoun 'we' and endowed with agency as the actor/doer of the action in the material process 'go'. One notable exception in the corpus is that the use of the extra mile works as a token in a relational clause.

(10)   Our outstanding quality and commitment to *going the extra mile* is your promise of a finished product that meets the brief and makes an impact

In this example, the extra mile is a token in a nominalised action embedded in a parallel construction of two pronominal clauses forming an equative sentence. The clauses contrast complementary nominalised actions of offer and need, projecting closeness between the actors (brand/customer) personalised by the possessive pronouns 'our' and 'your'.

sets us apart

As an ontological metaphor indicating orientation of the 'self' in a space deictically separated from others, this expression recalls models of difference that allow the construal of separation, in this case of the brand from the competition (again as an absent actor) by conceptualising the market as a space construct. Structurally, the expression is a phrasal verb where the actors are also present in the form of an object pronoun, thereby personalising the brand and collectivising its employees (van Leeuwen, 1996). The endowment of agency to actors shows an interesting variation when examining the grammatical role of the expression in the clause structure.

(11)   We *set ourselves apart* from the competition as the only fully integrated fire safety company in the UK
(12)   Our continuous, uncompromising devotion *sets us apart* from other contractors

In (11), actors are seen as active agents in the construction of the difference. The former is marked by both the first-person plural pronoun 'we' and the reflexive 'ourselves', the latter by the material process 'set apart'. In this reflexive construction, the actors and the goal are the same entity.

In the more frequent formula 'set us apart' or 'set + BRAND + apart' (12), we normally find self-attributed qualities, usually marked by the possessive 'our', or services in a nominal group actively affecting a more passively represented agent 'us' (or company name).

Money, Commerce and Affluence

a wealth of

Closely related in models evoked, this expression is highly prominent in the database to indicate abundance, in this case of qualities such as knowledge and expertise. It is structured metaphorically by reference to the KNOWLEDGE IS MONEY metaphor where wealth is mapped to such qualities.

(13) We have *a wealth of* experience in supplying a full turn-key package for our clients

(14) BRAND has developed *a wealth of* knowledge and experience to offer a comprehensive service

The main themes in the collocates are, unsurprisingly, qualities, mainly 'expertise', 'knowledge', 'experience' and the brand, identified by names or personalised by means of personal pronouns 'we', 'us' or collectivised, e.g. 'teams', both mostly engaged in relational (13) or material processes (14).

It is not uncommon to find a combination of clichés as attributes listed in a prepositional clause.

(15) In 2014, the BRAND Company was rebranded and BRAND was born, with an ongoing mission to be the leading supplier of pumps to the trade in the UK, with *first-class* service, *a wealth of* knowledge to share and a commitment to being *at the forefront* of innovation in the industry.

General and Abstract Terms: Importance

at the heart of

This is also a highly frequent cliché in the database structurally realised as a conventionalised conceptual metaphor whereby the business or organisation is conceived of as a (human/animal) body with a heart and personified as a living organism with body parts, with the heart being the central organ. This is consistent with the first-level semantic of meaning in the semantic tagging (the body and the individual). For this analysis, we decided on the general and abstract terms field given that the subfield 'important' was more in line with the contextual and metaphorical meaning of the cliché and the SCRs it evokes.

The expression 'at the heart of', within its HEART-AS-CENTRE metaphorical frame is used to emphasise the centrality of the main participants in the clauses featuring the expression. These are represented in the collocates themes as follows: personalised and collectivised actors ('families', 'communities', 'customer', 'group', 'you/your'), service ('value for money', 'comfort', 'safety') and values and/or qualities ('transparency', 'sustainability', 'simplicity'). Verb processes are mostly relational (i.e. sits, remains, lies and is/are) and there are some material ones (put, place).

The participants are construed both as token (16) or values (17) in relational processes and foregrounded or topicalised accordingly.

(16) *At the heart of* our business are the four core values which translate into everything we do

(17) Each customer is *at the* very *heart* of our business

(18) We place the communities we work in *at the heart of* our operations

Occasionally, the expression works as an obligatory locative circumstance in a material process (18) thereby highlighting the centrality of the participants involved (i.e. 'communities') as goal, or affected entities and the agency of the brand as personalised actors, foregrounded in the first-person plural pronoun 'we'.

It is not unusual to find a combination of two clichés. In fact, nearly 50 per cent of expressions featuring 'at the heart of' are followed by 'everything we do' or its variation 'what we do' normally as values in relational processes (e.g. 'remains', 'lie', 'are') where the values (e.g. 'comfort') and actors (e.g. 'customers') work as token and circumstance.

(19) Strategy, integrity and transparency lies *at the heart* of everything we do

at the forefront of

Positionality of the brand is also conveyed through the cliché *at the forefront of* which is lexicalised as an orientational metaphor mapping market RANKING in relation to the competition onto LOCATION IN SPACE. As a frequent expression in the corpus, its main collocates feature actors, mostly customers ('residents', 'their') and service ('products'), and interestingly, time references ('Tenth year', 'twenty years', '30 years', '40 years', 'still'). The latter is of significance in relation to verb processes and tense, as discussed later. Of special interest are also the verb processes that collocate with 'at the forefront of'. By examination of the co-text, we identified two groups.

In the first group, we found relational processes such as 'maintain', 'stay', 'functions', and various forms of the verb 'to be' (e.g. was, is, have been, being). Such relational verb processes are usually involved in representing a categorical position of superiority of the brand in relation to the competition or practice. These can be interpreted as markers of epistemic modality; that is, they express certainty and a high degree of confidence in such position. These are usually accompanied by time markers ('twenty'/30 years') and tense choice, such as simple past vs present tense with the adverb 'still' marking continuation (20), present perfect (21) and present continuous (22), and rhetorical devices, such as an antithesis contrasting the old and new reinforcing through both the present continuous tense and the time marker '30 years' the historical and current positionality of the brand (23).

(20) BRAND was, and still is, *at the forefront* of the industry
(21) BRAND has been *at the forefront* of retail finance technology and services for over *twenty years*.
(22) (we) are now celebrating our tenth year *at the forefront* of the retail-packed dried fruit...
(23) With a combined knowledge of over 30 years we are bringing fresh ideas to *the forefront* of a traditional and old fashioned trade

In the second group of verb process collating with 'at the forefront of', we found mental processes such as 'endeavours', 'aim', 'seek', normally followed by a form of to-infinitive ('to be', 'to grow'). These normally work to ascertain the desire to achieve the 'ideal self', functioning as deontic modal markers. The goals and actions set to achieve such positions are revealed in the circumstance and endowed with positive attributes ('work tirelessly').

(24) We aim to be *at the forefront* of the sector in empowering people with knowledge about their health
(25) BRAND always endeavours to be *at the forefront* of national best practice and works tirelessly to give the people it supports every opportunity to fulfil their potential

Emotional Actions, States and Processes: Contentment

we pride ourselves on

This is the second most frequently used cliché in the database. The semantic tagging also shows this expression within the emotional actions, states and processes semantic field indicating contentment, realised through discourse structures representing the mental or emotional state of the also represented actors in the expression; that is, the brand ('we', 'ourselves'). The field of names and grammatical categories is also prevalent due to the explicit presence of the pronouns 'ourselves' and 'we'.

The brand is personalised by means of the first-person pronouns and use of proper names (i.e. names of organisations). These also collectivise employees and endows them with agency as sensors of the mental process 'pride'. The latter also works as an evaluative item, indicating positive capacity within the appraisal framework (cf. Chapter 5) anchoring models of competence and confidence in the brand.

In terms of usage, the expression features prominently in the corpus.

(26) At BRAND *we pride ourselves on* being a forward-thinking transportation company

(27) *We pride ourselves on* our team and our commitment to our customers.

(28) *We pride ourselves on* the passion, knowledge and expertise of our team.

Unsurprisingly, the most prominent collocates relate to the brands, whether it is through naming (names of companies) (27), personalisation through plural forms of pronouns ('our') (28) and collectives by means of collective nominals 'group', 'team' and or representing actors such as 'shareholders', 'customer/client' (28) (van Leeuwen, 1996). Another collocates theme relates to skills or qualities, mostly attributed to the actors represented and all with positive valence. These include attributes such as being 'reliable', 'helpful', 'able to', 'unrivalled', 'forward-thinking' (26) and having 'passion', 'knowledge', 'expertise', 'commitment' (27, 28). The majority of such appraisal items belong to the category of judgement, under the sub-classification of capacity in the appraisal system (cf. Chapter 5).

Psychological Actions, States and Processes: Ability

a track record of

Within the macrostructure of psychological actions, states and processes, this cliché works as a marker ability or capacity. Textually manifested as BUSINESS AS SPORT metaphor that 'project(s) the experimental logic or value judgements associated with the scenario' (Boers and Stengers,

2008: 64), this expression works by mapping performance to participating in sporting events[6].

As an evaluative expression in itself (judgement/capacity in the appraisal taxonomy that appraises human behaviour), in using the cliché, the brands construe themselves as high performers by reference to quality ('success', 'innovation') and service ('profit growth', 'results') as the main themes in the collocates. The positive self-evaluation is strengthened by referencing past performance as an indicator of likely future practice. This is frequently achieved by graduating the focus of the evaluation through an epithet expressing attributes such as 'consistent', 'strong', 'proven' or by time references ('10/20 years'). In so doing, the expression instantiates models of expertise and success attributed to the brand.

(29) Our consistent *track record of* innovation and delivery has been recognised by multiple technology and industry awards
(30) NAME's powerful registry engine has more than 20 years' *track record of* uninterrupted service

The positive self-evaluative construal is either topicalised working as a carrier in a relational process (30) or as an attribute (31). The brand is represented collectively and is explicitly present in the form of plural personal or possessive pronouns.

4.5 Discussion

The analysis of clichés in the corporate discourse examined shows that the use of clichés serves to evoke SCRs of superiority and exclusivity, centrality, competence and confidence, ability and expertise as the main values through which brands project. These are consistent with semantic tagging revealing five macrostructures that frame such values: numbers and measurements; importance (general and abstract terms); emotional actions, states and processes; psychological actions, states and processes; and money and commerce. Such SCRs are evoked in two ways. Firstly, they are textually realised through the form the clichés take. Of the eleven most frequently used clichés examined, eight of them take the form of metaphorical models where brands evoke cognitive models by drawing on LOCATION metaphors, or by reference to highly conventionalised metaphors relating to basic aspects of human experience such as JOURNEY, FOOD, MONEY. Other clichés

---

[6] The expression is believed to have originated in horse racing to refer to the best time a horse has ever achieved at a particular track or over a particular distance. It also alludes to track and field records in athletics. Its figurative use dates from the late 1940s. www .idioms.thefreedictionary.com.

take the form of discourse structures representing emotional states ('pride',) or action processes ('do'). Secondly, SCRs are evoked through usage of the clichés in the co-text where SCRs are anchored by linguistic features such as transitivity choices, representations of actors, appraisal, tense and modality and metaphorical models, as demonstrated in the analysis.

From these findings, a number of aspects are worth discussing, starting with the main macrostructure which accounts for the largest number of clichés; that is, the numbers and measurements discourse field in the semantic tagger. We argued that these expressions, by virtue of the shared knowledge they carry, are used to evoke superiority, difference or wholeness of the brand. Hargraves (2014: 84) discusses similar expressions under the category of 'quantifying clichés' and argues that

these expressions veer into cliché when they are used hyperbolically, or without consideration of whether a more precise or less shorworn way of characterising the quantity might serve a better purpose [...] [I]t is often the case that the quantity presented with one of these cliches is surprisingly large.

Two aspects are of interest to this idea. Firstly there is an attitudinal juxtaposition between Hargraves's positioning towards clichés and cliché usage we found. The Hargreaves quote seems to indicate a negative evaluation of the use of expressions that aim to quantify experience without considerations as to whether such quantification is necessary. Interestingly, though, from a functional perspective, we found that a few clichés in this category are used to convey a 'self' assessment of performance of the brand and therefore interpersonally build a relationship of trust with the customer or stakeholder who is the ultimate addressee of the mission statements. Another aspect worth exploring is the 'hyperbolic' attribute assigned, arguably, exaggerations. In the context of mission statements, given the characteristics of the neoliberal market practices where these discourses function, and the element of competition in particular, it is no surprise that brands resort to quantifying clichés in an attempt to construe themselves in a competitive way. In this way, there seems to be a dialectical relationship whereby neoliberal market practices interdiscursively shape branding discourse manifested in quantifying clichés. From a sociocognitive perspective, these clichés evoke cognitive models where attributes such as superiority, difference or wholeness of the brand are purposefully 'exaggerated' and the quantity of such attributes being 'surprisingly large' is indeed the ultimate aim in the ideational construction of the brand.

Another aspect worth discussing is the conventionality of the clichés, mostly the metaphorical ones. Take, for example, *at the heart of*. According to Mussolf (2017), the 'heart-as-centre' concept is highly conventionalised and its metaphorical vividness, as relating to a bodily-organismic source domain, is minimal (p. 645). Despite being considered dead metaphors due to becoming so habitual in usage that have lost their figurative and imaginative value, rendering the initial imagery unrecalled (e.g. *mouth of the river*), some scholars (e.g. Gibbs 1993) have argued that dead metaphors still offer a subconscious mental mapping that evokes the initial imagery that is now seen at a distance. In that respect, clichés operate from the cognitive 'comfort zone', which allows them to evoke vivid imagery from a safe distance (Oswick et al. 2002: 294), hence offering a versatile, non-commitment and potentially vague angle of representation or construal, which could potentially be a good reason for resorting to clichés in the first place.

A further aspect is the result shielded by the cross referencing of clichés and industries in the mission statements corpus. Of the nine most frequently used clichés examined from this corpus, we find that most of them feature in the main industries: building and landscape services, engineering and construction, and manufacture. At this stage we are not in a position to venture any speculation regarding choice and usage of clichés without further enquiry into the demographics (e.g. education level) of the mission statement producers or even further detail about size, location, employees, etc. of the companies but we can venture into a speculation that such clichés are common usage within such CoPs, perhaps conventionalising their usage in the genres of mission statements and advertising, which, in a circular fashion, will then go on to constitute the discourse of such CoPs, as per theories of CDS (e.g. Fairclough and Wodak, 1997) propose.

All in all, the frequency and usage of (repeated) clichés in the corporate discourse examined, by virtue of the shared knowledge carried in such expressions, even if vaguely, allow brands to convey a common, yet reassuring, sense of service that serves as a benchmark for comparison within industries. Clichés thereby offer a mechanical, safe and shared resources constituting a framework to rely upon in the construal of self-ideations and the building and sustaining of relationships.

CHAPTER FIVE

Clichés as Politeness Strategies in Evaluation

5.1 Clichés in Interpersonal Relationships

We discussed in Chapter 2 that clichés fulfil an interpersonal function in that they allow the negotiation of interpersonal relations. In this chapter, we deal with the use of clichés in interaction. We therefore turn to the field of pragmatics, as the study of interpersonal relations are core and central to the study of one of the key fields in pragmatics, that is im/politeness.

The notion of im/politeness encompasses research and practice in the construction of both 'politeness' and 'impoliteness'. In terms of the former, 'politeness' can be seen to encompass 'linguistic behavior through which people indicate that they take others' feelings of how they should be treated into account'. (Kádár, 2017: online). This means that politeness is realised through instances where the interactants in a communicative event assess interactional behaviour in an attempt to build and maintain interpersonal relationships. In acting in what is considered or perceived as polite in a given situation, interactants endeavour to enact shared values within the speech community. In this way, 'the operation of politeness involves valences', which are seen as benchmarks reflecting the perceived moral order of an interactional context/event (Kádár, 2017: online). Conversely, impoliteness can be seen to encompass 'the communication of intentionally gratuitous and conflictive verbal face-threatening acts (FTAs) which are purposefully delivered' (Bousfield 2008: 72). Culpeper (2009: online) argues that 'impoliteness is a negative attitude towards specific behaviours [...]. It is sustained by expectations, desires and/or beliefs about social organisation' not being met.

We find two key concepts of interest in these definitions that are of relevance to this chapter. Firstly, that im/politeness involves attitude, and secondly, they are embedded and constrained by shared social practices. That is, discourse participants engage in expressing, co-constructing or interpreting attitudes that, as we discuss, have evaluative components and that are sustained by expectations, desires and beliefs revolving around social practices. We return to these aspects in Section 5.3. For now, we outline they key aspects of im/politeness research upon which we base our argument in this chapter.

A central concept to most approaches to im/politeness is 'face' (Goffman, 1967: 5), who defines it as:

the positive social value a person effectively claims for himself [*sic*] by the line others assume he is taking during a particular contact. Face is an image of self [which is] delineated in terms of approved social attributes – albeit an image that others may share, as when a person makes a good showing for his profession or religion by making a good showing for himself.

Brown and Levinson's model of politeness is predicated heavily on an evolution of Goffman's notion of face. They conceptualise face in two ways: (1) positive face relates to the positive consistent self-image or 'personality', crucially including the desire that this self-image be appreciated and approved of, claimed by interactants; and (2) negative face is the basic claim to territories, personal preserves, rights to non-distraction; that is, freedom of action and freedom from imposition (Brown and Levinson, 1987: 61).

Brown and Levinson (1987) base their approach to politeness not only on this understanding of face, but also on the notion of reciprocity. Through this, they effectively argue that interactants in discourse are more likely to maintain or enhance the face of other interactants if reciprocal attempts at maintaining face are made.

Based on this, politeness theories arising from, or evolving from Brown and Levinson's ([1978], 1987) seminal work seek to explore how the linguistic behaviour of interactants are shaped to manage or enhance utterances that might threaten the face of one or more of those interactants.

Later work exploring impoliteness (Culpeper, 1996; Bousfield, 2007a), linguistic aggression (Lachenicht, 1980), or rudeness (Terkourafi, 2008) seek to explore how and why linguistic behaviour is shaped to exacerbate or boost the threats to face inherent in conversing in order to damage the face of interactants for extra-linguistic or other situational reasons. Such face attacks (i.e. impoliteness) just like linguistic attempts to face management, mitigations and enhancements (i.e. politeness) can be typified by the linguistic constructions offered and, hence, of the explicit or implicit evaluations of interactants. This is a key point where we start to see links between im/politeness and evaluation, to which we return in subsequent sections.

5.2 Evaluation and Appraisal

Within linguistics, attitude has been interpreted as being 'first and foremost evaluations or evaluative responses towards some stimulus and (it is) characterised by a degree of positive or negative valence' (Bullo, 2014: 31). The term evaluation has been defined, also by linguists, as 'the expression of the speaker or writer's attitude or their stance towards, viewpoint on, or feelings about the entities or propositions that she or he is talking about' (Hunston and Thompson, 2003: 5).

Following the Systemic Functional Linguistics (SFL) tradition, Martin and White (2005) developed an analytical framework for the study of evaluation in discourse that focuses on the interpersonal aspect of meaning. This, as discussed, is concerned with the way in which people use lexico-grammar to construe and maintain interpersonal relations. The appraisal system realises tenor at the level of discourse semantics, that is, meaning beyond the clause (Martin and White, 2005: 10) and examines speakers' emotional attitudes expressed by lexico-grammatical items. As we discussed in Chapter 2, appraisal focuses on the way the text creates, negotiates and maintains relationships between interactants through a close examination of micro-level lexical choices expressing positive or negative valence towards people, things or situations. Such choices, are, in turn, seen to 'reflect and reinforce the ideological values of the culture' (Thompson, 2004: 76).

In working at a discourse-semantic level, appraisal allows for a structured text analysis of evaluative language choices by offering useful tools for text parsing. Such tools consist of structured systems that allow the categorisation of lexico-grammatical items. There are three main interacting domains considered in the appraisal taxonomy: 'attitude', 'engagement' and 'graduation'. Attitude is concerned with the expression of attitudinal disposition towards people and entities based on emotions or emotional reactions (as per the subcategory of affect), judgements of human behaviour (as per the subcategory of judgement) and evaluation of things and entities (as per the subcategory of appreciation). The domain of graduation is concerned with values by which speakers or writers increase or diminish feeling by 'graduating' the degree of intensity of an utterance (force) or blurring semantic categories (focus). The engagement system is concerned with sourcing attitudes and heteroglossic voices around opinions. This chapter focuses on the attitude system as it allows for a description of language that conveys evaluative disposition. Within the attitude system, we are able to categorise lexical selections for the evaluation of objects and entities are as follows: (a) affect examines lexico-grammatical items that indicate feelings and emotions towards an entity by an emoter; (b) appreciation examines evaluations of objects and the attributes or qualities of entities, that is the compositional or aesthetic features of the entity under scrutiny; (c) judgement describes evaluation based on moral or ethical values. Each subsystem has various categories. We address each of these as they appear in the data in Section 5.

5.3 Clichés and Politeness in Evaluation

We mentioned in the introduction to this chapter that a key aspect of im/politeness is that it involves attitude embedded and constrained by shared social practices. The latter is of key relevance to our argument given that, as we have discussed, clichés rely on their socially shared nature. This, in turn, allows them to 'work as tokens that nudge an evaluative positioning to be fulfilled by the recipient in interaction' (Bullo, 2019: 295). This is particularly interesting for the study of clichés in terms of facework and im/politeness and appraisal theory for the following reasons. Bullo (2019) goes on to argue that 'evaluation is directly motivated by a number of factors that need to be considered as underpinning such positioning. These include, for example, who the target of the evaluation is and on what grounds the evaluation is based' (p. 4). Similarly, White (2015: 1) notes that appraisal tools allow the analysis of evaluative choices 'by which the intensity or directness of such attitudinal utterances is strengthened or weakened'. This, in turns, permit an explanation of how such linguistic choices are used 'to manage interpersonal positioning and relationships' (White, 2005: online).

It is the very management of interpersonal relationships that are perennially key and central to all approaches to linguistic politeness. Indeed, politeness theories (e.g. Brown and Levinson and impoliteness theories (Bousfield, 2008; 2013) and Culpeper (1996; 2011) are all united in their aims to gain an understanding of what occurs at the interpersonal level. In fact, Spencer-Oatey's (2005: 97) definition of (im)politeness as 'an umbrella term that covers all kinds of evaluative meanings' with 'positive, negative or neutral connotations' that 'impact upon people's perceptions of their social relations and the rapport or (dis)harmony that exists between them', is indeed very fitting, aligning with White's definition of appraisal as an 'approach to exploring, describing and explaining the way language is used to evaluate, to adopt stances, to construct textual personas and to manage interpersonal positioning and relationships' in texts (White 2005: 1).

Despite the clear benefits of linking the appraisal framework and politeness models, there has been little research connecting them. Channell (2000), in a study of evaluative lexis, noted the need for evaluative language to be combined with studies of politeness, but as of yet very little research has explored this. Santamaría-Garcia (2014) looked at students' evaluative language on social networking sites, and how the students' evaluative assessments of others' posts on social media were realised as positive politeness strategies. She found that speakers 'rely heavily on expression of attitude to build positive face while doing relational work' (2014: 403) as 174 out of 181 positive politeness strategies used contained attitudinal meanings. Based on these findings, it appears as though speakers needed to exploit (others' capacity for the use of) appraisal resources to express attitude in order to fulfil the broad mechanisms for positive politeness, that is constructing common ground, conveying cooperation and fulfilling addressee's wants. This suggests that, as Spencer-Oatey notes, im/politeness deals with evaluative meanings and by establishing a better understanding of these meanings, by use of appraisal theory, we can get a better understanding of the interaction as a whole. Indeed, Brown and Levinson (1987: 256–258) in an oft ignored part of their wider thesis argued for just the sort of approach that Martin and White (2005) later provided. Brown and Levinson (1987: 256–258), Gumperz and Wilson's (1971) and Labov's (1972) 'social impingement on language' where social pressures in certain cultures or CoPs, in effect, leave an imprint on the grammatical structure and the patterns of grammatical usage of any given living human language. This, of course, is precisely where Martin and White's (2005) appraisal theory can be seen to make an important contribution to im/politeness.

Therefore, it seems obvious that understanding interpersonal meanings and speaker evaluations, from both discourse-semantic and sociopragmatic levels can provide a comprehensive insight into how interpersonal relationships are negotiated and, without forgetting the purpose of this monograph, provide further insights into the functions and rationales of cliché usage in linguistic constructions and their contributions to linguistic interaction.

The co-deployment of appraisal with im/politeness theories through looking at the evaluations made by a speaker allows a comprehensive understanding of (a) the choices made and their meanings at micro text level, and (b) of the speaker's apparent intentions and the likelihood of how the words, and the evaluations they contain impact the hearer(s). From a pragmatics perspective, it's worth clarifying that we are not claiming that speaker intentions can be 'recovered' from third-party linguistic analysis alone or even that speakers themselves are fully aware of their own extra-linguistic goals at all times (Grimshaw, 1990). However, we argue that a detailed analysis of im/politeness linguistic work via the appraisal framework can provide sufficient linguistic evidence to allow the reconstruction of speaker intentions, as argued by Grimshaw (1990). Further to this, we argue that the likelihood of more accurate speaker intentions being reconstructed increases when stock, common-currency or otherwise highly conventionalised in any given language, culture and CoP co-occur together, as is the case with clichés. Through this, we can then tie in the potential understanding of the hearer of what the speaker said, and the impact it can have upon the interactors' relationships.

5.4 Data and Methods

Clichés in Organisational Discourse

In this chapter, we contextualise clichés within organisational discourse. According to Grant et al. (2004: 3), organisational discourse refers to 'structured collections of texts embodied in the practices of talking and writing [...] that bring organisationally related objects into being as these texts are produced, disseminated and consumed'. It can represent collections of interactional data and communications such as emails. (Putnam and Cooren, 2004). Mumby and Clair point out that organisations are created by their members through discourse. It is through discourse that members create 'a coherent social reality that frames their sense of who they are'. (1997: 181).

Putnam and Fairhurst (2001) point out that rhetoric is infused with a variety of tropes in organisational discourse, mainly metaphor, synecdoche, metonymy and irony. Oswick et al. (2004) suggest that tropes are a prevalent feature of any form of discourse, and thus they are inevitable aspects of organisational discourse and life. For this reason, they are a significant area of study within organisational discourse. Many studies have indeed addressed tropes, and mainly metaphor, in organisational discourse in relation to particular phenomena. For example, Oswick and Grant (1996) examine the role of metaphor in organisational change. Koller explores the role of metaphors and social cognition in corporate mission statements (2008a) and branding (2008b). Anderson-Gough et al. (1998) investigate how clichés and slogans are used by organisational members for rhetorical purposes. They conclude that organisational clichés offer common structures of thoughts (beliefs, assumptions) that are drawn upon to normalise, reproduce, and constitute, organisational practices, and as such, they are 'enmeshed with the reproduction of relations of power and control in organisations' (p. 588).

In this chapter, we focus on attitude and im/politeness in communication taking place in organisational discourse but do not explore any aspects of organisational life that may frame the interactions we address. Rather, we use organisational communication as a discourse site to explore the ways in which clichés are used in interaction to construe interpersonal meanings. We chose organisation discourse as a discourse site where actors constitute a CoP, that is, they are engaged in a shared endeavour with conventionalised meanings, and, as such, this allows us to investigate the flow of cumulative meanings embedded in cliché usage.

In exploring how clichés are used as im/politeness strategies when conveying evaluation, we offer an innovative approach to organisational discourse and demonstrate the role clichés play in the maintenance and negotiation of interpersonal meanings.

Data Description

The data consisted of communications from an educational establishment, with individuals utilising common and previously agreed and negotiated shared linguistic behaviours in meetings and email communications. These consisted of gender-balanced staff interactions within a specific CoP (i.e. educationalists), with people performing similar roles with similar educational backgrounds in an age range between thirty and sixty years old. As such, this group fits the broad definition and understanding of a CoP that has been defined in Chapter 2.

The data deployed in this chapter have been selected on the grounds that they demonstrate the definition of clichés outlined in Chapter 2. Following the methods laid down by Bullo (2019), we identified the most recurrent clichés. At the end of the process, forty expressions fulfilling the criteria outlined earlier were recorded more than ten times during the process of data collection and used for analysis (Table 5.1). Due to confidentiality agreements with participants, it is not possible to include full stretches of conversation to more broadly contextualise the data, but rather selected illustrative co-text is provided.

Table 5.1 Most frequent clichés in organisational discourse

Clichés (in order of analysis)

1 We are not *moving forward*
2 We are *literally hitting a brick wall* here
3 After all the effort we put in, we are *back to square one*
4 We just seem to be *going around in circles*
5 We need to *go the extra mile* if we want to *make headway*
6 Don't just *talk the talk, you got to walk the walk*
7 We are *shifting the deck chairs* but not getting anywhere
8 We are shifting the deck chairs but *not getting anywhere*
9 I'm not sure *where we go from here*
10 We've *missed the boat* on this one
11 It makes me think whether it's time to *abandon the sinking ship*
12 The project has proved to be the team's *Achilles' heel*
13 I am aware that I am *punching above my weight* on this one
14 This is *way out of our league*
15 We are *barking up the wrong tree*
16 I am *biting off more than I can chew* by taking this on
17 Let's *think outside the box* for a minute
18 They've achieved this with *blood sweat and tears*
19 I'm not too sure about him, he's a bit of a *dark horse*
20 I heard it *straight from the horse's mouth*
21 We *started off on the wrong foot*, let's start over and forget it ever happened
22 His comment was *below the belt*
23 He's been *on cloud nine* all week
24 I was *in stitches* after he told the story
25 This report *is doing my head in*
26 It really *rattles my cage*
27 I am *beside myself* with rage over this
28 It *drives me up the wall* when I hear that
29 It's always a *glass half empty* for him
30 It would be wonderful *if you found it in your heart* to give me a second chance
31 *Not me ... been there, done that, bought the T-shirt*
32 He's got *a chip on his shoulder* so we need to be careful
33 We are stepping on a bit of a *grey area* here
34 They do produce *cutting-edge* research
35 It's been a *rocky road* so far
36 It's only a *half-baked idea* at this stage
37 We can't expect too much more, *it does what it says on the tin*
38 It is a *game-changer* for us
39 As interesting as it is, that is *the forbidden fruit*
40 That suggestion *is food for thought*, I hadn't considered that perspective actually

Analytical Tools

We followed two levels of analysis. At the first level, we coded clichés in terms of appraisal values by categorising the polarity (positive/negative) and appraisal category (affect, appreciation, judgement) and subcategories (e.g. dissatisfaction) through an examination of co-text. The full list of extracts with clichés and coding at both levels can be found in Appendix 2 of this book.

As an illustration of application of the appraisal taxonomy, let us consider the expression 'we are not moving forward'. As most expressions identified in this data set, the cliché takes a metaphorical form evoking the PROGRESS AS FORWARD MOVEMENT IN SPACE conceptual metaphor. This, according to Lakoff (1993), is indicative of the conceptualisation of a problem, entity, or situation as progress, or rather, as a lack of such progress. In this case, the speaker, as a member of a team addressing their team members, positions themselves as a member of a group (through the use of the group-inclusive first person pronoun, 'we') credited, or perhaps 'labelled', with the inability to make progress with a task thereby conveying explicit evaluation (cf. Section 5.5) as negative judgement of capacity, as per the appraisal taxonomy:

(1) *We are not moving forward*; (-), judgement: capacity

Appraisal is realised by the metaphorical expression, deemed so by establishing a contrast between the literal and contextual meaning, as recommended by the Metaphor Identification Procedure (MIP) by the Plagglejaz Group (2007).

The second analytical level consisted of an interpretation of im/politeness markers. We have illustrated this by providing an interpretation of (1). In im/politeness terms, then, this negative judgement of capacity conveyed through cliché can be seen as a criticism (see Bousfield 2008: 126). Criticisms attack both positive face wants (the desire to be approved of) and negative face wants (the desire to be unimpeded) simultaneously. This is because the critical metaphorical comment *we are not moving forward*, meaning we are not achieving what the speaker evaluates as valuable or necessary, demonstrates a considerable amount of disapproval – hence a threat to, or, in the right circumstances, attack upon the positive face needs of the recipients (the speaker may well be including themselves in an act of self-criticism, or, given the circumstances, may well not be doing so, either). Further, the fact that the previous, unsuccessful actions in pursuit of the metaphorical 'movement' (i.e. striving for success) have not been, to the speaker's evaluation, successful in making meaningful progress, is a further negative face threat designed to cease the current (level of) activities and to attempt something different, with a view to being more successful.

5.5 Findings

In this section we present the integrated findings of the analysis of the clichés through the co-deployment of the appraisal framework and face and politeness theory. The section is structured by reference to the first level of analysis, that is the appraisal findings. We present the findings according to appraisal category, starting with judgement as the biggest category. This is followed by affect and appreciation, respectively. We discuss each category and their subcategories at the beginning of each subsection. The examples of data discussed under each appraisal category are also interpreted by reference to the sociopragmatic theories of face and politeness outlined in Section 5.1.

Judgement

Within Martin and White's (2005) appraisal system, the category of judgement is concerned with attitudinal evaluation of human behaviour, either praising or criticising it, by reference to some set of social norms. The subcategory of social esteem refers to evaluations of capacity (i.e. ability), normality and tenacity of individuals in terms of their behaviour. When explicit, examples of each of the these could be attributes, in the form of, for example adjectives, such as 'in/efficient', 'weird' and 'stubborn', respectively. When it comes to clichés as formulaic expressions, most of which take the form of metaphors in this chapter, we refer to them as instances of evoked appraisal. That is a type of implicit appraisal; that is, where no explicit evaluative lexis is used as in the earlier examples, but rather the evaluation is implicitly embedded in various features of language, such as metaphors that function as tokens of evaluation. Economou (2012) considers that metaphors may evoke attitude by carrying ideological attitudinal meanings by reference to shared knowledge amongst the interlocutors in a CoP. Examples 2–19 refer to instances of the three categories discussed earlier, with most of them (2–17) being examples of appraisals of capacity (i.e. assessing human ability or performance), which is not surprising considering that the clichés were collected in a workplace context. In the context of the discourse-semantic evaluation of human behaviour, as manifested in appraisal of judgement/ capacity, we discuss the following examples in relation to the sociopragmatic function that they fulfil.

(2) We are literally *hitting a brick wall* here.

In im/politeness and face management terms, this utterance,[1] despite the apparently common misuse of the lexeme 'literally' when 'figuratively' is meant, can be interpreted as a complaint token from a speech act (Austin, 1962; Searle, 1975) perspective.[2] The face effects of a complaint token on the recipient can vary as to whether the complaint speech act is mentioned or aimed. If the former, then it can be seen as a mild expression of exasperation on the part of the speaker demonstrating, however inadvertently, a presentation of self and hence an invitation to face and identity construction (see Chapter 6) by the hearers.[3] In the case of (1), the complaint token is aimed as it functions as a mild and partially-face-managed criticism (Bousfield 2008: 126). The same is true of the following examples:

(2) we are not *moving forward*
(3) After all the effort we put in, *we are back to square one*
(4) We just seem to be *going around in circles*
(6) *Don't just talk the talk, you got to walk the walk*

Although criticisms were first identified as potential impoliteness strategies in Bousfield, (2008), in the case of our data, in using clichés to evoke appraisal of negative capacity, the speakers reduce or mitigate the positive face and negative face threats inherent in such critical commentary. Criticism as formulaic language (Culpeper, 2010), as in the case of clichés analysed here, works as a token of shared and oft used language within a CoP that seeks critique and challenge as a route to enhanced practice in a workplace setting. In short, it is an acceptable way to challenge others' face. For example:

(5) We need to go the *extra mile* if we want to *make headway*

---

[1] In line with the practice in the field of pragmatics, when referring to examples of data in this chapter, we will refer to them as 'utterances' as opposed to text, extracts, etc. as we have used in previous chapters.

[2] Uses of 'literally' in a figurative sense can be considered Illocutionary Force Indication Devices (IFID), or as emphatic 'boosters' (see Holmes 1984); that is, linguistic devices that enhance the emphasis of the main propositional content being conveyed.

[3] In some cases, the speaker can be seen as being on a scale between either legitimately airing a grievance in a single instance of concern to consistently giving a socially negative presentation of self as a complainer (and hence, a problem in professional or industry terms). This was not, we hasten to add, what was occurring in the situation through which we collected these data examples, but is highlighted here as we will pick this up again in Chapter 6.

The infamous 'extra mile' cliché, which in Chapter 4 was analysed as positive capacity, evokes a negative judgement in this example. This happens by virtue of the co-text with the conditional where the second cliché 'make headway' is embedded, indicating that the team have been unable to do so by performing the expected tasks. The core propositional content of this comment is that additional work, potentially beyond what might otherwise be expected or contractually required, seems to be required in order for the team to reach the negotiated goals and successes. It may also be a criticism (see discussion earlier) for not succeeding before now. In politeness terms, the former indicates that the cliché works to mitigate negative face threat because asking someone to do more than expected is primarily a negative face issue as it imposes on their rights and expectations to free time and freedom from imposition during such free time. The latter suggests that the cliché reduces positive face threat because a criticism is effectively a positive face issue where disapproval over someone's actions is expressed.

(7) We are *shifting the deck chairs* but not (8) *getting anywhere*

Positive face threat is reduced in a combination of metaphorical clichés in examples (7) and (8). In (7), as a take on 'moving deckchairs on the Titanic', the cliché works as a criticism that minor actions in pursuit of a specific outcome seem to be devoid of, or not cognisant of the wider context and situational perspectives of what is actually occurring, while in (8), the cliché suggests that any activity should, metaphorically, be progress ('getting anywhere'). Therefore, such lack of activity is criticism of wasted effort. In using the clichés the speakers evoke negative appraisal of capacity whilst mitigating the positive face threat inherent in the criticism as well as the potential negative face threat of a request some for change in performance.

(9) I'm not sure *where we go* from here

This is a fairly common cliché using the metaphor of PURPOSE IS DIRECTION. Similar to the discussion about examples (2), (3), (4) and (6), this can be construed as complaint, criticism or – what is different from those – a speech act of admission of limited suggestion, experience or ability, as indicated by the negative judgement of capacity. The latter can also be seen as a stark and higher-risk presentation of self that may be considered as an honest admission of (9). Again, the use of cliché – representing recognition and cognisance within a CoP of professionals – constitutes an efficient and lower-cost way of communicating this otherwise higher-risk admission, thereby saving positive self-face.

(10) We've *missed the boat* on this one

An extension of the PURPOSE IS DIRECTION metaphor, this cliché evoking negative capacity represents a SUCCESS IS VEHICLE metaphor, and OPPORTUNITY IS EMBARKATION metaphor – both at the heart of this cliché. In both cases, as with the discussions on (2), (3), (4), and (6), this represents – all contextual factors being equal – a criticism and/or a complaint that, again is either mentioned or aimed, with similar effects and outcomes intended.

(12) The project has proved to be the team's *Achilles' heel*

Another culturally shared and understood intertextual reference, this time to the Greek myth of Achilles, a hero of Greek antiquity who only perished as a result of being stabbed in the one vulnerable spot on his whole body – the heel of his foot. The metaphorical cliché conveys negative judgement of capacity whilst operating as a positive face-saving representation of the general resilience of the team referred to, and its general invulnerability (itself a metaphor for effectiveness).

(13) I am aware that I am *punching above my weight* on this one

Using a boxing sporting metaphor cliché, this example is an effective speech act of admission of operating beyond one's own assumed experience or capabilities. This ventures the speaker's own face through presentation of self (see Chapter 6) in a way that is a frank, honest and high-risk appraisal. In certain circumstances, it can, therefore, also operate as a polite, face-saving, highly indirect request for assistance, or be indirectly seeking advice or sympathy - both, again, high-risk face operations requiring careful linguistic constructions to achieve successfully.

(14) This is *way out of our league*

In face terms the use of the pronoun 'our', which Brown and Levinson (1987) have argued demonstrates that the speaker is claiming the speaker and hearer(s) are co-operators and is, hence, a positive face enhancement. However, the propositional content of the utterance, being similar to the effect in (13), makes this example an exposition of the speakers' appraisal of the limits of the whole team's experience or capabilities (negative judgement of capacity). This is therefore a use of a cliché to mitigate an expression of an impolite belief (Leech, 1983) to the assembled team.

(15) We're *barking up the wrong tree*

This self-referential animal metaphor cliché, also evoking negative capacity, suggests collective self-criticism of past and/or current actions. This is, therefore, a polite way of critically assessing said actions, and, as such, represents a polite way of engaging in criticism that, as earlier, threatens both positive face (as it disapproves of the actions taken to date) and negative face (as it requires a change of future actions to be imposed upon the team). The use of the personal pronoun plural 'we' again indicates the claim that speaker and hearer(s) are co-operators.

(16) I am *biting off more than I can chew* by taking this on

A cliché to do with not taking on more than one can temporally, physically, or conceptually deal with successfully (evoking negative (self) capacity), this is based on the metaphor EATING IS DOING. The use of the metaphorical cliché is a way of engaging in the speech act of admission, which, as noted earlier, is a high-risk presentation of self as something other, or less, than others expect. It is, in effect, a mitigated way of being self-critical through admission and may in fact serve to repair one's positive face, standing with one's interlocutor by simple fact of the admission.

(17) Let's *think outside the box* for a minute

Whilst seemingly an invitation to innovate, and hence a negative face threat, this utterance can also be seen as a positive face enhancement apparently demonstrating a polite belief in the abilities of the hearer(s) on the part of the speaker. This can also be a gentle, and linguistically politely expressed criticism for not previously engaging in innovative thinking (negative capacity), and/or for dwelling in unproductive thinking (cf. Chapter 4 for an analysis of this cliché from a sociocognitive perspective).

Still within the social esteem subcategory of the appraisal system, the examples that follow constitute cases of evoked judgement of tenacity and normality.

(18) They've achieved this with *blood sweat and tears*

This is a cliché with a clear if imperfect intertextual reference to the famous 'Blood, toil, tears, and sweat' speech that the then new prime minister, Winston Churchill, made on 13 May 1940 to the British House of Commons during dark and difficult stages of the Second World War following the fall of France and the occupation of much of Europe, and before the United States of America, or the Union of Soviet Socialist Republics had joined the conflict. As an intertextual reference to a significant point in British cultural and societal history, this is a powerful claim to a culturally shared set of experiences (even if few are alive, today, who lived through that period). The reference to the Second World War and the use of the cliché equating their efforts to strenuous activity to survive, maintain life and protect liberty might be equated with the metaphor EFFORT IS SURVIVAL AND FREEDOM IN EXTREME CIRCUMSTANCES, therefore evoking positive judgement of tenacity. In this case, this is another third-party reference that exaggerates the referents' efforts and hence represents a positive face enhancement for the absent third-party referents to the assembled recipients of the utterance.

(19) I'm not too sure about him, he's *a bit of a dark horse*

This animal metaphor cliché represents a judgement of normality. The minimalisation of 'a bit' is a classic Brown and Levinson (1987) linguistic politeness marker which poses that minimising the threat to positive face is more polite and more cognisant of the face needs of one's interlocutors than not minimising it. The animalisation in 'dark horse' cliché refers to the ILLUMINATION IS KNOWLEDGE and SEEING IS UNDERSTANDING metaphors as 'dark' means unknown. By referring to a horse, the animalisation element intertextually refers to the sport of horse racing. A dark (i.e. unknown) horse referred to a horse whose 'form' (or abilities on the current race track) were not known to the betting fraternity and the bookmakers, with a clear potential to surprise and reward the brave who choose to stake on said horse. As such, the reference to a person via the cliché of 'dark horse' is actually not normally negative socially. It can be an emotionally detached signal of admiration in British English usage – hence a positive face enhancement. However, the inclusion of the first clause 'I'm not too sure about him' seems to pre-modify the interpretation, steering it towards a more socially negative one, and therefore within the boundaries of 'normal' as per the appraisal of judgement/normality, which therefore seems to suggest that it's a positive face threat regarding the referent third party.

A second subcategory within judgement is that of social sanction, which is concerned with evaluations of human behaviour that have legal or moral implications. The examples that follow constitute cases of the categories of veracity (concerned honesty) and propriety (concerned with ethical behaviour).

(20) I heard it *straight from the horse's mouth*

This is another British colloquial cliché representing a claim to authority and judgement of veracity in order to mitigate the content of the message and hence mitigate, or shift the 'blame' or authorship of the producer of discourse (Thomas, 1984). As such, this is a way to mitigate any face threat that 'what was heard' might represent.

(21) We started off *on the wrong foot*, let's start over and forget it ever happened

The MOVEMENT metaphor again is used to provoke negative propriety. In this case, the foot is seen as a metonymy for the ability to walk and make progress. The trigger of the evaluation is the vehicle domain foot that gives access to the target domain of the person carrying out the action. This is a clear if figuratively realised, attempt at face repair and impression management through an invitation to co-construct a new relationship, devoid of a (presumably) troubled one in the past.

(22) His comment was *below the belt*

Another sporting metaphor cliché that can generally only be interpreted, *ceteris paribus*, as a criticism about a third party, presumably absent. The COMMENTS ARE PHYSICAL BLOWS metaphor is in effect here thereby constituting an intertextual reference to boxing in which punches below the waistline (metonymically associated with the belt) to the groin area are out with the rules of all regulated boxing matches and weights. As such, the cliché constitutes a criticism of the nature and style (i.e. judgement of propriety) of the comments the third party made. This is likely to invite the recipients to consider the referent socially negatively as it is a positive face attack on the referent.

(23) As interesting as it is, *that is the forbidden fruit*

Finally, within the category of judgement, a food metaphor is used to evoke propriety. This is achieved by means of a cliché drawing from biblical intertextual reference, the Adam and Eve species-creation belief of Christian faith. As such, this use of the culturally shared cliché is, again, a commonly used resource that appears to be deployed to politely decline or critique an earlier request or suggestion, declining or critiquing being inherently face-threatening to either or both positive and negative faces in a Brown and Levinson (1987) sense.

Affect

According to Martin and White (2005), affect is concerned with positive or negative emotional responses and dispositions towards people, things or situations that act as triggers of such emotion. The conscious participant experiencing the emotion is the 'emoter' and this can be the speaker/writer (referred to as authorial affect) or a second or third person (i.e. non-authorial) attributed with emotions. Affect is manifested in a number of ways, with different labels. We discuss each subcategory in the analysis that follows as we contextualise it within the sociopragmatic function of the clichés and their co-text.

The subcategory of un/happiness is concerned with emotions that relate to 'affairs of the heart' (Martin and White, 2005: 49). These feelings can be expressed as inner feelings or they can be expressed as directed towards a trigger such as liking or disliking something or someone. The negative variable of this category conveys feelings of misery or antipathy (e.g. sadness, hatred) whilst the positive valence expresses 'cheerfulness' or 'affection' (e.g. happiness, love). Let us consider the examples of appraisal of affect indicating un/happiness in terms of the sociopragmatic function they fulfil.

(24) He's been *on cloud nine* all week

This is an example of non-authorial affect indicating happiness whilst, at the same time, performing 'third-party' facework. In this case, unlike in examples (25) and (26) where the expression of own emotional states (or authorial appraisal) is at least partially proscribed in society, the representations of the perception of others' emotional states, especially positive emotional states, is much more welcomed. As such, the representation to the recipients of an absent third party's non-authorial happiness, especially over an extended one (indicated by the time period 'all week'), is used to build positive face understandings about the referent in the minds of the receivers, if that which 'he' is happy about is seen to be a socially desirable or acceptable state of affairs given the situation contributing to the positive emotional state.

(25) I was *in stitches* after he told the story

This cliché evoking positive authorial happiness represents the metonymic relationship between extreme exertion and physical pain in the side (a 'side stitch') referencing the assumption of extreme laughter being exceptionally exerting physically. The face-related nature of the comment is to raise the positive face of an absent third party (e.g. Toddington, 2014) who is recognised as a skilled raconteur. This is also interpretable as a form of presentation of self, a concept we cover in Chapter 6.

Another subcategory within affect is that of dis/satisfaction. This concerns the speaker's expression of 'achievement or frustration' regarding the activities they participate in both 'as participants and spectators'

(Martin and White, 2005: 50). Dis/satisfaction is conveyed through feelings of 'ennui' and 'displeasure' or 'interest' and 'pleasure'. Both examples (26) and (27) illustrate authorial dissatisfaction directly attributed to a trigger.

(26) This report is *doing my head in*
(27) It really *rattles my cage*

Similar in pragmatic face and politeness work to examples (2), (3), (4) and (6), examples (26) and (27) can be construed as mentioned complaints or criticisms and interpreted as requests for sympathy that is face-threatening for not only the recipient but also for the requester (as all requests arguably are). In (27), the speaker animalises themselves for effect. The cliché metaphorically operates as THE SPEAKER IS A CAGED ANIMAL, the emoter is mapped to an ANIMAL kept in captivity, presumably a ferocious one, and the object of the concern or complaint is a tormenter. In im/politeness terms, the onus for the cause or triggering lies more heavily on the causer than the experiencer, or emoter, of the negative emotions. See full discussion of this aspect in (28) and (29).

Dissatisfaction is also evoked by metaphorical clichés relating to SELF and SPACE. The former is generally used 'to conceptualise normal self-control by the subject and lack of it' (Lakoff, 1996: 110). In an upsetting situation, the subject perceives their location as outside the bounded region and hence lacking in self-control (Lakoff, 1996). In (28) the emoter locates themselves outside the bounded region of the body, seen as a CONTAINER, in an alternative location to evoke affect as dissatisfaction. Similarly, *it drives me up the wall* (29) evokes dissatisfaction in the emoter by comparing an upsetting situation to an external force causing displacement from the ground, which is considered positive or unemotional, to a vertical position that is mapped to a state of dissatisfaction.

(28) I am *beside myself* with rage over this
(29) It drives me *up the wall* when I hear that

In sociopragmatic terms, examples 28 and 29 imply a presentation of self's emotional state, with the cultural variable needing consideration as such expression of emotional states can be proscribed as making the hearers uncomfortable in a professional context. As such, it represents a threat to the utterer to engage in the speech act of admission of such a potentially socially sanctioned state. Example (28) can therefore act as an indirect, even implied, speech act of warning that the speaker is likely to seek redress for their emotional state (from the presumed trigger). This is likely to venture the speaker's positive face wants by exhibiting a prescribed state of being. Furthermore, it does so in order to demonstrate the threats to positive – and arguably negative – faces of the person who has triggered these emotions in the speaker (see Bousfield 2007b, 2008). Similar in pragmatic and facework role but to a culturally lower level of illocutionary force and hence risk to face, example (29) threatens the speaker's positive face in order to demonstrate threat to the causer's positive and negative faces as a result of the appraisal, by the speaker, of dissatisfaction with the state of affairs.

(30) It's always a *glass half empty* for him

Finally in the category of dis/satisfaction, (30) is a clear third-party criticism and hence an invitation to co-construct the future face of the third-party referent in a non-flattering way given the fullness, or emptiness of the metaphorical glass cliché where VOLUME IS OPTIMISM. The absence of, or perception of absence of fuller volume, is seen as a criticism (Bousfield, 2008: 62, 126) of the general personal or professional stance on optimism/pessimism, with the assumption that the referent defers regularly to the latter. Consistent positivity, regularly demonstrated in a low-key way, is often expected in professional settings whereas consistent pessimism, similarly demonstrated regularly, is proscribed.

Two more subcategories of affect that are found in the data to a lesser extent, include dis/inclination and in/security. The former concerns the speaker's intention with respect to a hypothetical stimulus. Martin and White (2005) suggest that the distinction between irrealis and realis (something that is known to be or not to be the case) is grammatically construed by desiderative mental processes for irrealis (e.g. I would like to) and by emotive mental processes for realis (e.g. I like to) (2005: 48). Irrealis affect implies a trigger and is realised by values of dis/inclination relating to 'desire', as in (31) and (32), non-authorial and authorial, respectively.

(31) It would be wonderful if you *found it in your heart* to give me a second chance
(32) Not me ... *been there, done that, bought the T-shirt*

From a sociopragmatic perspective, the cliché in (31) is a request speech act token, in this case a request for forgiveness, that is, inclination to an activity is attributed, or indeed requested, from the interlocutor. Requests themselves, being exceptionally culturally sensitive, are in every society more or less face-threatening. The linguistic choice of such prosaic cliché to make the face-threatening speech act of request is interesting insofar as the construction – being archaic – seems to suggest the requester is aware of the not inconsiderable gravity of their position and reason for making such a request. Requests, by their very nature at least primarily (if not wholly) impact on the negative face of the requestee. However, the use of the archaic cliché here deployed also puts the requestee's positive face under pressure for two crucial reasons. Firstly, the archaic, semi-formal and arguably ritualistic request for forgiveness is not easily dismissed without damaging the dismisser's face as being, potentially, unforgiving and hence damaging the dismisser's positive face, that is, their desire to be approved of for their actions. Secondly, the fact this was said in public further positions the requestee's face not only in relation to the requester but also the third parties present, too considering that face is 'on loan' from society (Goffman, 1959) and is, in current conceptualisation of the phenomena, co-constructed by members of that society or CoP (Eckert and McConnell-Ginert, 1992).

The cliché in (32) is complex metaphorically, simultaneously drawing on the LOCATIONS, ACTIVITIES AND PURCHASES ARE NOT-TO-BE-REPEATED EXPERIENCES metaphors. This cliché is a way of communicating refusal, and disinclination, to engage in future activities/experiences, which can be both positive and negative face threatening in multiple directions when declining a request or a reasonable instruction in a professional workplace.

Finally, (33) is an example of the affect subcategory of in/security. This is the speaker's expression of peace or anxiety 'in relation to the environs' (Martin and White, 2005: 49), which can also be authorial or attributed to someone else. Negative values, as in this example, are evidenced by feelings of 'disquiet' and 'surprise' while positive ones are manifested as 'confidence' and 'trust'.

(33) He's got *a chip on his shoulder* so we need to be careful

This cliché appears to function ostensibly as an attempt at third-party facework by representing to the minds of the assembled a critical comment about the referent. In facework and politeness terms, in attributing insecurity to a third party, this example also operates as a politely expressed speech act of warning to self and others in that semantic space ('we'). Warnings threaten both the negative face of the recipient (as they limit the future action environment of the addressee) and potentially also the positive face (by suggesting continued or past actions engaged in may be disapproved by the speaker or the third-party referent). The use of the inclusive 'we', putting the speaker as part of the same social group as the addressees, is a polite linguistic construction strategy (Brown and Levinson, 1987) suggesting addresser and addressee are co-operators. This coupled, again, with the cliché as formulaic, and hence shared language within the CoP, serves to mitigate the face threats inherent in the speech act of warning, which is strengthened by virtue of the negative valence of the appraisal of the third party attributed with emotions of insecurity.

Appreciation

The final category of appraisal, found to a lesser extent in the data, is that of appreciation, and is concerned with the positive or negative aesthetic evaluation (i.e. form, appearance, construction, presentation or impact) of objects, processes and state of affairs, and natural phenomena. Values of appreciation are properties attached to the entity or phenomenon under evaluation rather than the human subject doing the evaluation. However, in cases where the assessment does not directly focus on the correctness or incorrectness of human participants' behaviour but on qualities or 'aesthetic' features of human beings, values of appreciation are attributed. Thus, we may describe human individuals as 'beautiful', for example. In other cases, the evaluation of actions performed by humans may be seen as appreciation, as the appraisal refers directly to a non-human entity, for example, 'his actions were despicable'. In this case, the assessment relates to 'actions', which are 'things', and therefore theoretically any appraisal of things corresponds to the category of appreciation. However, as such actions were performed by a human being, they speak directly of the intentional behaviour of such human being. Therefore, in such cases, we consider examples like this as tokens of judgement. In general terms, appreciation can be divided into our 'reactions' to things, in terms of catching our attention and pleasing us, their composition and their overall value, such as innovation, or authenticity, for example.

The cliché in (34) is an interesting example of the blurry boundaries within appraisal, not only across categories but also within them and across subcategories.

(34) We are stepping on a bit of a *grey area* here

If we take the expression 'grey area' literally, then it falls within the subcategory of composition. However, there is not necessarily an appraisal in there as 'grey' as a colour has neutral valence. If we consider the figurative, and intended, meaning of 'grey area' where 'grey' is used metaphorically (colour is clarity/understanding), then we see an overall assessment of the 'area' or situation as somehow potentially problematic. In this case, we consider this an example of 'valuation'. The colour metaphor in the cliché is used alongside 'stepping', which is a

PHYSICAL MOVEMENT IS CONCEPTUAL ENGAGEMENT metaphor. In facework and politeness terms this is a politely constructed speech act of *warning*. As we argued earlier, the use of such clichés can – precisely because they are well used and shared resources – more efficiently mitigate face threat as a formulaic politeness construct (see Culpeper 2010). Another example of appraisal of appreciation as positive valuation of things is example (35).

(35) They do produce *cutting-edge* research

Pragmatically, this is a third-party oriented politeness cliché that invites positive face enhancement of the presumably absent referent in the recipients' minds. Taking this view, however, indicates that the appraisal relates to the people producing the research and therefore this could be considered a token of judgement, as discussed. The same is true of (23) and (23). Example (36) constitutes another example of an appraisal of appreciation under the subcategory of valuation whereby the overall experience being discussed is considered difficult,

(36) It's been *a rocky road*, so far

In im/politeness and face management terms, this utterance has a variety of functions ranging from the more likely expression of sympathy or empathy in line with Brown and Levinson's 'strategy 2' (1987: 104–105); to the less likely implied admonition for not controlling, anticipating or managing the situation more widely (cf. 'criticise' Bousfield, 2008: 126), dependent on the wider contextual factors. In the instance being considered here, the appraisal framework value of valuation (appreciation) contextualises the utterance within the former. That is the expression of empathy and, secondarily, sympathy for the shared experiences of the addressee by the utterer. As such, this operates as a positive face enhancement strategy by showing approval of the resilience and determination or professional 'survivability' of the team being addressed, thereby demonstrating the value of the co-deployment of both approaches.

Below are two examples of clichés evoking appraisal of appreciation within the category of composition, that is, evaluation in relation to the complexity of an entity.

(37) It's only a *half-baked* idea at this stage

Within the food metaphor, this cliché indicates that the idea is unready (i.e. food unfit for consumption as it still requires cooking). This appraisal of appreciation suggests over-hasty action or activities requiring more thought and activity to be successful. As such, this can be seen as a way of communicating positive face-threatening comments in a potentially more palatable way.

(38) We can't expect too much more, it *does what it says on the tin*

Similarly, in (38) the cliché referring to the 'what-you-see-is-what-you-get' English idiom evokes an appraisal of appreciation (potentially ambivalent in valence) indicating, perhaps, simplicity (hence coded as 'composition'). In pragmatics terms, the cliché operates as a speech act of advising (to manage one's own expectations) or warning (not to over expect). This is therefore a contender for linguistic politeness seeking to manage the positive and negative faces of the recipients of the message, that is, to manage them now so as to avoid greater face damage later should over-inflated expectation not be met, especially if the recipients had sought to invest their professional faces in that concept referred to in (32).

A final subcategory within appreciation is that of reaction impact. This is concerned with the qualities of an entity that make it captivating to the onlooker or not. Explicit values in this category are encoded in adjectives such as 'arresting', 'captivating' or 'tedious', for example. The cliché in (39) represents a good example of implicit (or evoked) appraisal within this category.

(39) It is a *game-changer* for us

This example represents another sporting metaphorical cliché where PROJECTS OR ACTIONS ARE GAMES. Subject to context, this can be either positive or negative, socially, for the referents in 'us'. In either case, the positive and negative faces are under scrutiny via any such utterance.

Finally, though another food metaphor, cliché (40) also evoked appraisal of judgement in terms of the impact an entity has.

(40) That suggestion is *food for thought*, I hadn't considered that perspective actually

Lakoff and Johnson (1980) noted that food metaphors might be expected to be socially positive metaphors. Presumably, this is due to the bodies we have, and the sorts of experiences we have as a shared species where the consumption of food is a universal shared experience. In light of that, (40) could be interpreted as a mix of the metaphors FOOD IS FUEL, in both metaphorical and biologically literal terms, and the FUEL FOR THE MIND-ENGINE metaphor. Such figurative language, especially when we consider this final utterance, is interpretable as a positive face

enhancement, of the recipient, by the speaker, given the speaker's obviously socially positive evaluation and appraisal of the recipient's prior
suggestion.

5.6 Discussion

In this chapter we focused on how clichés can be used for negotiating
interpersonal relationships in organisational discourse. We conceptualise
clichés as im/politeness strategies in the expression and management of
evaluative meanings regarding an interactant either directly, or indirectly
(by association with an aspect, event or situation to which they are connected). Given their reliance on socially shared knowledge as carried by
their formulaic nature, we pose that clichés allow the conveyance of evaluation of people or situations whilst also enhancing or mitigating the impact
of such evaluation on facework and assumed identity. The study of clichés
as interpersonal devices as explored in this chapter encompasses a multidimensional investigation co-deploying two complementary approaches: a
systemic functional approach, utilising the appraisal framework, and sociopragmatic approaches in the case of im/politeness, and face theory.

The majority of the clichés examined consist of metaphorical and metonymical expressions and some are intertextual references. The main
metaphors identified in clichés relate to movement or journeys, self in
space, food, games and animals, showing consistency with cognitive linguistics theories that argue that language is not structured arbitrarily but
motivated and grounded in bodily, physical, social and cultural experience (e.g. Johnson, 1992). The findings therefore indicate that the conceptualisation of life in this organisational setting and assessment of its
people and events is indeed grounded on basic aspects of human experience. This is also an indication of the conventionality, and hence reason,
for the widespread use of clichés as socially shared resources.

In order to explore how evaluation functions linguistically in the data,
this chapter proposed two analytical levels. The first level consisted of
examining clichés at discourse-semantic level in order to identify their
evaluative function as per the attitude system of the appraisal framework. The second level consisted of an interpretation of the evaluation
from an im/politeness and face perspective.

Using appraisal allowed for an understanding of the subtle patterns
of evoked evaluation in clichés usage. The data reveals that the majority of appraisal instances have negative valence and relate to the assessment of behaviour of human entities, manifested in values of judgement,
with the subcategory of capacity having the highest frequency of use. The

second largest cluster relates to the subsystem of affect. Clichés within this category also relate to emotions caused by elements in the work environment, with frustration and anger being the most predominant emotions identified. The predominance of judgement and affect is significant given that they refer to human entities or behaviour and as such they have the potential for hindering interpersonal relationships. Therefore, as demonstrated in this chapter, clichés come in as handy im/politeness strategies.

By drawing on face theory and speech act theory, we were able to identify that most clichés were complaints and/or criticisms, warnings, admissions and refusals. Interestingly, we found that the vast majority of clichés are used to mitigate, repair or enhance positive face threat in the interlocutors in said speech acts via appraisal clichés as negative face-saving devices.

The most important findings from a sociopragmatics perspective is the preponderance of third-party im/politeness. Clichés are used to appraise a third party and therefore enhance, co-construct or even critique the positive face of a third party not present in the exchange. These cases mostly refer to evaluations under the category of affect and are realised as what is referred to as non-authorial affect. The latter label is well established within the appraisal system but the pragmatic effect of considering a third-party face wants is not a vastly researched area in the field, therefore identifying a gap that grants further research.

The co-deployment of both approaches has yielded positive outcomes in a number of ways. The majority of clichés, and in particular those identified as expressing judgement of capacity do, in fact, have a face-saving function especially when they are embedded in a work environment. In a way, this should come as no surprise. However, exploring clichés from both perspectives has allowed seeing *both sides of the coin*, as it were, especially the third-party im/politeness instances. Take for example (25) *I was in stitches after he told the story*. The cliché indicates authorial appraisal of affect as happiness therefore pointing at the positive appraisal of the emotion conveyed by the speaker. This is a classic example of authorial affect as per the appraisal taxonomy. However, the face-related aspect of the cliché invites us to look past the emoter/speaker and consider the third party causing the emotion, who is considered funny though the appraisal does not extend to this third party. It is by virtue of the sociopragmatic layer of analysis that the contextually absent third party comes to be linguistically present and we see how the cliché aims to raise their positive face. This is an interesting case that makes the co-deployment of both approaches worthy of pursual in other contexts of study.

Clichés, by carrying shared knowledge, are able to convey appraisal, say, through inherent metaphorical entailments or similar mechanisms while still preserving a safe detachment from the propositional content of the literal words, which allows the utterer to attend to the face wants of the community. As posed by Zijderveld (1979), their 'mechanicity' renders clichés useful resources for negotiating interpersonal relationships. Saying that something or someone *rattles* one's *cage* for example conveys a more effective appraisal of distress in the emoter than the literal 'I am angry' form. The interlocutor gets a sense of the emotional state of the emoter due to the reference to angry animals that is assumed to be shared knowledge. The encyclopaedic knowledge of the interlocutor not only encompasses the image of the angry animal but also the potential consequences or entailments (as per conceptual metaphor theory by Lakoff and Johnson, 1980), hence maximising the semantic value of the appraisal. At the same time, by using the cliché instead of the literal expression, or even an insult, the speaker saves (positive) face whilst, at the same time, potentially mitigating the positive face threat of the third party causing the anger or behind the situation leading the speaker to such an emotional state. Evaluative clichés, therefore, allow speakers to share feelings and generate social belonging (Martin, 2004). The same is true of clichés used as requests or criticism of performance manifested as judgements of capacity. Say that a cliché is used to convey the imminent need for improvement of performance, for example the recurrent *we are shifting the deck chairs but not getting anywhere*, which works by conveying a sense of the severity of the situation and urging a change in the current actions in order to improve performance. In this way, the cliché works to both mitigate threat to positive face at the inherent criticism for poor performance and mitigate the negative face threat of the request for improving work practices. As such, clichés are a useful 'aspect of rhetoric' (Anderson-Gough et al. 1998: 566) and, as such, strengthen the appraisal of judgement whilst attending to positive and negative face wants inherent in both speech acts. In fact, this is the case for the majority of clichés identified as expressing judgement of capacity, which is no surprise given the nature of the discourse under investigation in this chapter.

Further to this, the shared nature of clichés as available structures of knowledge in a particular CoP, as in a particular workplace, also allows them to work cumulatively, over various situated conversations and exchanges. By this, we mean that the data for this chapter was collected over various instances of organisational communication (as per our definition of organisational discourse earlier). However, we still see a coherent prosody of interpersonal meanings working cumulatively to create semantic interdependence across the corpus (Martin, 2004). Such prosodic effects texture the evaluations and create a flow of evaluative patterns across various instances of interaction (Oteiza and Pinuer, 2013: 48) demonstrating interdependence and construing a local community of values (Lui, 2018).

The prosodic effect of clichés as im/politeness devices allows the transfer of patterns of evaluative meanings to different discourses within a CoP by virtue of their conventionalised, formulaic nature, therefore contributing to the negotiation and maintenance of interpersonal relationships.

Finally, a note on the co-deployment of both approaches. In general terms, we might argue that the desire for approval is, in effect, and in Martin and White's (2005) terms, an expectation of and desire for positive appraisal, be it affective, aesthetic or the assessment of things, circumstances or events people relate to, or of behaviour (as per the three appraisal categories). Additionally, but rather more indirectly, the desire for freedom of action and freedom from imposition similarly assumes an expectation of at least the avoidance of negative appraisal of these aspects, though none of them are represented lexically.

Another aspect that needs considering is an exploration of face as proposed by Scollon and Scollon (2001: 48), who note that 'any communication is a risk to face'. Indeed, this is an evolution of the point Tracy (1990: 221) makes in her argument that there is no faceless communication. In effect, where there is communication, face is an issue. To this we add, where there is communication there is also attitude towards the contributions interlocuters make by the co-construction of the communication, both directly as a real-time interactant and indirectly as a post facto interactant. Hence, appraisal theory is inextricably tied to the notion of face, which, in terms other than in Goffman's approach, is our 'public self-image' (Brown and Levinson, 1987: 61).

When making evaluative choices of the world around us in interaction, we establish our own face and manage the faces of others. Take, for example, complimenting someone's car, even if evoked by means of a metonymical cliché, as in *nice wheels*. Here the speaker is evoking appraisal via a valuation (appreciation) of their possession. Furthermore, in so doing, the speaker is performing what Brown and Levinson (1987: 103–129) call 'show or intensify interest in h, h's goods, values or belongings', and thereby the complimenter is (all other things being equal) enhancing the face of the hearer by use of positive politeness (via a positive appraisal), and enhancing their own face by showing that they are a kind and thoughtful person. This is effective relationship management vis-à-vis appraisal meanings realised through a selection of discourse-semantic resources conveying attitude as well as through linguistic politeness devices which appear, for the most part, designed to simultaneously manage the face of both recipient and author of the message. Therefore, the co-deployment of both approaches allows a more holistic understanding of the construal of interpersonal relationships in discourse by facilitating the examination of not only the evaluative choices – including triggers, intentions and meaning potential, as per appraisal as an SFL rooted approach – but also of the contextual aspects of the interaction and the impact that the interaction has on interpersonal relations, as per sociopragmatic approaches.

CHAPTER SIX

Clichés as Identity Markers

6.1 Clichés in Face and Identity

This chapter investigates the role that clichés play in the construction and articulation of face and identity by examining and analysing transcripts from TV show *The Apprentice* utilising insights from SFL (e.g. Halliday, 1978) and Brown and Levinson's (1987) approach to politeness and positive face.

We see individual identity as a fluid construct (Giddens, 1991) which is negotiated through and within social systems and cultural norms but is not predetermined by them (Jenkins, 1996; Goffman, 1959). In this way, self-identity can be (co)constructed as a constant self-endeavour by reference to a framework for social negotiation (Giddens, 1991; Jenkins, 1996). Goffman's (1959) self-presentation theory compares identity construction to an individual 'performance' where actors project the desired image in interpersonal interaction. Interaction is compared to a front stage where an actor is aware of being observed by an audience and therefore performs observing certain rules and conventions. Failure to do so results in face loss. The actor's behaviour in private is compared to backstage where no performance is necessary. Goffman's (1959) thespian metaphor for one's self-presentation as a continual process of complex negotiation between the front and back stages stands for the multitude of presentation strategies that a person strives to manage when balancing the individual goals and the 'self' that they assume the audience, or interlocutors, desire (Leary and Kowalski, 1990).

Joseph (2013: 35) poses that 'identity and face have much in common, each is an imagining of the self or another, within a public sphere involving multiple actors'. He goes on to argue that in the same way participants in any interaction can engage in facework (co-construction of own, or of others' faces through primarily linguistic means), they, too, can engage linguistically in social identity construction in the same way (Joseph, 2013). This is crucial to our argument in the following ways:

Firstly, Joseph (2013) cites Tajfel (1978: 63) who, as one of the leaders of social identity theory, defines identity as a social construct, that is '[t]hat *part* of an individual's self-concept which derives from his [*sic*] knowledge of his membership of a social group (or groups) together with the value and emotional significance attached to that membership' (*emphasis* in original). As we have noted earlier (cf. Chapter 5), when considering social behaviour, especially linguistic behaviour (which is, of course, a subset of social behaviour), and emotional significance of that behaviour, then we are engaging in the negotiation or maintenance of interpersonal relationships.

Secondly, in terms of groups and group membership, especially in terms of how members of the group interact and harmonise their behaviours, Lave and Wenger (1991) theorise and demonstrate the concept of a community of practice (hereafter CoP). As defined in Chapter 2, a central component of a CoP is shared concern for an endeavour and 'they do and learn how to do it better as they interact regularly'. (Lave and Wenger 1991: 98). The examples they go on to give would therefore also include both business as CoPs and entrepreneurial activities as CoPs (as a sub-nested set of business ones). The key point to note here, of course, is the role language use or linguistic behaviour plays in the co-construction *of*, and claims *to* membership of any CoP, clichés being, of course, common currency and heavily concretised instances of language behaviour.

Thirdly, with Tajfel (1978) and those following in the social identity tradition, recognising that identity is intrinsically engaged with group membership, we can therefore contextualise and theorise the specific reasons for the usages of the linguistic behaviour (especially, for our purposes, through the use of clichés) by reality television, (RTV) contestants as they introduce themselves. Clearly the contestants' linguistic choices are shaped precisely by their desire to represent their fitness for inclusion in the notoriously competitive CoPs for business in general and entrepreneurialism in particular. In effect, clichés as used by the contestants on BBC's *The Apprentice* in their introductory scenes effectively operate with an ideational function in that they are linguistic resources used by the contestants in the attempt to construct their own identities as entrepreneurs and hence their fitness for inclusion in the CoP of not only business, but business with Lord Sugar. All of these aspects relate directly to the concept of identity. As we noted earlier, and following Joseph (2013; see also Bousfield 2013), identity and face must be theorised together and cannot be theorised alone, at least from the perspective of studies on language use and behaviour. To put it another way, we can first compare, then contrast the concepts of face and of identity.

Face in this study is understood in the fundamental sense proposed by Goffman, which we outlined in Chapter 5 and which refers to the value claimed by an individual in interaction vis-à-vis the interactants assumptions regarding such individual's positioning and by reference to approved social norms.

Identity on the other hand is here understood in the sense of Joseph's (2013) approach. Joseph argues that '[i]dentity relates classically to who individuals are, understood in terms of the groups to which they belong, including nationality, ethnicity, religion, gender, generation, sexual orientation, social class and an unlimited number of other possibilities' (p. 36).

Citing these very quotations, Bousfield and McIntyre (2018: 47) argue that '(t)hese "other possibilities" alluded to by Joseph must also involve the notion of "profession" included by Goffman'. Profession, being an aspect of identity is not, we feel, a terribly contentious claim to make, especially when the contestants in *The Apprentice* are attempting to begin or continue a business profession as an entrepreneur. In effect then, both identity and face – as linguistically constructed – are important to the contestants in order for them to utilise such linguistic resources as clichés.

In terms of our unfolding argument, here, Bousfield and McIntyre (2018: 48) make a potentially pertinent point:

Neither face nor identity are static entities but are, rather, transitive (in the sense that, primarily through interaction, they can be changed). The relationship of face to identity is that through discursive interaction, face can be threatened, enhanced, saved or damaged, resulting in longer-term impacts on identity both in terms of Self and Other construction and recognition of those identities. Essentially, then, we argue that the notions of face and identity are discrete but linked concepts. We accept that identity is durative and that face is punctual, but also argue that face is iterative in that it needs to be made and constantly remade in interaction.

Goffman (1955) argues that face is on loan from society which implies that it has to be formed in some (even non-verbal) interaction. This links back to what we discussed in Chapter 5 where, following Scollon and Scollon (2001) we suggested that there cannot be interaction without face being an issue. Taking this to an extreme, Terkourafi argues that face only exists in interaction between two or more interactants and face does not exist in isolation or outwith interaction (Terkourafi, 2008). Despite broadly agreeing with this view, we would argue, following Bousfield (2018) that face expectations (of self and of our interactants) can be formed prior to interaction and that we can start the interaction by carefully phrasing and framing our words in order to try to make them land in a way that we see as desirable to ourselves and the co-construction of mutual aspects of face. It follows, then, that both schemata and preparatory linguistic behaviour can contribute to the construction of such face expectations, by which we mean the schemata of our interactants based on: previous experience and interactions with them; cognitive-schematic expectations of the type of person we are talking to (based on socially acquired schematic expectations of how they behave), and the role that they have to play both in society and in the interaction at hand.

In explaining these terms in more detail, Goffman (1959) pointed out that social roles play a part in shaping identity. Such roles become an 'institutionalised set of social expectations, with stereotypes emerging as a more fixed form of meaning and stability – in other words an ideal type that may constrain experience as well as inspire the crafting of new meanings' (Down and Warren, 2008: 5).

In terms of the concept of schema or schemata (also referred to as script), this was first posed by Bartlett (1932) who then refers to them as 'structured patterns of information stored in memory' which can explain 'associative processes' (Mazzone, 2011: 2148) and indeed the choices of linguistic repertoires during identity performance, as will be discussed later in this chapter.

To further support our argument of the role of clichés as membership-oriented linguistic resources, Down and Warren (2006: 5) propose that the role of the entrepreneur corresponds, in fact, to a stereotypical cultural script considered as an 'ideal type' by shared cultural narratives. Examining narratives of self-presentation, Down and Warren (2008) show how clichés, as presumed commonplace linguistic devices, can be used to frame self-narratives as heroic, successful and self-sufficient. In so doing they illustrate the juxtaposition of 'ordinary public narratives' with 'extraordinary' self-attributed qualities for the purposes of construing the desired entrepreneurial identity (p. 18). This echoes our findings in Chapter 4 in which we conclude that the use of clichés in branding discourse evokes superiority and difference of the brand by virtue of the shared knowledge they carry. This links to Culpeper's (2010) argument that certain concretised formulaic constructions can actually carry pragmatic weight, even if they move from one context to another. In being formulaic constructions with set meaning, clichés function as common currency that are less susceptible to the context in which they are uttered than are novel linguistic construction and resources.

We would now argue further that, given there are, or at least can be, face expectations prior to face co-construction in and through interaction, then it is (as we will show in the examples here) entirely feasible and legitimate that contestants, even when ostensibly alone (though they are, technically, interacting with the camera crew as they introduce themselves to camera – see our discussion on double articulation later in this chapter), in a recorded situation may attempt to invite socially positive construction of their faces given that 'since face being punctual is more malleable [this means] it is, in effect, a route into identity' (Bousfield and McIntyre, 2018: 48). The significance of this point, and the differences between the concepts of face and identity to our study on clichés, are perhaps best captured in the following quotation from Garcés-Conejos Blitvich and Sifianou (2017: 235):

a. Face is a social attribute; identity is an individual one.
b. Face is relational, the result of a non-summative process; identity is the property of monadic individuals, the outcome of a summative process.
c. Face is a punctual phenomenon; identity is a durative one.
d. Face is invested with emotion; identity is not.

In short, part of the argument we are making here is that although the contestants speak to a (from the audience's perspective, an apparently,) silent camera crew, this is still a multiplicitous form of interaction. As such, their attempts at choices of clichés to construct their identities as core members of business-related CoPs represent instances of their own attempts to construct, or invite the construction of their positive (approval-based) faces in a highly desirable (to themselves) way.

6.2 Reality TV and Broadcast Discourse

According to Scannell (1991: 1) broadcast discourse is the 'communicative interaction between those participating in discussion, interview, game show or whatever and, at the same time, is designed to be heard by absent audiences'. Broadcasters, therefore, work to meet the assumed demands of such audiences. Dubrofsky (2011) discusses that RTV participants have become used to publicly displaying the self for entertainment purposes. Walters (1995: 6) calls RTV 'symptomatic texts' that are evidence of cultural practices. Therefore, an analysis of such 'symptoms' provides insights into larger cultural practices (Walters, 1995: 10).

Working on impoliteness in exploitative RTV, Lorenzo-Dus, (2009) examines the 'doubled' nature in the way in which the participants' linguistic contributions of BBC's show *Dragon's Den* are presented. Here Lorenzo-Dus (2009) poses that the first stage of articulation, is in effect, what the participants choose to say, or they wish to construe in their instances and examples of self-representation. The second stage, or layer of articulation, is dependent on how the editorial team in the production company decides to edit the much longer interactions on the show in order to portray a certain 'angle', 'slant' or perspective on the interaction and, crucially, the participants themselves. The double articulation relies on voyeurism, and audiences are therefore presented with a strategically selected proportion of the filmed material for each episode in instances of interaction that make frequent use of 'unmitigated face-threat' (Lorenzo-Dus 2009: 62). The latter is often maximised through various semiotic devices (e.g. verbal wit, verbal and non-verbal face-threatening behaviour, categorical evaluation), coupled with strategic angles of representation, for entertainment purposes (see Culpeper 2005). In line with the argument of this study, we propose that the single and double articulation of the representation of the use of clichés by the contestant of *The Apprentice* is an example of self-presentation; and that this example of the use of clichés as self presentational resources by the contestants can therefore be seen to perform ideational and interpersonal functions (cf. Chapter 2). At the first level of articulation, participants resort to clichés to construe or attempt to construct their version, or identity, that best represents the stereotypical role or schema they see fits them (as candidate or actual members of relevant business CoP). That is, there is an ideational component (cf. Chapter 2) as they use these resources to construct a preferred version of reality. Further to this, the double articulation, in being strategically edited for entertainment purposes by the programme's editorial team, appeals to the audience's emotions, attitudes or stance, and as such works to create a position for the audience that, in most cases, provokes some kind of (dis)affiliation with the represented characters, thereby fulfilling an interpersonal function, at macro level.

When speaking to camera, and there is technically no other immediate interactant present, face expectations are still present through double articulation. In this way, as Bousfield (2013) suggests, these instances are in effect an attempt to shape the future ways in which people interact with the 'self' and therefore construct their face. In effect, these introductions to camera offer the contestants the opportunity to presage others' face expectations of them and thus, at least theoretically, smooth the way to achieving their desired identity as the ideal entrepreneur and, hence, the preferred candidate of Lord Sugar. It is at this point that double articulation becomes a matter of interest in RTV and broadcast discourse because what the candidates tend to do or say and what the editorial team actually then go on to choose to represent may well clash, thereby offering a potentially face-threatening broadcast of contestants as their attempts at later face management (through, amongst other things, their use of their clichés) are subverted by the editing process.

That is what we aim to demonstrate by examining, presumably and almost definitely, heavily edited and carefully orchestrated self-presentations of contestants in *The Apprentice* show where their self-presentations heavily comprise clichés. Whilst we should be exceptionally wary of assuming all or even most communication in such RTV interactions is naturalistic, it is undeniable that, unless staged for linguistic purposes, participants' linguistic practices are indicative of their presence in discourse. In effect, and more simply put, the contestant actually says these clichés in relation to themselves. We pose, therefore, that an examination of clichés in reality shows is worth pursuing as clichés can indeed be seen to constitute indicators of larger cultural practices embedded in linguistic behaviour.

6.3 Data and Methods

Data

The data for this chapter were collected from episodes of *The Apprentice*, seasons 11, 12 and 14, which were chosen owing to the accessibility of the full seasons. *The Apprentice* is a British BBC business-styled reality that has run since 2005 (we are aware of *The Apprentice* format being operated in other countries and cultures, of course). The BBC programme focuses on a group of entrepreneurs competing in a series of business-related challenges set by British businessman Lord Alan Sugar in order to win the competition and win a £250,000 investment. Lord Sugar is assisted by two close business associates who act as observers. Each season runs for fifteen episodes.

The show starts with the selected candidates meeting Lord Sugar after having handed in business plans that they would like to carry out upon the show's conclusion with the help of Lord Sugar's investment. The selected candidates are divided into two teams which compete against each other. The teams are given a series of team-oriented tasks which test candidates' skills in conducting business. The competitive nature of the show means that candidates, despite being expected to work together, often focus on raising their individual profiles and increase their chances of winning the competition.

Once a task is finished, the candidates report back to Sugar at a staged boardroom to review the task, discuss its outcomes and how it was conducted. After careful scrutinisation of each team and each team member by Lord Sugar, his aides and the candidates themselves (when reviewing team members performance during the tasks), Lord Sugar and his aides decide which candidate or candidates from the losing team will leave the show by being 'fired'. The winning team is rewarded with a prize, the losing team left to wait back at the candidates' shared house.

In the final episode only two or, maximum, three candidates go through to the final task where one of the three candidates will be the winner. The series were watched fully and clichés were manually recorded as they appeared in the conversations with immediate context. As we were looking for clichés relating to identity, we selected instances from episode 1 of each series where the contestants talk to the cameras about themselves.

Out of 152 clichés collected and scrutinised, we were left with fifteen expressions that fit the criteria we were looking for: (a) they fit the *definition* of cliché outlined in Chapter 2; (b) they constituted an instance of referential self-presentation. This was decided by searching for clichés in extracts with self-referential devices, mostly the first-person singular personal and possessive pronouns (marked in the transcribed examples). The data were retrieved from shots that lasted 5–10 seconds. The shots were intersected with scenes of the team in action. When a participant was foregrounded during team interaction, this was then followed by an individual shot of the participant talking to the camera about themselves. The extracts were transcribed and collated for analysis.

Methods

We analyse each extract (fifteen in total) featuring clichés in terms of what identities are construed by clichés and how they construe the participants' (desired or actual) entrepreneurial identity by reference to Goffman's self-presentation theory.

At the first level of analysis, we prioritise the way in which clichés are seen as choices the speakers make to construe the version of the identity they wish to perform at the point of filming. This is what we refer to as single articulation. At this point, we do not concentrate on the interpersonal aspects of clichés, that is, the relationships they are seen to enact, as we will discuss that in the following section. Our main analytical tool for clichés is CMT, first introduced in Chapter 4 of this book.

The second level of analysis discusses the juxtaposition between the interpersonal functions clichés fulfil in the self-presentation extracts and in the representation of such self-presentation. In order to avoid confusion potentially caused by multiple analytical levels, when analysing the self-presentation extracts we do not analyse the interpersonal function by reference to the analytical tools proposed by SFL at this level (cf.

Chapter 2), but rather focus on the facework carried out, by reference to Brown and Levinson's (1987) framework outlined in Chapter 5. Further to this, we analyse the interpersonal aspects of the ways participants are represented when using clichés after the editorial process has taken place, by reference to Lorenzo-Dus's (2009) work, as outlined earlier. We refer to this as double articulation.

6.4 Findings

In this section, we present the findings of the analysis of clichés contestants use to talk about themselves, that is, the single articulation level. The first part of this section is structured in relation to the identities clichés are seen to facilitate for the contestants. Extracts are clustered under the label indicating identities inferred. Each label then contains the corresponding extracts and brief explanation of how clichés contribute to such identity construction.

Confrontational and Fear Inducing

(1) Joseph: when I was 14 I was expelled from school […] but I *turned my life around* […] I'm now *the godfather of* business […] and I'm here to make Lord Sugar *an offer he cannot refuse*

Within this example, there are three clichés, the latter two of which are intertextually and interdiscursively linked to their famous (arguably) source materials, that is Scorsese's Godfather films. Through the first one, in the form of the ACTIONS ARE DIRECTIONS metaphor within the wider LIFE IS A JOURNEY metaphorical frame, *turning my life around*, speaks of the identity construction of someone who realises their (presumed, implied) mistakes. In so doing, Joseph is informing us that he purposefully ceased engaging in self-destructive practices and engaged in those sorts of practices that he schematically understands or believes are viewed positively, at least by those members of the CoPs within society with which he wishes to associate, one in which business acumen and achievement stand as socially approved success measures. As such, the cliché seeks to generate an effective positive face enhancement. His latter two clichés, however, introduce a rogue and dangerous element to his attempts at identity construction.

By explicitly invoking the concept of *The Godfather*, and qualifying this (as the mafia related meaning, rather than the socially-religiously related meaning) with the last cliché an *offer he cannot refuse*, Joseph

introduces the identity construction of a dangerous, ruthless and powerful individual, with an entailment of fear. What he presumably did
not intend is that the invocation of such source material may well have
inadvertently brought across into the meaning construction space
the criminal elements that go with such a reference. His usage here
of these three clichés is to presumably demonstrate he is a capable,
self-reflective, ruthless, determined, powerful and vaguely dangerous
or risky individual, all adding to the 'bad boy' identity he may well be
playing up to.

    (2) Aleksandra: The sheer energy that *I* am going to bring is going to
        mimic that of a nuclear explosion [...] *once* I *lock myself in on the*
        target [...] *they do not stand a chance*
    (3) Dillon: basically I'm king of the truth bomb [...] that means that
        I'm going to tell you how it is whether you like it or not

Both Aleksandra and Dillon utilise clichés in the form of military metaphors to construe confrontational identities. Aleksandra's PURPOSES ARE
WEAPONS, PERSONAL OBJECTIVES ARE MILITARY TARGETS and OPTIONS
ARE CHANCES metaphors construe a narrative of success where she pres-
ents herself as defeating her opponents.

    Dillon's uses power (king) and military metaphors (bomb) to pre-empt
the threat inscribed in the cliché *I'm going to tell you how it is whether
you like it or not*, inducing fear and construing a confrontational identity in ideational terms. Both contestants also construct, in Brown and
Levinson's terms, their own positive face.

    (4) Paul₁: *I* definitely *don't shy away from* conflict [...] *make no mis-*
        take about it [...] *I'm here to win*

'Shy' in its predicator form, in the sense of 'moving away from, or
staying away from', is becoming archaic in general English usage.
As such, the codification of shy in *don't shy away from* in Paul's cliché here is evidence of the ossification effect of clichés within lexical chunks, which then operate independently (if conventionally) of
their original lexical terms. The first of three clichés that Paul uses
construes a brave, confident and even fearless identity ready for
confrontation, and is a cliché used to pre-qualify the following two:
make no mistake about it and *I'm here to win*. Added to the brave,
confident and fearless identity is, therefore, the self-presentation as
determined and focused, indicating predisposition and readiness. The
ideational function of clichés here, as elsewhere, is therefore to construe aspects of professional identity in a way that reflects the values

of the entrepreneurial community he aspires to belong to by winning the competition.

(5) Jackie: <u>my</u> game plan is to *pick off the competition one by one* [...] <u>I</u>'m completely ruthless and <u>I</u>'d be surprised if Lord Sugar doesn't already have a cheque with <u>my</u> name on it

A complex set of conventionalised metaphors are used here by Jackie's clichés. The PURPOSES ARE WEAPONS metaphor is qualified by the intertextual invocation of the SHOOTING IS RESOLVING metaphor. The clichés work to create a version of reality in which her identity is that of the confrontational, calculating and confident contender.

(6) Jessica: A lot of people underestimate <u>me</u> [...] and then *I pull out the big guns* and *I* always tend *to get my way*

Jessica's introductory statement sets herself up as defiant of expectation. However, through her use of PURPOSES ARE WEAPONS and BIG IS BETTER metaphors, Jessica's first cliché construes herself as confrontational and fear inducing to them, through the second cliché *I always ... get my way* as another LIFE IS A JOURNEY metaphor, demonstrating her skills as a determined, confident and commanding individual and engaging in self-enhancing face behaviour.

Uniqueness

(7) Grianne: I think everyone thought 'oh she's just a make-up artist' [...] but I'm a make-up artist who wants *to think outside the box*

The use of the infamous *to think outside the box* cliché invokes the socially positive persona of an original thinker, and an innovative and effective problem solver. Grianne, therefore, uses this cliché, arguably, to create an identity that she sees as socially positive. She is, in effect, schematically referring to the concept of original thinkers being prized and lauded in society at large. The conjunction 'but' suggesting a counter argument, and the mental process 'wants' preceding the cliché indicate a predisposition to actively strive to be different (presumably from other make-up artists), which helps the candidate present herself as unique and defiant of expectations.

(8) Richard: I've got a unique concept and a business plan that's really *cutting edge* [...] he'd be crazy to pass by Richard Woods

Cutting edge is an interesting cliché utilising the metaphor SLICING IS PROGRESS and the cutting edge, therefore, is the leading element of the process of slicing, hence the contestant's proposal to lead, and cause, the progress to be made. Relying on encyclopaedic knowledge of business and entrepreneurial CoPs valuing catalysts of progress and positive change, he uses this cliché to construct his desired identity through enhancing his positive face and presenting himself as having a unique product. The construction of uniqueness is also reinforced later in the narrative where he includes himself as an actor in his self-presentation (what van Leeuwen calls 'personalisation'), which helps Richard present himself as explicitly different and standing out from the other contestants, reinforcing the uniqueness being construed.

> (9) Karthik: *I don't walk the path that others walk* [...] *my way is a separate superhighway*

In this example, the use of the LIFE IS A JOURNEY (Lakoff and Johnson 1980) metaphor through the *walk the path* cliché, which is then extended to Karthik's use of his own *superhighway*, is an attempt to also construe uniqueness based on independence, originality and speed (with a QUICK IS SUCCESSFUL PROGRESS metaphor) and hence to suggest he is more successful than others.

Tough and Controlling

> (10) Dan: If you *cross me* [...] then *it's like hitting a brick wall* [...] you're never going to get past

The first cliché in this extract means to defy, challenge or frustrate. Any of these could be seen to be a threat to Brown and Levinson's (1987) concepts of both negative face (the desire to be unimpeded) and positive face (the desire to be approved of). Hence, to cross someone in effect – to offend in some way – may well be intentional or incidental. The use of this cliché, then therefore demonstrates an ideational attempt by Dan at self-identity construction of a specific reality that he is claiming about both the latitude and respect that he expects, and, especially when considering the second cliché, the response he will provide if not afforded such latitude and respect. It amounts to the construction of, or addition to the construction of a tough business entrepreneur identity. The second, *it's like hitting a brick wall*, references the well-known and common currency simile-clichés by means of the metaphor ACTION IS MOVEMENT and SUCCESS IS AN OPEN PATH. Again, by attempting to construct his identity-as-entrepreneur in this way, Dan is engaging in self-directed face construction as a hard and unyielding business operator, presumably as he sees these aspects as central to the identity of a successful entrepreneur, noting that undesirable action on the part of others will not be successful and will be definitively and irrevocably stopped.

(11) Paul$_2$: I've got no problems stepping up and being a project manager on any of the tasks [...] the way to *fend off* your strongest rivals is to not let them see you coming [...] I'm just going to sit there and *pull the strings* and *do what I need to do* to *get through to the end*

Fend off as a predicator (meaning 'to push away') is used in conjunction with the *pull the strings* cliché allowing Paul to construe himself as a strategic, powerful and strong figure able to push his opponents and achieve success. The latter is evidenced in the LIFE IS A JOURNEY and SUCCESS IS DESTINATION metaphors in the cliché.

(12) Kayode: When it comes to business [...] I don't *just grab the bull by the horns* [...] I put it in a headlock and squeeze every opportunity that comes out of him

The classic PROBLEM IS A POWERFUL ANIMAL metaphor as a cliché, here Kayode is constructing an identity as a fearless tackler of issues, and someone who turns challenge into opportunity. Again, from an ideational function perspective, he is attempting to construct the identity of the ideal entrepreneur.

Ambitious

(13) Alex: *money makes the world go round* [...] and to me [...] it is my world [...] I'm like a cash machine [...] if *you push the right buttons* [...] I will give you money

(14) Daniel: money is the *be all and end all* [...] some people say *money can't make you happy* [...] but I'd rather cry in a sports car than cry in a banger

In (13) Alex's use of the MONEY IS A POWERFUL FORCE metaphor through the *money makes the world go round* cliché, when coupled with the PERSON IS A MACHINE metaphor and KNOWLEDGE IS REWARD metaphor, we see the attempt at creating an ambitious, powerful, rewarding and machine-like identity. These constitute linguistic evidence of what Alex sees as positive traits for a member of the CoPs of business and entrepreneurship. Similarly, in (14) Daniel extends the understandings of MONEY IS EVERYTHING metaphor and MONEY INVOKES EMOTION metaphor by implied metonymic reference to sports cars (costing a lot of money) and bangers (being very old, unreliable, cheap second-hand cars).

Ready for Business

(15) April: I'm there [...] I'm where it needs to be [...] *I'm suited I'm booted* [...] come on

The cliché *I'm suited, I'm booted* utilises the metonymic and intertextual references to the uniform of business, the business suit complete with smart and formal footwear. The reference to being *suited and booted* is also an implicature (via Grice's (1975) maxims of relation and possibly manner) that April is ready and capable of operating effectively within the CoPs that regularly require such a wardrobe. April is seeking positive affirmation, and hence positive face enhancement, via the identity construction of herself as prepared for business. This means her cliché serves the ideational function of creating a reality in which she is already successful and is prepared for such success.

All in all, every cliché we have explored in this data set aims to create an identity that is assumed by the contestants as desirable in the CoP of entrepreneurs to which they (aspire to) belong. In presenting themselves as confrontational and fear inducing, unique, tough and in control, ambitious and ready to their intended audience, their use of clichés can be considered an attempt to co-construct positive face with those in the CoPs they wish to operate within. The audience they aim for, however – i.e. members of business and entrepreneurial CoPs in general, and Lord Sugar as the ultimate arbiter and decider of who wins *The Apprentice* – is not necessarily the audience who sees the construction of the linguistic clichés here. As we argued earlier, the editing team for *The Apprentice*, in making any form of editing choice, introduce the double articulation effect. On a practical level, the reality is that there are many more hours of filmed behaviour than can make it into an hour's weekly episode. Lord Sugar himself has noted that the boardroom scenes where he makes decisions on which contestants stay and which leave the process, and which is never more than thirty minutes of screen time, actually take at least three hours to film, and usually longer. Further, entertainment like its subset, drama, needs conflict in order to pique the public or audience's interest and keep them engaged (as per Culpeper, 2005). The extra-linguistic aim of the contestants is to win the competition, the extra-linguistic aim of the TV production company is to entertain, and conflict is a necessary component of such entertainment. It is therefore no surprise that what the contestants aim for ideationally (i.e. the identity they construe) and how their messages land interpersonally (with the audience, with Lord Sugar, or with the other contestants) may clash, as per the TV company's aim of entertainment. It then follows that those scenes that are seen to represent a contribution to some form of clash in terms of ideational function and interpersonal effects are arguably more likely to be selected, precisely because conflict is a form of entertainment (Culpeper 2005).

6.5 Discussion

In examining the construal of entrepreneurial identities by the contestants, we focused solely on the clichés used as ideational resources in terms of their metaphorical form. SFL considers these lexical metaphors (e.g. Halliday and Matthiessen, 2004) whilst we analysed them by reference to CMT, thereby examining the conceptual mappings between source and target domains, which allowed us to unveil the metaphorical entailments in the clichés (e.g. fear) and how they work to construe the desired identity (cf. Chapter 4; Lakoff and Johnson, 1980; Kovecses, 2002). We are, however, aware that such choices prevented us from focusing on other aspects of the construal of experience, losing some analytical depth. This is particularly the case when not examining the interpersonal function of the clichés and their co-text at lexico-grammar level where certain choices at this level reinforce the identities construed (or performed, in Goffman's terms) and help the overall competitive positioning. An example of this is the selection of pronouns usually construing the first person in direct opposition (i.e. confrontation) with a generic second person, marked by the personal pronoun ('you') or third person ('they'). In so doing, their opponents are construed as 'the other', be they other competitors, the people they sell products to in the shows' tasks or actual or potential customers (e.g. (2) and (3)). Other interpersonal resources include the imperative mood (e.g. (4)) and the reported speech in extract (7) in the construction of uniqueness.

Another aspect worth discussing is the role of Lord Sugar in the contestants' identity construction process via clichés. Sugar's public identity is predicated on the fact that he comes from a working-class background in East London, and his accent and linguistic repertoire, which includes clichés, are important aspects of this public identity. Albeit not explored in detail in this chapter, we acknowledge the possibility that, in using clichés, the contestants may be interpersonally trying to align themselves with that aspect of Lord Sugar's identity to gain his approval. Having said that, Lord Sugar as an entrepreneur does indeed constitute a member of the desired CoP we have discussed.

In taking a CMT approach to clichés, we could unveil other significant aspects. Despite the running argument of this study being that clichés are highly conventionalised – even dead metaphors which partly explain their ubiquitous characteristic – in this data set in particular, we see a manipulation of clichés by extending conventionalised metaphors.

By this we mean that contestants extend the conventional metaphor in a way that shows a conscious choice to do so for the purposes of identity construction in self-presentation. In (9), for example, the contestant extends and exploits the LIFE IS A JOURNEY metaphor (*superhighway*) to construe himself as unique but also to demonstrate his competitive position. In other words, there is a claim to shared knowledge but with a novel interpretation (14) or extension (12). This novelisation goes vis-à-vis the schemata of what entrepreneurs do, especially in a competitive setting where they have to resort to their imagination to be able to come up with solutions that will allow them to succeed in the tasks that have been set for them and stay in the competition. In 'novelising' the cliché by extending it (e.g. 14), they also show their ability to challenge established practice and therefore perform different identities. Take for example extract (14) where we see two angles on entrepreneurial identity. Firstly the contestant uses the clichés to present himself as ambitious and convey the idea that he will do whatever it takes to succeed. This is a reflection of what is perceived as being common currency within the CoP. But also in innovating or extending the metaphor ('I'd rather cry in a sports car than in a banger'), the contestant conveys an idea of differentiation, which positions the contestant in a different identity, that of 'uniqueness', therefore showing that the concept of identity is not fixed but fluid and can be performed by linguistic choices at various levels. Having said that, the fact that the editing of such self-presentation focuses on a highly conventional and established cliché can be seen to subvert the contestant's positive face enhancement and the attempt to create the idea of the innovation in his representation, and by extension, threaten his positive face presentation at the second level of articulation and anchor the contestant's identity as 'ambitious'. Therefore, in focusing on the double articulation we see how the editors position themselves interpersonally with the audience and invite the public to (dis)align with the contestants by relying on surrounding discourses (containing attitudes) around clichés and perceptions of entrepreneurs as striving for money. This, in turn, creates an inherent clash and the potential for drama upon which the entertainment relies. We conclude therefore that the single and double articulation dyad goes hand in hand with the ideational and interpersonal functions of the discourse, the latter understood as having both a micro level (what the contestants say) and at macro level (the representation of what they say by editors).

CHAPTER SEVEN

Concluding Remarks

Throughout this study, we have made a number of original, significant and rigorous contributions to the field(s) of linguistics in particular and to the study of clichés in general.

In this study, we conceptualised clichés as strategies used in discourse to fulfil a number of functions. Despite addressing clichés as formulaic sequences (e.g. Wray, 2002), we do not claim this work to be placed within the field of formulaic language. However, we do acknowledge the premise, and widely agreed view, that clichés have an important role in allowing economy of speech production and decoding, as important psycholinguistic evidence has concluded (e.g. Miller and Weinert 1998; see also Wray 2002).

For our purposes, we approached discourse as language use in speech and writing, 'as a form of social practice' (e.g. Fairclough and Wodak, 1997: 258), as a multidimensional social phenomenon whereby social reality is constructed and made real through discourse. We worked with van Dijk's (2009: 65–66) definition of discourse as presented in Section 2.3 and explored clichés as ways of social interaction (e.g. comments to online news in Chapter 3 and organisational interactions in Chapter 5). We also explored clichés as forms of social representations (e.g. Chapter 4) and actions (face-threats/enhancements) in cultural products (BBC RTV show in Chapter 6). In so doing, we extended our study of clichés as formulaic sequences in discourse into a number of disciplines. We borrowed, or co-deployed, tools from SFL, appraisal theory, sociocognitive discourse analysis, discourse-historical approach, corpus linguistics, sociopragmatics and im/politeness, interactional sociolinguistics and identity theory. In placing this study within the broad discipline of discourse studies, we explored a number of dimensions of clichés in discourse as 'naturally occurring' language use by real language users, focusing on larger units of language and the study of interaction (Wodak and Reisigl, 2009: 2).

Our basic premise was that clichés can be explored by reference to the sociosemiotic environment (as per Halliday, 1978) in which discourses operate, and focused on exploring how clichés, as language choices, work to fulfil ideational and interpersonal metafunctions that correspond to the contextual parameters of field and tenor, as posed by SFL (cf. Section 2.4). In other words, we argue throughout the book that clichés are sociosemiotic resources of language and that people use them in different contexts for a variety of purposes in discourse, which we unveiled by co-deploying tools from 'special-purpose approaches' that helped us explain how clichés work as multidimensional phenomena (Matthiessen, 2012: 444).

We posed that clichés perform an ideational function in discourse in that they help construe aspects of reality, as per Halliday's (1978; 2014) definition in Section 2.4. This, we proposed, is achieved by virtue of the fixed meanings attached to them that carry unchallenged knowledge assumptions. In Chapter 3, for example, by reference to Wodak (e.g. 2015), we conceptualised clichés as topoi that work as 'common sense reasoning schemes' (van Dijk 2000: 98) carrying ideational components that allow language users to put forward a point of view, or version or reality, in argumentation. We also showed how, in some cases, the same clichés were used to build different arguments and construe different versions of the same phenomenon, thereby proving their ubiquitous character. Similarly, in Chapter 4, taking a sociocognitive perspective, we saw clichés as offering a mechanical, safe and shared framework that brands rely upon in the construal of self-ideations, which positions them as benchmarks for comparison within and across industries whilst engaging in a dialectical relationship with neoliberal market practices and discourses. Finally, in Chapter 6, we explored the role of metaphorical clichés in the construal of entrepreneurial identities, examining data from competitive BBC TV show *The Apprentice*.

Our second premise was that clichés fulfil an interpersonal function. We explored this in Chapter 4, where we found that clichés allow the construction of emotional or rational appeals in advertising and brand positioning, therefore building a relationship of trust with stakeholders. In conceptualising them as im/politeness strategies in organisational discourse, in Chapter 5, we were able to account for how clichés perform face-work in the expression and management of evaluative meanings demonstrating their value in the enactment and maintenance of interpersonal relationships. Finally, in Chapter 6, we saw how clichés work at a metalevel in the double articulation process represented by the careful staging or editing of the RTV show (i.e. the contestants will either have been told to say something 'soundbitey' about themselves, or the editors will have chosen the most 'soundbitey' bit). As such, clichés work as tools for the enactment of relationships between the programme producers/editors and the audience by relying on the public's knowledge of the negative discourse about clichés which makes the show 'watchable'.

Even if fundamentally we sought not only to interrogate the role, nature and use of clichés, we also, albeit more indirectly, explored their effective perception within society. As we have shown throughout, we found that there is a mismatch between the generally negative *perception* of clichés' usage, and their *actual* usage. Whilst their socially negative perception persists, clichés (cf. Chapter 1), when realised in specific contexts of use, can be creative and shared resources. This allows for the ideational functions of language in terms of facilitating the construal of a version of reality, through which, for example, identity is constructed or at least attempted to be constructed. Further, clichés in such usage, as we have argued in Chapter 2, and shown in Chapters 5 and 6, are linguistic tokens with a significant interpersonal function, where their use as shared resources available to members of a CoP is to enact and maintain relationships.

The ideational and interpersonal functions of clichés in certain genres and CoPs are also evident in the second aspect of originality we have introduced through our work and presented in this book. As we have argued and shown in Chapters 5 and 6, clichés operate pragmatically in regards not only to ideational identity construction but also (via cliché users' invitation) to co-construct face, and associated phenomena, including linguistic politeness. In doing so, we have, to our knowledge, encapsulated the combination of, and potential for the future fruitful alliance of two hitherto disparate areas of linguistic scrutiny and professional scope: systemic functional linguistics and pragmatics (in both the pragmalinguistic and sociopragmatic senses). In doing so, we hope we have opened the door to future more in-depth explorations of the fertile cross-pollination of these areas, in studies ranging far beyond clichés to other forms of language use in general. Indeed, we can foresee a thorough reconciliation of appraisal theory along face and identity lines; and further, not only a new and richer, more explanatory approach to linguistic politeness, with a view to consolidating the plethora of voices and approaches in this area of academic scrutiny, but also a more systematic reimagining of the aims and aspirations of pragmatics (at least pragmalinguistics) and SFL through alliance and rapprochement, in the same way as SFL and critical discourse studies have found a way to bridge micro-patterns of text level analyses to the macro-patterns of society (Matthiessen, 2012) and cognition (van Dijk, 2009), as discussed in Chapter 2 and partly demonstrated in Chapters 3 and 4.

Further, given the natural, if currently underexplored alliance between the approaches co-deployed in this book, we are effectively utilising constituent mechanisms and primary approaches from each field to interrogate and support each other, thereby contributing to the rigour, not only of this study, but also to the overarching superordinate field of linguistics as it connects to society and which seeks to illuminate, explain and even predict interaction and its outcomes more specifically.

Future exploration of, for example, the SFL–pragmatics interface and arguably their interdependency, is especially important given the other contributions to originality and significance that we contend this study represents. Indeed, this study and the present book re-open the discussion around clichés, challenging the prevailing received and lay perspective of the concept as negative in general, and arguing for a more positive perspective given the introduction of the ideational and interpersonal functions we propose they serve. Given that clichés are formulas and hence they represent a set of linguistic resources that communicate the same or similar meanings in a quick, efficient and shared way within a CoP, or genre, and even as contextualising facts may vary, we can see other applications and explorations for their use in disciplines such as health and medical discourse, political discourse and other forms of institutional discourse. In other words, it could be applied to disciplines where the purpose of cliché usage might not ultimately only be efficiency, but also, as in this book, for face and identity co-construction and belonging, membership-claiming within a given CoP, enactment of textual personas and dis/engagement with other's positions, all of which make communication, action and success (whatever those success measures may be) possible and where clichés are just one set of linguistic resources which licence discourse participants to these ends.

Limitations to the study, however, remain. In the main these include the fact that we have not resolved (nor sought to resolve) the definitional distinction and the boundary between concepts under the umbrella of formulaic sequences, and in particular that of clichés and idioms. The fact is that, in regard to the latter and in light of our argument in Section 2.2, we could easily and convincingly argue that the difference between clichés and idioms is, in no small part, one based on perception, both of their usage and their existence-in-being. After all, if a consensus is not reached by reference to the many attempts at differentiating them by formulaic language specialists (e.g. Moon, 1998; Wray and Perkins, 2000; Grant and Bauer, 2004; Wood, 2020 as discussed in Chapter 2, Section 2.2) then, we may venture, an idiom vis-à-vis a cliché, is an idiom if it is seen to be positive or at least neutral by lay users and their general perception at large. After all, idioms, too, are also taken to hold, or claim a source of general truth about the human condition and the human experience, at least within similar sorts of situations relating to that in which they are invoked, and as such are capable of performing similar functions to clichés. A cliché, however, is often perceived to be an eye-rolling example of unoriginal, cheesy and lazy language behaviour devoid of originality in use or thought (cf. Chapter 1). However, this is in the eye, or rather, the ear of the beholder, at the time, and in the situation where they receive or otherwise experience the idiom/cliché dilemma. As such, we hypothesise that different interactants, even if cognitively explicitly considering the idiom/cliché candidate as either, will likely come to different opinions and conclusions as to whether the token is either. Again, we hypothesise that this will be as a result of how the discourse participants appraise the candidate idiom/cliché token, given their emotional response to it, the propositional content of the message in which it is embedded, and potentially, the social acceptance of the interpersonal function it is seen as enacting. Clearly then more in-depth research is needed here, not only in terms of finding a consensus on linguistic difference between idioms and clichés, but also, and more related to the aims of this book, in terms of societal – and individual – terms of perception. It would, as a continuation study, also be important and interesting to explore, once differentiated from clichés, how or whether both are similarly complicit and utilised as shared linguistic resources, accessible by members of a CoP and across various genres for the functions clichés have been demonstrated to fulfil in this book.

Additional considerations need to be stated here, too. We are not, through this study and within this book, claiming that our exploration and studies of the clichés, and their ideational and interpersonal functions and discourse sites and/or CoPs are exhaustive or even unproblematically applicable to other discourse sites, genres and CoPs, though future research will need to explore this latter aspect comprehensively in those communities and sites we identified.

From a more sociolinguistic perspective, future research will also need to explore the wide footprints, or currencies of usage of particular clichés, including the ways in which cliché usage stimulates or enables CoP fluidity, evolution and general pressures of change. It perhaps seems an irony that such unchanging, formulaic aspects of language should be considered agents, or at least facilitators of a changing CoP as the members seek to re-orient, renegotiate and restate their purposes for being in response to external stimuli and happenstance necessitating change and evolution. We would consider, therefore, clichés to be catalysts – provoking or facilitating change, whilst remaining (largely) unchanged themselves. However, the fact remains that clichés, whether catalysts or not, are as much component parts of CoP behaviour as they are resources/tools – and re-useable tools at that – for negotiating tasks, aims and the change that is inherent in any healthy community.

Furthermore, exploration of the processes of what we might tentatively call *enclichélisation* is also an area for future research and research consideration. An exploration of how novel phrases come into common currency and how regularised usage (as identified in Chapter 3 in relation to the Brexit context) is subsequently applied across multiple discourses, CoPs and genres to become more common linguistic and communicative currency is clearly needed. In effect, how do new phrases become common clichés? How do they relate to notions of, and originate from perspectives of cultural dominance? In exploring the relationship of cliché to CoPs and power within that space, how do clichés also relate, therefore, to the expression, consolidation or contestation of power? Some clichés, at least, are evidently originating from idiolectal sources (arguably all do but this, too, is an area for future research), others from event or circumstance-driven neologisms but how, and under what pressures of communication or circumstance do these become widespread, then institutionalised and eventually conventionalised as common currency in certain CoPs? How do these communities, and their behaviours share, donate, or forcibly colonise other communities, and what cliché (and other) linguistic resources are utilised and deployed, or adopted and adapted in order to facilitate this connectivity and colonisation? What role do clichés play in the relationship and negotiation of the superordinate CoPs and the subordinate CoPs, in both use and perception, and again, how do these relate to the expression, assumption, challenge to, and resistance of assumed power hierarchies within CoPs, and by collective CoPs in relation to each other?

Finally, future research has to explore the attitudes towards the current negative perceptions, but enthusiastically positive (and arguably subconscious) adoption and use of clichés. The actual and effective use of clichés shows they are and will remain in common currency for the reasons stated, and it remains a conundrum that such effective tools of communication, as sociosemiotic resources, would be as reviled and bedevilled by negative opinion as clichés are. Future research and future meta-research may well need experimental studies and methodologies involving comprehension, as well as perceptual attitude and efficacies – both anticipated and actual.

In this study, using data from a variety of sources of language in use, we re-interrogated and re-imagined the function of clichés and identified the ways they are used in communication and interaction, explaining their ubiquity and widespread usage.

Appendix 1: Clichés in News Comments

Data set 1: *The Guardian*, 20 March 2019
Article title: 'Nine Days from "Brexit Day", does anybody have a clue what's happening'. https://www.theguardian.com/commentisfree/2019/mar/20/nine-days-brexit-clue-extension-liechtenstein (Last accessed April 2021)

Data set 2: *Daily Mail*, 31 March 2019
Article title: 'Revoke Article 50 petition calling on the Government to cancel Brexit hits 6 million signatures'. https://www.dailymail.co.uk/news/article-6869939/Revoke-Article-50-petition-hits-six-million-signatures.html (Last accessed April 2021)

Data set 3: *BBC News* (online), 1 April 2019
Article title: 'Article 50: MPs debate six-million-signature petition'. https://www.bbc.com/news/uk-politics-47772682 (Last accessed April 2021)

Below, we present a selection of additional comments containing clichés from each data set. The clichés listed here have not been included in the Chapter 3 discussion. In this section, we present them by topoi. For ease of reading, we do not present them in the original table form used in the analysis. Instead, we list the clichés in the extracts where they featured originally under the heading corresponding to the topoi they have been allocated. The platform where they were extracted from is offered (in brackets) at the end of each extract. This is followed by a contextual analysis and interpretation of the purpose of the clichés in each numbered extract. The extracts have been kept verbatim as they appeared in the original platforms from where they were taken so they may present language errors.

Authority

1. *Let's take back control* and revoke article 50 (BBC)
   Contextual analysis/purpose: legitimises revoking Article 50 as it restores a sense of authority to the government.

2. The best vote we've had of the British people was the referendum and the majority who voted, voted to leave and leave we must!! *END OF.* (BBC)

   Contextual analysis/purpose: the result of the referendum provides the authority needed to leave the EU in any way necessary.

3. Yes first past the post system.in this country! *Leave means leave* (*Daily Mail*)

   Contextual analysis/purpose: the authority provided by the vote to leave legitimises Brexit.

4. Odd how the 0.4% of the population who voted DUP now *run the show* isn't it? (*Daily Mail*)

   Contextual analysis/purpose: others the DUP by claiming they have disproportionate control over the government.

Authority; Common Sense; Reality

5. (a) *enough is enough* well what an argument like leave means leave , brexit means brexit ? really do you know what you voted for ? the problems are so easy to solve ? really thats why 3 yeas later nobody knows so great leave without a deal fantastic like (b) *shoot yourself in both feet* ... please *get a grip on* reality. (*Daily Mail*)

   Contextual analysis/purpose: 5 (a) highlights the authority provided by the Leave vote, legitimising Brexit; (b) argues that those who are pro-Brexit are lacking in common sense and are not based in reality, legitimising opposition to Brexit.

Burden

6. Everyone is sick of Brexit but the only way to stop hearing about it every day for the next 10 years is to revoke it. *Let's put us all out of our misery.* (BBC)

   Contextual analysis/purpose: revoking Article 50 would remove the burden that Brexit is placing on the country.

7. I am *sick to death* of hearing about Brexit (BBC)

   Contextual analysis/purpose: legitimises ending the Brexit saga one way or another as it has become a burden on the country.

8. Never mind the 'Will of the people', what about *'Losing the will to live'*? (*Guardian*)

   Contextual analysis/purpose: legitimises opposition to Brexit by arguing that Brexit is a burden on the country and the people.

Burden; Elitism

9. Two things are certain, whatever the outcome it will be the little people who will once again be called upon to *bear the burden* and as she
steps down or is forced out TM will walk away *smelling of roses*, and
oh yes don't forget the *gold plated pension* and all the after dinner
speaking. (*Guardian*)
Contextual analysis/purpose: legitimises opposition to Brexit by
arguing it is a burden to the UK. Argues that those involved in implementing Brexit do not care as they are already financially well off.

Certainty

10. Yes clearly. We can hear the right wing idiots *loud and clear*. Even if
they shut up we can still hear them. (BBC)
Contextual analysis/purpose: highlights the strength of the apparent
ignorance of right-wing voters.

Certainty; Elitism

11. *Fact of the matter* is Leave voters already had their say in the referen-
dum.so why would they feel the need to sign another worthless piece
of garbage? *Sour grapes* an all that (BBC)
Contextual analysis/purpose: asserts that the Revoke Article 50
petition is irrelevant as in reality people already voted to Leave in
the referendum. Those signing the petition are behaving as if their
opinion is more important than the opinion of those who voted
Leave.

Common Sense

12. This means nothing. All you need to sign a government petition is
an email address, and there is no limit to how many of those you can
have. Total *no-brainer,* I'll bet there is only a fraction of 'real' signa-
tures on it! (*Daily Mail*)
Contextual analysis/purpose: questions the authenticity of the revoke
Article 50 petition, legitimising opposition to it.
13. Anyone who signed does not believe in democracy, *pure and simple*
(*Daily Mail*)
Contextual analysis/purpose: others those who signed the revoke
Article 50 petition as undemocratic.

Denial

14. Oh well done to them. But until it reaches 17.4 million and one I'm not interested. *Jog on* (*Daily Mail*)
    Contextual analysis/purpose: legitimises opposition to the petition by denying its importance.
15. Fake signatures, *fake news.* (*Daily Mail*)
    Contextual analysis/purpose: questions the authenticity of the petition by claiming it is not true, therefore legitimising opposition to it.
16. Fake signatures, all *a load of rubbish*!!! (*Daily Mail*)
    Contextual analysis/purpose: denies the authenticity of the revoke Article 50 petition, legitimising ignoring it.
17. Please don't be fooled by this Petition. Six million?? *You're having a laugh*. I have never heard anything so ridiculous in my life!! (*Daily Mail*).
    Contextual analysis/purpose: refutes the idea that the revoke Article 50 petition authentically represents the people, legitimising ignoring it.

Desperation

18. *Stop clutching at straws*. Personally, I've never been more confident that this is the end, the termination of Brexit. (*Guardian*)
    Contextual analysis/purpose: argues that those who are in favour of Brexit are desperate.
19. We would be better off in the EU but this *clinging on* in the hope it wont happen, is making a the situation worse. (*Guardian*)
    Contextual analysis/purpose: legitimises opposition to Remain by suggesting that it is adding to the uncertainty of the situation and making things worse.

Elitism

20. the tory voters must be *choking on their tea and crumpets* this morning knowing another mp has resigned, its now officially a brexit dictatorship with no peoples vote and a huge dismissal of a general election, now we have this petition which the brexiteers will hate as they don't support the democratic values we believe in (BBC)
    Contextual analysis/purpose: suggests that Tory voters are posh and aren't really representative of the 'real people' who are predominantly working-class.
21. *Who do BREXITERS think they are.* (BBC)
    Contextual analysis/purpose: suggestion that Brexit voters believe they are morally/intellectually superior due to their stance on Brexit.

22. so maybe that tells us from where the *strings are being pulled*......
(*Guardian*)
Contextual analysis/purpose: argues that certain people are working behind the scenes to further their agenda.

Elitism; Authority

23. *Who do REMAINERS think they are.* PLEASE REMEMBER THAT LEAVE WON. LEAVE NOW WITHOUT A DEAL. *LEAVE MEANS LEAVE* (BBC)
Contextual analysis/purpose: argues that Remain voters believe themselves to be morally/intellectually superior to Brexiteers. The authority gained from the referendum result legitimises leaving in whichever form is chosen.

Elitism; Strength

24. Are some people *living in a bubble* or are the *snowflakes* to thick to see whats going on with France hungry Italy. Poland Lithuania, Wait til France have an Election. My bet is Mari Le Penn will win. (*Daily Mail*).
Contextual analysis/purpose: accuses pro-EU people of being a part of the elite that is unaware of what is going on in ordinary people's lives, as well as being weak.

History

25. Older brexiteers are stuck in a world before globalisation and inward investment. *The past is the past.* It isn't coming back. (BBC)
Contextual analysis/purpose: argues that Brexit is an idea that is based in the past rather than the present/future, legitimising opposition to it.

Immaturity

26. How OLD are you, 6? Biggest crisis since 1939 and yous want to make losers of us all? Seems to me it is the biggest petition yet, blurt. Giro jockeys more likely to be kwitters as they want a nemesis. Now just *grow up* (BBC)
Contextual analysis/purpose: others one side as immature and implies that the other side is better and more mature.

27. Nick Boles has a *hissy fit* because he can't get his own way... (BBC)
Contextual analysis/purpose: accuses remain MP Nick Boles of being immature and cannot accept the result of the referendum.

28. *Stop chucking your toys out your pram.* Guess what...... If there's another vote then your precious 17.4m who voted leave can STILL VOTE LEAVE! SHOCK HORROR. or are you worried that a majority of them have realised they were completely lied to and likely to change their mind if there's another vote? How about the people who were underage to vote back in 2016 having their say? You're boring and quite clearly scared that you're likely to become one of the MINORITY. So *wind ya neck in* (*Daily Mail*)
Contextual analysis/purpose: others those opposing the petition as immature; others those supporting Brexit as arrogant and immature.

Immaturity; Threat

29. Nick Boles sums up remainer temperament perfectly. If you don't get your own way, *stamp your feet* and refuse to co-operate like a spoilt child. When the losing side refuse to co-operate with the result of a democratic vote, democracy ceases to function. The alternative is far worse that leaving the EU without a deal, so *careful what you wish for.* (BBC)
Contextual analysis/purpose: suggests that Remain MPs and voters are acting like children in refusing to accept the referendum result. Suggests that by being uncooperative, Remain MPs are risking an outcome worse than what is currently available; implied protest and/or violence.

Immaturity; Strength; History

30. Still around 60,000,000 citizens of the U.K. have NOT signed this pathetic petition so it's 10 to one against the *remoaners* so why not stop wasting your time and do something useful to make *Britain Great Again* and a proud independent democratic nation. (*Daily Mail*)
Contextual analysis/purpose: others Remain voters by arguing they are immature by refusing to accept the result of the referendum; legitimises Brexit by suggesting it will make the country stronger and bring back its historical success.

People

31. *Mickey mouse* has voted 50,000 times.... (Used on multiple occasions) (*Daily Mail*)
Contextual analysis/purpose: argues that the revoke Article 50 petition lacks authenticity and does not represent the views of the British public.

32. An uncontrolled petition whereby *any person and their dog* can vote
    is no reflection on true life. (*Daily Mail*)
    Contextual analysis/purpose: argues that the petition is not an authen-
    tic representation of the UK electorate and therefore opposition to
    it is legitimate.

Reality

33. Brexit you are a minority. *Please get that into your head.* (BBC)
    Contextual analysis/purpose: accuses Brexiteers of being too stupid/
    stubborn to recognise that they are no longer a majority view, sug-
    gesting Remain voters are more intelligent and representative.
34. There are far more non EU immigrants coming into this country today.
    Look up the figures *Wake up get real!* (BBC)
    Contextual analysis/purpose: argues that people don't realise that
    there are more non-EU migrants than EU migrants, potentially
    attempting to legitimise EU membership.
35. Leave cheated *get over it.* (BBC)
    Contextual analysis/purpose: legitimises ignoring the referendum
    result as in reality the Leave campaign cheated, therefore the refer-
    endum result is invalid.
36. While a march by 1m people for another referendum, and a petition
    from 6m people for revoking Article 50 is not, and should not, overturn
    the 2016 referendum result, *it is a wake up call.* It cannot be ignored.
    (BBC)
    Contextual analysis/purpose: argues that the pro-Remain protests
    and petitions legitimise a potential rethink regarding the govern-
    ment's Brexit strategy.
37. Leavers *lost big time* on the issue of immigration (BBC)
    Contextual analysis/purpose: justifies a pro-immigration stance as
    have Leave voters have lost the argument.
38. Go now. Remainers sorry but you lost *get over it* (BBC)
    Contextual analysis/purpose: argues that remain voters need to
    accept the result of the referendum.
39. The pre and post Brexit studies clearly name influx of migrants as the
    BIGGEST single reason for leaving. Oh the irony, *you just could not
    make it up!* (BBC)
    Contextual analysis/purpose: argues that the findings of academic
    research into Brexit justifies the argument that migration played a
    big role in the vote and accuses those that disagree of lying.

40. *Bottom line* is we are leaving, sorry chaps but that is what will happen, I am not one for gambling but I am risking a pound on it (A pound rather than a euro because lets be straight we never really joined) (*Guardian*)
    Contextual analysis/purpose: argues that the reality is the UK is leaving the EU, so there is no point trying to oppose it.

41. *At the end of the day*, the EU announced that they had received no letter from the PM outlining her request, let alone an actual plan. (*Guardian*)
    Contextual analysis/purpose: argues that the prime minister is trying to dodge reality in the negotiation process, legitimising opposition to her.

42. *Bottom line is*, the brexiteers have been had! We are not leaving, at least not with a no deal to exit! The madness of May in my view was to frustrate and confuse, all with the intent to remain! (*Guardian*)
    Contextual analysis/purpose: argues that the reality is that Brexit voters have been misled, which legitimises opposition to Brexit.

43. -CANCEL BREXIT NOW-*in your dreams* cupcake (*Daily Mail*)
    Contextual analysis/purpose: the argument that cancelling Brexit is an unrealistic expectation, legitimising opposition to it.

44. *Not in a million years* this Petition was signed by the British people (laughable!!) By the way Tusk, what about the 17 million + 'leavers' that have been betrayed. Go away, you fool. (*Daily Mail*)
    Contextual analysis/purpose: questions the authenticity of the revoke Article 50 petition, legitimising ignoring it.

Reality/Immaturity; Strength; Immaturity

45. Anyone with multiple email addresses anywhere in the world can vote on this for as many email addresses they have. It's all rubbish really. The vote was had. (a)*You can't have your own way* all the time. Learn how the rules work and (b) *suck it up*. What a bunch of (c) *bell shafts* (*Daily Mail*)
    Contextual analysis/purpose: (a–c) others those signing the petition and accuses them of being weak and immature, legitimising opposition to the petition.

Responsibility; Threat; Responsibility

46. Somebody in the government needs to (a) *stick their neck out* and admit brexit is impossible to deliver. As true as it is (b) *it would be political*

suicide, nobody is going to (c) *throw themselves under the gravy train* (BBC)
Contextual analysis/purpose: (a) urges politicians to face the consequences of their actions and (b/c) accuses them of being unwilling to do the right thing as they would rather preserve their career than the interests of the nation.

Strength

47. Remainers shoud back brexiteers UK independence and support No Deal 12th April' *Over my dead body.* (BBC)
    Contextual analysis/purpose: argues that Remain voters will go to extremes to prevent a no deal Brexit. Highlights the strength of feeling about opposing no deal.
48. *we went from strength to strength* (BBC)
    Contextual analysis/purpose: argues that what was being referred to was beneficial and therefore should be continued and supported.
49. People who make economic decisions beyond what to buy from lidl are looking at the collapse of inward investment (down by half on last year), market activity indices (all down) consumer spending (on the rocks) and growth (almost 0). *Weak to weaker.* (BBC)
    Contextual analysis/purpose: argues that Brexit is having a negative impact on the UK's economy and therefore should be opposed.

Strength; Urgency

50. Yep – if we have another vote and it's leave I'll *'suck it up'*. So let's roll (*Daily Mail*)
    Contextual analysis/purpose: others those who want another referendum as weak.

Threat

51. The ONLY reason *Brextremists* don't want a 2nd ref is because they KNOW they will LOSE! (BBC)
    Contextual analysis/purpose: poses that Brexit voters are a threat to the prosperity of the country; legitimises opposition to Brexit in the sense that the majority of the people are now opposed to it; others Brexit supporters accusing them of having extreme views.
52. Very cleverly, the EU have refused a short extension, so the choice is: a longer one, with EU elections – and what democrat would want to

forego an opportunity to test anti-EU sentiment in the UK – or just *go over the cliff* with No Deal. (*Guardian*)
Contextual analysis/purpose: poses that the uncertainty and the threat that no deal Brexit brings legitimises opposition to it.

53. Notice to all Brexiteers! Remain is running out of steam before they stamped up 16,141,241 votes. This time with the help of the Russians a putrid 6 million. Lots of their voters must have changed sides. Well remainers from the *dark side*. (*Daily Mail*)
Contextual analysis/purpose: others Remain voters by suggesting they have questionable motivation].

54. Of the 17 million that voted leave at least 50% have changed their mind now that they see it's not the easiest deal ever. That's why brexiters are *scared to death* of a second vote. (*Daily Mail*)
Contextual analysis/purpose: legitimises the idea of a second referendum by suggesting that Brexiteers are threatened by it because they think they will lose.

Threat; Strength; Immaturity

55. *No pain no ultimate gain.* Please remember, Sunderland had the highest leave percentage in the country!! You mentioned Nissan, I think??? Nissan in Sunderland, I think?? *Get over yourself* like the rest of you *spineless remainers*!! G-d forbid should there be another war, we can't rely on you weak lot. (*Daily Mail*)
Contextual analysis/purpose: argues that despite the threat Brexit poses, it is still legitimate to favour it as ultimately it will be beneficial; others remain voters as immature and weak.

Threat; Burden

56. Her strategy is to protect her bickering Tory Party and let the country *pay the price.* (*Guardian*)
Contextual analysis/purpose: argues that opposition to Brexit is legitimised as it poses a threat to the country; others the Conservative Party by saying they are responsible for this threat.

Uncertainty

57. For the record I voted leave and am now *on the fence* between revoke and no deal. Hard to see what would be best for future (BBC)

Contextual analysis/purpose: people are unsure about what is the best way forward regarding Brexit.

58. h @Friday, did I trigger you?.....don't bother asking for any apology from me, there won't be one. Make you a deal, free education? sure, once you get the college and university professors to work for 'free', *good luck with that* (*Daily Mail*)
Contextual analysis/purpose: the other person's argument requires luck to work and is therefore uncertain to work, legitimising opposition to it.

Urgency

59. The government said quite clearly that they would obey the result of the referendum! thats called democracy so *get on with it* (BBC)
Contextual analysis/purpose: the implementation of the referendum result by any means necessary is legitimised due to the urgency of the political situation.

60. *Give it up*, its time to leave without a deal. The EU has not been interested in giving us a decent deal from minute one, and why would they? *just get it done!* (BBC)
Contextual analysis/purpose: urges to complete Brexit arguing that too much time has been wasted and that no deal is legitimised owing to this.

Usefulness

61. keep it up remoaners the *gift that keeps on giving* (BBC)
Contextual analysis/purpose: suggests that Remain voters are actually playing into the hands of the Leave campaign, making a negative implication about their intelligence.

Uselessness

62. U.K. is only in this mess because the Remain MPs foisted a Remain PM on the electorate. She let the career minded civil servants (a) *get bowled over* by the commission. She chose a mostly Remain cabinet and made out she had changed her spots. (b) *COMPLETE STITCH UP* (BBC)
Contextual analysis/purpose: (a) blames the civil service and government for not getting a good deal in the negotiation, (b) argues that

the opposition have worked together to sabotage Brexit and the people who voted for it.

63. Could end up relying on USA for trades but may have to give way to backstop as USA is a signatory to GFA. *Back to Square 1.* What's the point of no deal? (BBC)
    Contextual analysis/purpose: argues that the current Brexit strategy does not work, legitimising opposition to it.

64. You're clearly *not the sharpest tool in the box!* (*Guardian*)
    Contextual analysis/purpose: others the opposite side by arguing that they lack intelligence.

65. So the best plan is to go full steam ahead, wreck the economy and continue to be the world's *laughing stock* (*Guardian*)
    Contextual analysis/purpose: argues that Brexit and those who advocate for it are an embarrassment to the UK and therefore it should be stopped.

66. Click bait is so easy! To click on a campaign takes no effort at all. *Lazy gits!* (*Daily Mail*)
    Contextual analysis/purpose: others those who have signed the revoke Article 50 petition as lazy.

Uselessness; Immaturity

67. They just *can't get it into their thick skulls* can they? You lost *get over it* (*Daily Mail*)
    Contextual analysis/purpose: others 'them' through arguing that they lack intelligence and by suggesting that they lack maturity.

Uselessness; Common Sense

68. it's easy to see what is happening. The liars have lied, the lies were believed, the lies are now just washing away the people who embraced them and those that rejected them. It's *not rocket science* (*Guardian*)
    Contextual analysis/purpose: others those who have advocated for Brexit by arguing that they lack intelligence; legitimises the anti-Brexit position by claiming it is just common sense.

Appendix 2: Clichés in Corporate Mission Statements

In this section we present further extracts from corporate mission statements featuring the most frequently used clichés in the database analysed in Chapter 4.

The data are organised by cliché in alphabetical order.

Under each cliché heading, we provide the discourse field yielded by semantic tagging of the corpus, the SCRs inferred to invoke and the main collocates of the clichés in their co-texts. These are also highlighted in the numbered extracts listed in each section where we also offer a description of the grammatical function of the clichés in their immediate co-text. The clichés are highlighted in **bold**. Collocates are shaded in grey. The grammatical features the clichés fulfil are <u>underlined</u> and discussed underneath each extract. Other relevant grammatical features in the co-text are marked in *italics*.

a track record of
Discourse field: psychological actions, states and processes: ability
SCRs invoked: capacity
Collocates: quality, service, *graduating devices*

1. Our *consistent* **track record of** innovation and delivery <u>has been recognised</u> by *multiple* technology and industry awards.
   Grammatical function: circumstance in a mental process
2. BRAND <u>is</u> a UK-focussed specialist property REIT with **a** *strong* **track record of** delivering value enhancing retail and leisure asset management.
   Grammatical function: circumstance in a relational process
3. We <u>have</u> **a track record of** delivering complex asset management and development initiatives, enhancing assets through refurbishment and extension.
   Grammatical function: attribute in relational process
4. BRAND <u>has achieved</u> **a** *100 per cent* **track record of** DNS availability for domains delegated to it IPv6 support.
   Grammatical function: goal in a material process
5. BRAND powerful registry engine <u>has</u> more than *20 years'* **track record of** *uninterrupted* service.
   Grammatical function: attribute in a relational process

6. We <u>have</u> **a** *proven* **track record** and *long experience* **of** supporting brands successfully.
Grammatical function: attribute in a relational process
7. Our senior management <u>are</u> an experienced team with **a** *proven* **track record** in planning, development and construction.
Grammatical function: attribute in a relational process
8. Experts in corporate acquisitions and a long-term investor in successful companies, we <u>have</u> a proven operational management team and **a track record of** *consistent* profitability demonstrated *over a number of years*.
Grammatical function: attribute in a relational process
9. We have provided tailored solutions for *over 20 years* and <u>have</u> **a** *proven* **track record** of delivery, driving process improvements and efficiency savings whilst ensuring continuity of service.
Grammatical function: attribute in a relational process
10. Key to our market position <u>is</u> *continuing* our *strong* **track record of** profit growth.
Grammatical function: value in a relational process
11. We <u>have</u> **a** *proven* **track record of** delivering a *consistent* supply of professionally sorted and graded rough coloured gemstones to world markets through a programme of private auctions.
Grammatical function: attribute in a relational process
12. We <u>maintain</u> **a(n)** *excellent* **track record** in Health, Safety, Quality and Environment.
Grammatical function: goal in a material process
13. Adopting this ethos and business style <u>has helped</u> BRAND develop **a(n)** *impressive* **track record** and an excellent reputation.
Grammatical function: goal in a material process
14. We <u>have</u> **a** *proven* **track record of** delivering results and a truly quality service.
Grammatical function: attribute in a relational process
15. We have **a** *strong proven* **track record of** success working in partnership with some of the UK's leading brands.
Grammatical function: attribute in a relational process

a wealth of

Discourse field: money and commerce: affluence
SCRs invoked: abundance
Collocates: qualities, brand
16. BRAND <u>has developed</u> **a wealth of** knowledge and experience to offer a comprehensive service
Grammatical function: goal in a material process

17. We have **a wealth of** knowledge of the supports industry built up over many years of experience
    Grammatical function: attribute in a relational process
18. Over the last 5 years we have also started to supply a number of national retail giants and this has blessed us with **a wealth of** experience with meeting the demands of all sized businesses.
    Grammatical function: attribute in a relational process
19. BRAND benefits from **a wealth of** expertise and knowledge built up over many years.
    Grammatical function: goal in a material process
20. Our clients benefit from reduced overheads, flexibility through a choice of equipment, and **a wealth of** knowledge from our experienced staff.
    Grammatical function: goal in a material process
21. With **a wealth of** experience to draw on, our reputation is excellent and is achieved by genuine teamwork.
    Grammatical function: circumstance in a relational process
22. We have developed **a wealth of** experience in developing and implementing mechanical, electrical and renewable solutions.
    Grammatical function: goal in a material process
23. Everyone in the BRAND team brings **a wealth of** expertise from industry and a passion for keeping pace with a market that is constantly evolving.
    Grammatical function: goal in a material process
24. We have **a wealth of** experience in supplying a full turn-key package for our clients.
    Grammatical function: attribute in a relational process

at the forefront of

Discourse field: general and abstract terms: importance
SCRs invoked: importance
Collocates: brand, customers, competition, service, *time references*

25. We put people and their wellbeing **at the forefront of** our design thinking with the belief that thoughtful, sustainable designs generate positive outcomes for our clients.
    Grammatical function: circumstance in a material process
26. With over *30 years'* experience of manipulating the surface chemistry and crystalline properties of calcium compounds, we engineer and manufacture products **at the forefront of** calcium technology.
    Grammatical function: circumstance in a material process

27. We aim to be **at the forefront of** the sector in empowering people with knowledge about their health status.
    Grammatical function: phenomenon in a mental process
28. BRAND was, and *still* is, **at the forefront of** the industry, whether this be pioneering new products or opening and educating new markets around the world.
    Grammatical function: attribute in a relational process
29. We *have been* **at the forefront of** the sector in capitalising on the opportunities arriving from technological change.
    Grammatical function: attribute in a relational process
30. Our research and development team *have ensured* our products are **at the forefront of** our field.
    Grammatical function: phenomenon in a mental process
31. We*'ll always* look to improve wherever we can and this is driven by our unrelenting desire to maintain our position **at the forefront of** our industry.
    Grammatical function: circumstance in a material process
32. BRAND *always* endeavours to be **at the forefront of** national best practice.
    Grammatical function: phenomenon in a mental process
33. The company seeks to grow through a combined organic growth and acquisition strategy, *always* with the customer **at the forefront of** its considerations and providing best of breed payment acceptance solutions to retailers in every market sector.
    Grammatical function: phenomenon in a mental process
34. BRAND *has been* **at the forefront of** retail finance technology and services for over twenty years.
    Grammatical function: attribute in a relational process
35. With a combined knowledge of over *30 years* we are bringing fresh ideas **to the forefront** of a traditional and old fashioned trade.
    Grammatical function: circumstance in a material process
36. BRAND are *now* celebrating our *tenth year* **at the forefront of** the retail-packed dried fruit and nuts business in Britain.
    Grammatical function: phenomenon in a mental process
37. We stay **at the forefront of** business by keeping abreast of new market developments.
    Grammatical function: attribute in a relational process
38. BRAND has been **at the forefront** of setting standards in glass engineering for over *three decades*.
    Grammatical function: attribute in a relational process

39. Our friendly team members are proud to be **at the forefront of** technology to ensure our solutions offer the best functionality in an ever-evolving industry.
    Grammatical function: phenomenon in a mental process
40. We place the rights of residents **at the forefront of** our philosophy of care.
    Grammatical function: circumstance in a material process

at the heart of
Discourse field: general and abstract terms: importance
SCRs invoked: importance
Collocates: service, values or quality, people (customer, brand actors)
41. **At the heart** of our business are the four core values which translate into everything we do.
    Grammatical function: token in a relational process
42. Customer Service: Putting the customer **at the heart of** everything we do
    Grammatical function: circumstance in a material process
43. We place our Health, Safety, Environment and Quality **at the heart of** our business.
    Grammatical function: circumstance in a material process
44. The BRAND has sustainability **at the heart of** its operations.
    Grammatical function: attribute in a relational process
45. **At the heart of** what we do is engaging people to create better business and a brighter world for all.
    Grammatical function: token in a relational process
46. BRAND's values lie **at the heart of** everything we do.
    Grammatical function: attribute in a relational process
47. We are proud of our reputation; each customer is **at the** very **heart of** our business and we appreciate that the purchase of a new home is not taken lightly.
    Grammatical function: attribute in a relational process
48. BRAND puts you **at the heart of** decision making, ensuring the company continues to meet and exceed customers' expectations.
    Grammatical function: circumstance in a material process
49. Customer care and value for money are **at the heart of** our business
    Grammatical function: attribute in a relational process
50. BRAND create bathroom products with your Relaxation **at** their very **heart**.
    Grammatical function: circumstance in a material process

51. Inspiration and a constant drive for improving your comfort are **at the heart of** what we do.
    Grammatical function: attribute in a relational process
52. As a regional developer, we place the communities we work in **at the heart of** our operations.
    Grammatical function: circumstance in a material process
53. This desire to strive for excellence and quality is still **at the heart of** BRAND today.
    Grammatical function: attribute in a relational process
54. The company is committed to placing the customer **at the heart of** the operation.
    Grammatical function: phenomenon in a mental process
55. Community is **at the heart of** everything we do
    Grammatical function: attribute in a relational process
56. Innovation remains **at the heart of** BRAND.
    Grammatical function: attribute in a relational process
57. Respect for our residents' privacy, dignity and individuality is **at the heart of** everything we do.
    Grammatical function: attribute in a relational process
58. Each PIG has its own identity, each evolved rather than too designed, but each putting the kitchen garden **at the** very **heart of** the operation.
    Grammatical function: circumstance in a relational process
59. Strategy, integrity and transparency lies **at the heart of** everything we do at BRAND.
    Grammatical function: attribute in a relational process
60. Project Management is **at the heart of** our core services.
    Grammatical function: attribute in a relational process
61. That's why it is so important to our continued success that we continue to place our people and with it, our brand, very much **at the heart of** the way we do business.
    Grammatical function: circumstance in a material process
62. A business model that places the tenant's needs **at the heart of** everything we do.
    Grammatical function: circumstance in a material process
63. Some good solid values are **at the heart of** what we do.
    Grammatical function: attribute in a relational process
64. We make sure that simplicity remains **at the heart of** what we do.
    Grammatical function: attribute in a relational process

everything we do
    Discourse field: measurement and numbers: entirety

SCRs invoked: comprehensiveness
Collocates: service, people, values, standards

65. A business model that <u>places</u> the tenant's needs *at the heart of* **everything we do** and delivers positive outcomes for everyone we collaborate with.
Grammatical function: circumstance in a material process

66. At the heart of our business <u>are</u> *the four core values which translate into* **everything we do**
Grammatical function: value in relational process

67. BRAND has been built on a set of fundamental values that <u>are</u> embodied *in* **everything we do**.
Grammatical function: circumstance in a relational process

68. BRAND values <u>lie</u> *at the heart of* **everything we do**.
Grammatical function: circumstance in a relational process

69. BRAND's success is rooted in collaborative, long-term relationships with clients and a recognition that our people and our supply chain <u>are</u> key to excellence in **everything we do**.
Grammatical function: circumstance in a relational process

70. Community <u>is</u> at the heart of **everything we do** and we strive to go above and beyond to make a difference.
Grammatical function: circumstance in a relational process

71. Customers <u>are</u> central to **everything we do**.
Grammatical function: circumstance in a relational process

72. **Everything we do** <u>stems</u> from our common goal to help people affected by challenging diseases.
Grammatical function: carrier in a relational process

73. **Everything we do**, from the content we create, to the services we deliver, and the products we stock, <u>is</u> designed to help people enjoy their passions
Grammatical function: token in a relational process

74. Founded in 1920 by BRAND, we are still as passionate about plants as we were 90 years ago and we <u>are</u> committed to reducing our impact on the environment in **everything we do**.
Grammatical function: circumstance in a relational process

75. In **everything we do** we <u>*strive*</u> to find the simple answer.
Grammatical function: circumstance in a material process

76. Innovation <u>is</u> at the core of **everything we do** – that's why we're committed to the continuous evolution of our technology.
Grammatical function: circumstance in a relational process

77. It's our attention to service that's allowed us achieve Grade A BRC Certification, a standard that ensures that **everything we do**, and that you receive, <u>is</u> of the very highest quality.
Grammatical function: token in a relational process

78. Our mantra is Innovation, Dedication & Passion and we <u>apply</u> these standards *to* **everything we do.**
    Grammatical function: circumstance in a material process
79. Our personalised services include [...] *A personal approach to* **everything we do.**
    Grammatical function: circumstance in a relational process
80. Putting our customers <u>is</u> at the heart of **everything we do.**
    Grammatical function: circumstance in a relational process
81. Respect for our residents' privacy, dignity and individuality <u>is</u> at the heart of **everything we do.**
    Grammatical function: circumstance in a relational process
82. Strategy, integrity and transparency <u>lies</u> at the heart of **everything we do** at BRAND.
    Grammatical function: circumstance in a relational process
83. The very first seed sown in the ground in 2011 has <u>led</u> the way *to inform* **everything we do** *at BRAND.*
    Grammatical function: circumstance in a material process
84. To achieve this, we will <u>invest</u> in our BRAND *to improve* **everything we do** *and empower everyone to deliver growth.*
    Grammatical function: circumstance in a material process
85. To improve patient health by <u>putting</u> patients *at the centre of* **everything we do.**
    Grammatical function: circumstance in a material process
86. We are dedicated to the highest professional standards and <u>believe</u> in acting with honesty, fairness and clarity **in everything we do.**
    Grammatical function: circumstance in a relational process
87. We'<u>re</u> always <u>looking</u> for ways *to improve* **everything we do.**
    Grammatical function: circumstance in a material process
88. We've been awarded some impressive certifications, but don't worry, we've not let this go to our heads – we'<u>re</u> as passionate about **everything we do** as we ever were.
    Grammatical function: circumstance in a relational process

first class/first-class
Discourse field: measurement and numbers: linear order
SCRs invoked: superiority
Collocates: brand, service
89. At BRAND we <u>pride</u> ourselves on being a forward thinking transportation company, whilst believing in traditional values of **first-class** customer care and attention.
    Grammatical function: phenomenon in a mental process

90. Businesses want to work with us because we have: [...] **First-class** customer service.
    Grammatical function: attribute in a relational process
91. From distribution development and expansion, through to innovative product creation; development of cutting-edge technology or provision of **first-class** customer servicing, we are here to help.
    Grammatical function: circumstance in a relational process
92. In 2014, the NAME was rebranded to come under the NAME banner, and BRAND was born, with an ongoing mission to be the leading supplier of pumps to the trade in the UK, with **first-class** service, a wealth of knowledge to share and a commitment to being at the forefront of innovation in the industry.
    Grammatical function: circumstance in a material process
93. Our **first-class** service, outstanding quality and extensive product range set BRAND apart from other companies in our sector.
    Grammatical function: actor in material process
94. Our mission is to maximise a contractor's take home pay whilst ensuring a 100% compliant payroll solution and **first-class** contractor care.
    Grammatical function: value in a relational process
95. Our trading partners enjoy a **first-class** service whilst also benefitting from a level of 'exclusivity' that our competitors in London struggle to provide.
    Grammatical function: phenomenon in a mental process
96. Our unique and rewarding approach means we have **first-class** relationships with our key delivery partners – including institutional investors, commissioners in local authorities, Clinical Commissioning Groups and developers.
    Grammatical function: attribute in a relational process
97. These surgeries include seven referral practices providing **first-class** specialist treatment.
    Grammatical function: circumstance in a relational process
98. Together we have the skills required to deliver a **first-class** service to every one of our clients.
    Grammatical function: circumstance in a relational process
99. We've been providing our customers with a **first-class**, professional and flexible service each and every day for over the last 30 years.
    Grammatical function: goal in material process

go the extra mile
Discourse field: measurement and numbers: quantities
SCRs invoked: effort
Collocates: customer, service, company, values, thought, action

Grammatical function: material process clause, action

100. Through many years of hard work BRAND has emerged as Ireland's foremost number plate provider and has **gone the extra mile** by providing customers with a wide variety of branded automotive products to support their business.

101. We're hungry and a close-knit team, when we say we **go the extra mile**. We don't think twice about taking a demo unit to the other side of the country.

102. BRAND understands that without quality, reliable products we would not be the company we are today, which is why we **go the extra mile** to make sure safety is not compromised.

103. At BRAND we strive to offer new products regularly, which meet our customers requirements. We are always willing to **go the extra mile**.

104. Our staff are professional, knowledgeable and dependable and we **go the extra mile** to make sure that our patients receive the high standard of care that they deserve.

105. We take responsibility to get things right and **go the extra mile**.

106. We **go the extra mile** to ensure compliance, increase efficiency and minimize waste.

107. Our core values: [...] **Going the extra mile**. BRAND believe that it is important to be part of the community; we have a policy of using local labour & materials wherever possible, helping to create a positive economic impact.

108. Our outstanding quality and commitment to **going the extra mile** is your promise of a finished product that meets the brief and makes an impact. [nominalisation as token in a relational process]

pride [ourselves] on
Discourse fields: emotional actions, states and processes: contentment
SCRs invoked: satisfaction
Collocates: brand, customers, quality
Grammatical function: mental process clause, thought.

109. Whether that means sourcing sustainable raw materials or investing in the latest machinery and livery, it is something the group **prides itself on**.

110. We are a market leader in the supply of bedding and flowering pot plants and **pride ourselves on** our quality of products.

111. We **pride ourselves on** our team and our commitment to our customers.

112. We **pride ourselves on** being a specialist tower crane firm, offering expert knowledge to our clients.

113. We **pride ourselves on** taking care of our customers because your opinion matters to us.
114. We **pride ourselves on** our power to innovate.
115. We **pride ourselves on** supplying a prompt, reliable and helpful service at all times.
116. We **pride ourselves on** offering a friendly, helpful and professional service, designed to support you in your drive for improved production and performance.
117. As such, it should come as no surprise that we **pride ourselves on** being able to find whatever bricks, blocks, tiles, slates or paving stones you need.
118. BRAND **prides itself on** the highest level of service
119. We **pride ourselves on** never forgetting a face – everyone gets a warm welcome and soon feels part of the BRAND family.
120. We **pride ourselves on** manufacturing high quality, reliable and ethical products in several different markets.
121. We have been involved in every mainland UK cellular network delivery and upgrade programme since 1996 and we **pride ourselves on** delivering safe and right first time telecom logistics so our customers reputation for safety, reliability and a trusted service is preserved at all times.
122. We care for some of the most vulnerable in society and our highly experienced team **pride themselves on** being able to deal with almost any dental emergency or condition which comes through our doors.
123. We **pride ourselves on** delivering an unrivalled experience and portfolio of services to our UK wide client base.
124. We **pride ourselves on** having the largest collection of Preowned Rolex watches in Herefordshire.
125. We **pride ourselves on** the passion, knowledge and expertise of our team.
126. BRAND **prides itself on** being an independent aggregate producer that offers the widest range of products possible.
127. We use our expertise and experience to identify efficiencies across your IT environment and **pride ourselves on** delivering strategic, high-value, innovative change.
128. The company **prides itself on** unrivalled levels of service, selection of products and technical knowledge.
129. We **pride ourselves on** a tailored service with you being in control every step of the way.
130. We **pride ourselves on** delivering quality developments to our clients and we value our shareholders.

131. We **pride ourselves on** delivering quality, well engineered solutions that not only address current requirements, but also those of the future.
132. BRAND **prides itself on** prioritising patient care so profits can go towards extra nurses.
133. Since its formation, BRAND have progressed into an organisation that **prides itself on** its ability to deliver a quality service to all its clients.
134. We **pride ourselves on** being easy to work with, a fact that's backed up by the many long-term relationships.

set us apart
Discourse field: measurement and numbers: distance
SCRs invoked: difference
Collocates: brand, competition, service
135. We **set ourselves apart** from the competition as the only fully-integrated fire safety company in the UK.
    Grammatical function: brand as actor in construal of difference
136. Our onsite installation teams whom are all employed directly, **set ourselves apart** from of our competitors.
    Grammatical function: brand as actor in construal of difference
137. A closely controlled design and manufacturing process plus in-house Research and Development is all managed by a proficient engineering team that **sets us apart** from the competition.
    Grammatical function: attributed qualities construing difference
138. Our first-class service, outstanding quality and extensive product range **set** BRAND **apart** from other companies in our sector.
    Grammatical function: attributed qualities construing difference
139. What **sets** us **apart**: Independent: A family-owned, independent business, built on trust. Unique: The only manufacturer to offer the full range of CL and IOL materials. High standards: Award-winning, clinical laboratories, ISO7 clean room, state-of-the-art manufacturing facilities. Pioneering: The leading developer of biocompatible polymers. International: Worldwide presence, including offices in the UK, US and China and distributors around the globe.
    Grammatical function: attributed qualities construing difference
140. In-house development, direct network connections and technology that consistently satisfies our customers, **sets us apart** and coincides with our belief that 'every message matters'.
    Grammatical function: attributed qualities construing difference
141. To us, jewellery is art, not fashion'. This truly **sets** BRAND **apart** as storytellers, as well as jewellers.

Grammatical function: attributed qualities construing difference
142. We believe that our pursuit of excellence combined with our long-term future objectives, **sets us apart** from our competitors.
Grammatical function: attributed qualities construing difference
143. Our continuous, uncompromising devotion **sets us apart** from other contractors.
Grammatical function: attributed qualities construing difference
144. We strive to always find the simplest solution to a client's problem, an approach which has often **set us apart** from our competitors.
Grammatical function: attributed qualities construing difference

Appendix 3: Clichés in Evaluation

In this section we present the extracts analysed as having evaluative clichés in Chapter 5. The data are organised following the order presented in Table 5.1 outlining examples of the most frequently used clichés in the data set. All clichés are presented in *italics*. Each cliché identified as an evaluative item in the extracts is coded in terms of the appraisal category, subcategory they realise, the valence and with the target of the appraisal. This is followed by the propositional content the clichés carry and the face-oriented strategies they fulfil.

It is important to bear in mind that the words 'positive' or 'negative' in the context of appraisal refer to attitudinal valence. This is not to be confused with the words positive or negative preceding the type of face that the face-work is seen as performing, that is positive face refers to the desire to be accepted whilst negative face refers to the desire not to be imposed, as per the Brown and Levinson (1987) approach. Neutral or ambivalent valence instances have been left unmarked.

1. We are not *moving forward*
   Appraisal category: judgement
   Valence and appraisal subcategory: negative capacity
   Target of appraisal: self and team
   Propositional content: functions as the speech act of 'complaint'
   Face-oriented strategies: positive face threat to those addressed in the use of the inclusive 'we', and also a negative face threat; this complaint speech act also functions as a criticism (see Bousfield 2008) of the group's level of progress. Hence it threatens positive (approval) face by suggesting a level of disapproval for lacklustre progress made so far; and negative (freedom from imposition) face by suggesting current modes of working and effort expended are not sufficient and will need to change.
2. We are literally *hitting a brick wall* here
   Appraisal category: judgement
   Valence and appraisal subcategory: negative capacity
   Target of appraisal: self and team
   Propositional content: criticism

Face-oriented strategies: positive face and negative face threat. This is another criticism (which may also secondarily be a complaint) which functions similarly in terms of threats to both aspects of face as in example 41.

3. After all the effort we put in, we are *back to square one*
Appraisal category: judgement
Valence and appraisal subcategory: negative capacity
Target of appraisal: self and team
Propositional content: criticism
Face-oriented strategies: positive face and secondary negative face threat. This, again, threatens both the individuals' and the collective team face (as in 41 and 42), a rather more off-record criticism, this nevertheless still threatens the desire of approval (positive face) as it shows disapproval at apparent lack of metaphorical progress (assuming MOVEMENT IS SUCCESS); and the desire for freedom from imposition (negative face) as it implies current practices must change if 'progress' is to be made.

4. We just seem to be *going round in circles*
Appraisal category: judgement
Valence and appraisal subcategory: negative capacity
Target of appraisal: self and team
Propositional content: criticism
Face-oriented strategies: positive face and secondary negative face threat. This example works, pragmatically, in the same way as example 43.

5. We need to go the extra mile if we want to make *headway*
Appraisal category: judgement
Valence and appraisal subcategory: negative capacity
Target of appraisal: self and team
Propositional content: complaint
Face-oriented strategies: positive face threat and potential secondary negative face threat. This complaint, as with the immediately previous examples, challenges and threatens positive and negative face by being critical about the lack of metaphorical 'progress'. This seems to suggest the clichés used for complaint tokens of this metaphorical nature are elegant variations on a well-worn theme.

6. Don't just *talk the talk, you got to walk the walk*
Appraisal category: judgement
Valence and appraisal subcategory: negative capacity
Target of appraisal: other
Propositional content: criticism

Face-oriented strategies: positive face threat and negative face threat. This example is directed at a (presumed, idealised) 'other'; where if the other cannot achieve the metaphorical 'walk' and 'talk' (LIFE IS A JOURNEY; SUCCESS IS DIALOGUE), then the criticism takes effect. This criticism, in effect, suggests the positive face wants (of approval) and negative face wants (of freedom from imposition) will be unmet by the speaker if not achieving the metaphorical objectives.

7. We are *shifting the deck chairs* but not getting anywhere
Appraisal category: judgement
Valence and appraisal subcategory: negative capacity
Target of appraisal: self and team
Propositional content: criticism
Face-oriented strategies: positive face threat and secondary negative face threat. This, again, as with examples 41–46, is both team- and self-oriented and attacks individual and collective team face. The criticism shows disapproval (positive face) of current activities and secondarily suggests current actions (negative face) need to change to make 'progress' in future.

8. We are shifting the deck chairs but *not getting anywhere*$_2$
Appraisal category: judgement
Valence and appraisal subcategory: negative capacity
Target of appraisal: self and team
Propositional content: admission and implied criticism
Face-oriented strategies: positive face threat and negative face threat. The explanation of which is covered in example 47.

9. I'm not sure *where we go from here*
Appraisal category: judgement
Valence and appraisal subcategory: negative capacity
Target of appraisal: self
Propositional content: self-critical or admission
Face-oriented strategies: positive face save. An admission which also operates to lower one's own face in the positions of the interlocutors, the speaker is demonstrating lower approval of own face than might have been expected earlier by their interlocutors.

10. We've *missed the boat* on this one
Appraisal category: judgement
Valence and appraisal subcategory: negative capacity
Target of appraisal: self and team
Propositional content: complaint and implied criticism
Face-oriented strategies: positive face threat and negative face threat. The speaker, as with the examples 41–46, threatens self's and team's

notions of face (both positive and secondarily negative) by suggesting disapproval (by missing an opportunity for success via the SUCCESS IS MEANS OF TRANSPORT metaphor), and suggests better actions in future are needed.

11. It makes me think whether it's time to *abandon the sinking ship*
    Appraisal category: judgement
    Valence and appraisal subcategory: negative capacity
    Target of appraisal: self
    Propositional content: admission
    Face-oriented strategies: positive face threat. Perhaps inadvertently this casts the speaker in a 'less-than-leader' role (Captains as leaders are schematically and traditionally expected to go down with their literal ships (to avoid the face loss of failure)) by admitting willingness to abandon current activities; and also casts the speaker in the role of a 'rat', again given the schematic assumptions of the clichéd saying 'rats leaving the sinking ship' as rats will attempt to save their own lives from imminent and immense danger. Neither interpretation casts the speaker in any socially positive light, and invites disapproval, especially from those where responsibility and accountability rank highly (such as in business CoP).

12. The project has proved to be the team's *Achilles' heel*
    Appraisal category: judgement
    Valence and appraisal subcategory: negative capacity
    Target of appraisal: self and team
    Propositional content: admission
    Face-oriented strategies: positive face save. This suggests the current activities are the only activities in which the speaker and their team could have failed. This is referencing, intertextually, the ancient Greek myth of Achilles, who could not be killed except by being stabbed in his heel (the only part of him not immersed in the invulnerability-giving-powers of the River Styx when he was a baby) and hence being the only way he could be defeated. This is an attempt to save positive face of self and team whilst admitting failure to achieve necessary objectives.

13. I am aware that I am *punching above my weight* on this one
    Appraisal category: judgement
    Valence and appraisal subcategory: negative appraisal of capacity
    Target of appraisal: self
    Propositional content: criticism
    Face-oriented strategies: positive face save. Suggesting, using the metaphors of boxing from that sport's 'weight' classes, the TASK IS A

BOXING OPPONENT, meaning 'above my weight' means 'an area where I was not expected to operate let alone do so successfully'. This seems to be an attempt to save or even enhance positive face given the scale of challenges attempted.

14. This is way *out of our league*
    Appraisal category: judgement
    Valence and appraisal subcategory: negative appraisal of capacity
    Target of appraisal: self
    Propositional content: admission
    Face-oriented strategies: positive face threat. This is nearly identical to the example in 53, but referencing either football or baseball opponents rather than boxing opponents. It is implied the football/baseball opponents are of a 'higher' ranked league and therefore are more challenging to overcome.

15. We're *barking up the wrong tree*
    Appraisal category: judgement
    Valence and appraisal subcategory: negative appraisal of capacity
    Target of appraisal: self and team
    Propositional content: criticism
    Face-oriented strategies: positive face threat and secondary negative face threat. As with the other examples of criticism, and following the observations made in Bousfield (2008: 126), this shows dispraise of the self and associated team and suggests other actions should be taken in future. This threatens both positive and negative face of self and team. The SELF/TEAM AS DOG(s) metaphor is secondary, here, and simply maps unthinking (over-) excitement leading to wrongful action to the interpretation.

16. I am *biting off more than I can chew* by taking this on
    Appraisal category: judgement
    Valence and appraisal subcategory: negative appraisal of capacity
    Target of appraisal: self
    Propositional content: admission
    Face-oriented strategies: positive face threat utilising the ACHIEVING IS EATING metaphor where smaller elements are more successfully dealt with in terms of mapping. This admission threatens the speaker's own offer of their own position in terms of positive (approval) face needs.

17. Let's *think outside the box* for a minute
    Appraisal category: judgement
    Valence and appraisal subcategory: negative appraisal of capacity
    Target of appraisal: self and team

Propositional content: warning or request

Face-oriented strategies: positive face enhancement of a third-party or negative face threat. This is dependent on the THINKING IS CONSTRAINED metaphor especially where this is overcome for positive (socially positive) outcomes or opportunities. This can therefore suggest, when used in general terms, a call to arms for innovative thinking beyond the norm (a positive face enhancement); or a negative face threat through suggesting current self-limited thinking/action has led to lacklustre progress.

18. They've achieved this with *blood sweat and tears*

Appraisal category: judgement

Valence and appraisal subcategory: positive appraisal of tenacity

Target of appraisal: others

Propositional content: compliment

Face-oriented strategies: positive face enhancement of a third party. Heavily utilising the intertextual speech to Winston Churchill in the Houses of Parliament in 1940, when the UK stood nearly alone against the assembled forces of tyranny, the use of this cliché is a reference to extreme effort and sacrifice in the face of near overwhelming adversity. A positive face enhancement through complimenting.

19. I'm not too sure about him, he's a bit of a *dark horse*

Appraisal category: judgement

Valence and appraisal subcategory: appraisal of normality

Target of appraisal: other

Propositional content: warning

Face-oriented strategies: positive face threat of a third party. Through the PERSON IS HORSE metaphor, where (presumably at night) a 'dark horse' was not seen coming, and therefore was an unintended and surprising contender for achievement and success. This is not an approving term in British English cliché usage, and suggests warning, and hence sense of disapproval, more than anything else.

20. I heard it *straight from the horse's mouth*

Appraisal category: judgement

Valence and appraisal subcategory: positive appraisal of veracity

Target of appraisal: self

Propositional content: representative speech act

Face-oriented strategies: positive face save. Utilising a clichéd metaphor of ORIGINATOR IS HORSE metaphor, hearing it direct from them, means getting the honest and unvarnished truth. This suggests a desire for approval, for having the means of access to, and wherewithal to access, this source of truth.

21. We *started off on the wrong foot*, let's start over and forget it ever
    happened
    Appraisal category: judgement
    Valence and appraisal subcategory: negative appraisal of propriety
    Target of appraisal: self and other
    Propositional content: admission
    Face-oriented strategies: positive face repair of a third party. A SUC-
    CESS IS A DANCE metaphor, where starting off 'on the wrong foot'
    means every step or move thereafter is wrong. An admission (as
    partnership dancing takes at least two) of partial guilt seems to act as
    positive repair of face of third party, rather than blame for the rela-
    tionship not working/being successful.
22. His comment was *below the belt*
    Appraisal category: judgement
    Valence and appraisal subcategory: negative appraisal of judgement
    of other
    Target of appraisal: other
    Propositional content: criticism
    Face-oriented strategies: positive or negative face threat. A DISCOURSE
    IS BOXING metaphor, the comment made was 'below the belt' meant
    out of the 'rules' of the interaction. As a criticism, this threatens
    both positive face (by showing disapproval of the comment) and sec-
    ondarily negative face (by implying such comments should not be
    repeated or tolerated).
23. He's been *on cloud nine* all week
    Appraisal category: affect
    Valence and appraisal subcategory: positive appraisal of happiness
    Type of appraisal: non-authorial
    Propositional content: third-party representative speech act
    Face-oriented strategies: positive face enhancement of a third party.
    This is a speaker's report of another's socially positive emotions and
    behaviours. These, in turn, suggest (all other things being equal) a
    high degree of approval is being proffered with this third-party rep-
    resentative speech act.
24. I was *in stitches* after he told the story
    Appraisal category: affect
    Valence and appraisal subcategory: positive happiness
    Type of appraisal: authorial
    Propositional content: compliment
    Face-oriented strategies: positive face enhancement of a third
    party. A cliché referring to the pain in the side of the torso that can

come from overexertion, on the understanding that experiencing great physical mirth can give rise to such overexertion. This cliché is, then, metonymic and, given the socially positive view of mirth making and mirth creation, this is highly likely in most contexts to be viewed as a positive face enhancement through the representation of approval for the humorous nature in which 'he' tells his narratives. It therefore represents a positive face enhancement of a third party.

25. This report *is doing my head in*

Appraisal category: affect

Valence and appraisal subcategory: negative appraisal indicating dissatisfaction

Type of appraisal: authorial

Propositional content: complaint

Face-oriented strategies: positive face threat. Utilising the metaphor of the REPORT IS AN ASSAILANT; in most cases this will be seen as a self-oriented positive face re-adjustment 'down' to a less favourably-than-usually-expected positive face construction, due to expressing extreme exasperation with the nature/complexity/effort required on interacting with the report. Additionally, this may be seen as a cry or plea for support or sympathy, both of which risk the speaker's own positive (approval) face.

26. It really *rattles my cage*

Appraisal category: affect

Valence and appraisal subcategory: negative appraisal indicating dissatisfaction

Type of appraisal: authorial

Propositional content: complaint

Face-oriented strategies: positive face threat, with the construction of the clichéd metaphor SPEAKER IS A DANGEROUS ANIMAL, where rattling the cage of the animal can make the speaker agitated and aggressive. All of which suggests lack of greater control over one's emotions which in British English settings traditionally is seen with varying degrees of disapproval. As such, this represents a self-oriented positive face threat.

27. I am *beside myself* with rage over this

Appraisal category: affect

Valence and appraisal subcategory: negative appraisal indicating dissatisfaction

Type of appraisal: authorial

Propositional content: complaint

Face-oriented strategies: positive face threat. Not entirely dissimilar in self-face-orientation and effect as in example 66, this example uses a clichéd metaphor of SPEAKER IS ANOTHER PERSON (oft cited in 'I'm not myself, today' when feeling unwell, for example). The being 'beside myself with rage' comments suggests extreme anger which disembodies the speaker such is the rage felt. Again, as with example 66, the admission/complaint of lack of emotional control suggests disapproval is likely from the recipients.

28. It *drives me up the wall* when *I hear that*
Appraisal category: affect
Valence and appraisal subcategory: negative appraisal indicating dissatisfaction
Type of appraisal: authorial
Propositional content: complaint
Face-oriented strategies: positive face threat of a third party. Example 68 is similar to examples 67 and 66; difficult to express in TARGET IS SOURCE terms, this clichéd metaphor is, nevertheless, used to express, again, being pushed beyond one's abilities to limit one's negative emotions from erupting and being demonstrated as a result of an external trigger. As such, this functions as a positive face threat of self, and also, more explicitly a third party for causing the emotional loss of control.

29. It's always a *glass half empty* for him
Appraisal category: affect
Valence and appraisal subcategory: negative appraisal indicating dissatisfaction
Type of appraisal: non-authorial
Propositional content: criticism
Face-oriented strategies: positive face threat; where SITUATION IS A GLASS OF WATER metaphor is used to suggest that the referent has a focus more on what's not there (what's socially negative) in the situation, than what is there (what's socially positive); that is, that the referent is overly pessimistic. As alluded to previously, the expression of negative emotions, in British English society at least, usually and stereotypically attracts disapproval (perhaps unsurprising from a culture at least partially expected to 'keep calm, and carry on' in the face of extreme adversity). As such, the third-party criticism of the referent is likely to offer a positive (approval) face re-evaluation lower than before the comment. Ironically, such a critical expression can also have backwash on the speaker, who risks being seen, too, as expressing negative emotion, with predictable outcomes as a result.

30. It would be wonderful *if you found it in your heart* to give me a second chance
    Appraisal category: affect
    Valence and appraisal subcategory: positive inclination
    Type of appraisal: non-authorial
    Propositional content: request
    Face-oriented strategies: positive face threats and negative face threat. Reliant on the age-old metaphorical metonym of THE HEART AS THE LOCUS OF EMOTION, this clichéd use of figurative language suggests the intended recipient/hearer of the requester has the ability and perhaps the will to forgive and give permission for future actions. This is negative face-threatening for the hearer (with an arguable secondary positive face threat implied if they don't agree); but is also positive face-threatening for the speaker who risks disapproval for asking for such a favour/chance.

31. *Not me... been there done that bought the T-shirt*
    Appraisal category: affect
    Valence and appraisal subcategory: negative appraisal indicating disinclination
    Type of appraisal: authorial
    Propositional content: refusal
    Face-oriented strategies: positive face threat of a third party or negative face threat of a first person (singular or plural). SUGGESTION IS MASS-MARKET, PACKAGE TOURISM metaphor, seems to suggest what is being referred to or suggested is a well-trammeled and unoriginal approach to mundane levels of 'success' or what is sought to be achieved. This therefore operates as a refusal (evidenced by 'not me') with the metaphorical reason why offered as the 'account'. This is rather dismissive given the mappings of unoriginal, boring and well-trammeled routes to achievement and, as such arguably expresses an opinion likely to co-construct positive face at a lower level of approval than sought; and negative face hindrance, as it suggests, limiting the proposed actions or activities.

32. He's got *a chip on his shoulder* so we need to be careful
    Appraisal category: affect
    Valence and appraisal subcategory: positive security
    Type of appraisal: non-authorial
    Propositional content: warning or criticism
    Face-oriented strategies: positive face threat. Another cliché with a difficult to map TARGET IS SOURCE metaphor, this traditionally represents the referent as having unnecessary or continuous issues with

suggestions, recommendations, or other challenges often resulting in 'him' (in this instance) acting unreasonably and/or disproportionately given the stimuli. This, again suggests the expression of negative social emotions, or actions not in keeping with harmonious long-term relations and suggests, therefore, that this will represent the desire for approval as lower than otherwise might be anticipated.

33. We are stepping on a bit of a *grey area* here

Appraisal category: appreciation

Valence and appraisal subcategory: negative valuation

Target of appraisal: situation or entity

Propositional content: warning

Face-oriented strategies: negative face threat or positive face enhancement of a third party. This is oblique reference to WHITE IS CORRECT; BLACK IS INCORRECT metaphors, themselves iterations of LIGHT IS GOOD; DARK IS BAD metaphors in much of human experience and cognition (in terms of ILLUMINATION only, we hasten to add). The notion of a 'grey area' is one that, metaphorically, suggests things are neither right nor wrong; and the allowability or not is vague and unknown. This seems to act as a warning which is primarily a negative face threat (warnings restrict unfettered freedom of action), though used in situations where outcomes and success are prized more highly than following the letter and the spirit of the 'rules', this can be seen as a positive (approval) face enhancement to such risk-taking and innovation.

34. They do produce *cutting-edge* research

Appraisal category: appreciation

Valence and appraisal subcategory: positive valuation that works to implicitly invoke judgement of capacity

Target of appraisal: product

Propositional content: compliment

Face-oriented strategies: positive face enhancement. A SLICING IS PROGRESS metaphor, this is a positive (approval) face enhancement as it suggests admiration for the clear, concise and effective way in which research is conducted and disseminated for positive social effects.

35. It's been a *rocky road* so far

Appraisal category: Appreciation

Valence and appraisal subcategory: negative valuation

Target of appraisal: situation or circumstances

Propositional content: complaint or admission

Face-oriented strategies: positive face threat. An iteration of the LIFE IS A JOURNEY metaphor so often clichéd in many and varied ways. Most often this would occur either as an admission (of a situation found challenging) or complaint (where another is implied to be the cause of the less-than-smooth progress).

36. It's only a *half-baked idea* at this stage
    Appraisal category: appreciation
    Valence and appraisal subcategory: negative complexity
    Target of appraisal: idea at stake
    Propositional content: criticism
    Face-oriented strategies: positive face threat and secondary negative face threat. SUCCESS IS BAKING metaphor, which clearly suggests that 'half-baked' is not successful or likely to result in success. This is a criticism which threatens both positive (approval) face and secondarily negative (freedom from imposition) face; as in the latter aspect, it suggests the idea needs to be completed/rethought more fully before success can be achieved.

37. We can't expect too much more, *it does what it says on the tin*
    Appraisal category: appreciation
    Valence and appraisal subcategory: negative complexity
    Target of appraisal: entity at stake
    Propositional content: advice
    Face-oriented strategies: negative face threat. An allusion to an age-old cliché similar to *what you see is what you get* which suggests that the limits of what's achievable are evident to all to see. This is likely to operate a negative (freedom from imposition) face threat, or rather a reconceptualisation of ones freedom to expect great(er) things.

38. It is a *game changer* for us
    Appraisal category: appreciation
    Valence and appraisal subcategory: negative reaction / impact
    Target of appraisal: situation or circumstance
    Propositional content: admission
    Face-oriented strategies: positive face enhancement and secondary negative face enhancement. A SUCCESS IS A COMPETITIVE GAME where the notion of a 'game changer' is always used as an opportunity for better 'players' to be utilised for better and greater effect than currently. This is therefore a positive face enhancement by showing approval of (future) possibilities. This could secondarily be seen as a rare enhancement of negative face (negative face is almost always *mitigated* for threats, rarely *enhanced* by the acquisition of new

spaces of freedom of action), as the possibilities for future action are less limited and more open.

39. As interesting as it is, that is *the forbidden fruit*
    Appraisal category: appreciation
    Valence and appraisal subcategory: negative valuation, (implicit) propriety
    Target of appraisal: action or idea at stake
    Propositional content: refusal or criticism
    Face-oriented strategies: positive face enhancement of a third party and/or negative face threat; utilising intertextually the reference to the apple in the Garden of Eden sampled by Adam and Eve, the notion of the forbidden fruit almost inherently suggests a limit of possible or permissible action (and hence a negative face threat); however, as alluded to previously, where success is valued more highly than following the rules, especially where the rules may not be clear, or set, then this can be seen as a positive face enhancement of the consumer of the metaphorical forbidden fruit.

40. That suggestion *is food for thought*, I hadn't considered that perspective actually
    Appraisal category: appreciation
    Valence and appraisal subcategory: reaction / impact
    Target of appraisal: idea proposed
    Propositional content: admission
    Face-oriented strategies: positive face threat. A THOUGHTS MUST BE NOURISHED metaphor (a THOUGHT IS AN ANIMATE ENTITY derivative), operates as a positive face enhancement (by expressing approval), which in this case is further strengthened by the admission the suggester is more insightful than the speaker (a further positive face enhancement of the hearer).

Appendix 4: Clichés as Identity Markers in BBC's Reality TV Show, The Apprentice

The extracts in this section represent the contestants introducing themselves on camera at the start of the new season. These self-presentation shots are intersected with shots of the contestants meeting for the first time, meeting Lord Sugar in the boardroom, preparing and performing the tasks set for them and discussing the tasks afterwards. Each episode is 60 minutes long.

The data presented here contains all extracts identified as containing clichés. All clichés are presented in *italics*.

The extracts are listed as they appear in the analysis section in Chapter 6. They indicate the identity type they are seen to construct. Each cliché in the extract (if more than one) is then separately analysed in terms of the language feature they represent and the pragmatic function they fulfil.

(1)   Joseph: when I was 14 I was expelled from school [...] but I *turned my life around* [...] I'm now *the godfather of* business [...] and I'm here to make Lord Sugar *an offer he cannot refuse*
      Identity type: confrontational and fear inducing

(1.a) *I turned my life around:*
      Language feature: ACTIONS ARE DIRECTIONS conceptual metaphor within the wider LIFE IS A JOURNEY metaphorical frame with the WRONG DIRECTION IS FAILURE metaphor, too and hence turning around effectively maps the connotations of moving away from failure and towards success.
      Pragmatic function: The ability to recognise success, and to self-reflect and want to move away from perceived failure, are widely considered, far beyond business CoP, to be aspirations and activities across many walks of life and ways of working. As such, this is an effective attempt at the presentation of himself that Joseph engages in, serving to offer his positive (approval) face wants at a high and admirable level. His comments thereafter in this opening self-presentation pitch scene serve to hone in on the business CoP that he appears to want to be identified with more closely.

(1.b) *I'm the godfather of* business:

Language feature: interdiscursive reference to crime/mafia cultural texts. which serves to operate as a BUSINESS IS CRIME metaphor.

Pragmatic function: ironically, although crime is considered a societal negative, the intertextual, interdiscursive reference to the *Godfather* films seems to map socially positive notions of 'coolness' connotations from the main protagonists of the film to Joseph. The connotations of fierce, edgy, cool, ruthless – being synonymous connotations with business – can be seen as attempts to represent his own positive (approval) face wants in a highly enhanced manner.

(1.c) *Make [...] an offer he cannot refuse*

Language feature: intertextual reference to Scorsese's *Godfather* films that further reinforces the concepts we're invited to map from the Godfather to Joseph, because he seems to consider them socially positive aspects and acquires expectation of approval from these.

Pragmatic function: this is essentially a continuation of the preceding attempt to enhance his own positive face (desire for approval) through continued intertextual reference to the *Godfather* film(s).

(2)   Aleksandra: The sheer energy that I am going to bring is going to mimic that of a *nuclear explosion* [...] *once I lock myself in on the target* [...] *they do not stand a chance*

Identity type: confrontational and fear inducing

(2.a) The sheer energy that I am going to bring is going to mimic that of a *nuclear explosion*

Language feature: WEAPONS ARE PURPOSES and BUSINESS IS WARFARE. These metaphors have the mappings of objectives in business are objectives in warfare, to be met (metaphorically) with huge explosive energy, power and effect. This suggests an ENERGY IS NEARLY BOUNDLESS metaphor which Aleksandra is claiming for herself, energy being a positive social trait in most walks of life.

Pragmatic function: the mappings suggest that Aleksandra considers boundless energy applied indiscriminately to all aspects of the business objectives she will be seeking, is a positive social trait, or group of traits, valued by members of business CoPs. This therefore serves as her attempt to present her own face as a set of enhanced positive (approval) face wants/needs and capabilities.

(2.b) *once I lock myself in on the target*

Language feature: MILITARY TARGETS ARE PERSONAL OBJECTIVES and BUSINESS TARGETS ARE MILITARY OBJECTIVES. Similarly to the explanation in 2.a, this maps near identical meanings and entailments from the source domain of weapons onto Aleksandra as target domain. This means that she is representing herself as ALEKSANDRA IS A WEAPON. The explicit naming of herself as a weapon, however, would be inadvisable as this is often used in some British English dialects as an insult (for the reasons of causing hurt and destruction).

Pragmatic function: despite the risks in identifying herself as a weapon, Aleksandra is seeking to map the notions of an uncontained powerful force onto herself, as she presumably sees such traits and aspects as being welcomed by members of a business CoP, and this functions to enhance her positive face wants (want for approval) by members of that CoP.

(2.c) they do *not stand a chance*

Language feature: metaphors CHANCES ARE OPTIONS and BUSINESS IS COMPETITION with the mappings of assumptions of winning the competition inherent in business operations.

Pragmatic function: positive face self-enhancement and negative other threat. This seems to suggest that the confidence in winning the competition of the speaker is such that they will be effortlessly successful, suggesting positive (enhancement) face of self further assuming traits prized by the business CoP. That this is oriented to a non-specific 'other' counts as a generic negative face threat to that other that their options to operate freely towards success are so curtailed by the speaker's presumed actions, meaning they are not free to succeed or even given opportunity to do so.

(3)   Dillon: basically *I'm king of the truth bomb* […] that means that *I'm going to tell you how it is whether you like it or not*

Identity type: confrontational and fear inducing

(3.a) basically *I'm king of the truth bomb*

Language feature: TRUTH IS A HIERARCHICAL KINGDOM metaphor and the TRUTH IS AN EXPLOSIVE, with the mappings of the former being those of assumed authority, control and respect; and the mapping of the latter being sudden and potentially damaging.

Pragmatic function: such mappings are evidently Dillon's attempts to construct face through identity construction via representation of the traits of authority, control, respect, rights, and potentially damaging (for purposeful effect within a wider BUSINESS IS WARFARE metaphor) as assumed positive social traits within a business context and CoP. As such, this is an evident attempt to construct identity through self-positive (approval) face enhancement.

(3.b) that means that *I'm going to tell you how it is whether you like it or not*
   Language feature: declarative speech act (as the speaker is declaring their intent for the upcoming speech event), and a commissive (as the speaker then commits themself to that speech event); from this we can also deduce this is an implicature, as this flouts Grice's (1975) maxims of quantity (the speaker could have just told the hearer how it was without prefacing it), and manner, and is, therefore, an implied threat/warning.
   Pragmatic function: negative face threat, primarily, with secondary positive face threat inherent. The admonition that the speaker is going to tell the listener 'how it is' means there is limited scope for the hearer (without challenge to the speaker) to avoid the freedom of action that a pseudo-lecture of this type entails – it imposes on the hearer's freedom of imposition. The fact that the 'whether you like it or not' is used as a semblance of, and assumption of incidental rather than intentional face damage-at least on the surface, but operates in either case to secondarily impact positive (approval) face wants as it implies the hearer is at least partially responsible for the reason for the pseudo lecture, either through disapproval of past action or past inaction.

(4)   Paul₁: *I* definitely *don't shy away from* conflict [...] *make no mistake about it* [...] *I'm here to win*
   Identity type: confrontational and fear inducing

(4.a) *I* definitely *don't shy away from* conflict
   Language feature: PEOPLE ARE SKITTISH ANIMALS, metaphor, where what's mapped is the opposite of the fact skittish animals will 'shy' away from perceived threat or danger.
   Pragmatic function: Paul is trying to represent the construction of his own face as one in which he is not afraid of threat or danger, and he has the characteristics of confidence, fearlessness and determination; Paul is effectively seeking positive face (approval) enhancement on the assumption that these factors are welcomed by members of business CoPs.

(4.b) *make no mistake about it*
   Language feature: illocutionary force indicating device (IFID) which gives a reiteration of 4.a.
   Pragmatic function: is effectively a reinforcement and reiteration of 4.a. It is a pragmatic repetition for the purposes of foregrounding for effect.

(4.c) *I'm here to win*
   Language feature: an assertion speech act which acts as a BUSINESS IS CONFLICT metaphor with the nested metaphor of SUCCESS IS WINNING

THE CONFLICT, and all that this entails mapped onto Paul from the concepts of success in conflict.

Pragmatic function: as with the other metaphorical and other non-metaphorical clichés in the self-presentation scenes, the speaker – in this case Paul – is attempting to construct and offer a highly (presumed) approved version of his identity as core member of any given business CoP. From this, we can deduce Paul's assumptions about the model or idealised member of said CoP, as we can in all other cases.

(5) Jackie: my game plan is to *pick off the competition one by one* [...] I'm completely ruthless and I'd be surprised if Lord Sugar doesn't already have a cheque with my name on it
     Identity type: confrontational and fear inducing

(5.a) my game plan is to *pick off the competition one by one*
     Language feature: PURPOSES ARE WEAPONS metaphor. intertextual invocation of the SHOOTING IS RESOLVING metaphor, mapping the concepts of being accurate, carefully positioned, methodical, and ruthless especially when we consider the use of JACKIE IS A SNIPER metaphor inherent in 5.a
     Pragmatic function: Such mappings as those in these metaphors are likely, in Jackie's eyes, at least, to be seen to be concepts which are prized by members of a business CoP In this way she appears to be assuming the conceptual traits of accuracy, careful selection of positioning, methodical, patience and ruthlessness are central ones to a business CoP.

(5.b) I'd be surprised if Lord Sugar doesn't already have a cheque with my name on it
     Language feature: the cheque is metonymical with money / funding; as is the name on the cheque in this construction.
     Pragmatic function: Jackie is making the self-presentational claim that she considers she's already won the competition, this level of confidence being prized as a trait in successful businesspersons and their identities in business CoPs.

(6) Jessica: A lot of people underestimate <u>me</u> [...]and then *I pull out the big guns* and *I* always tend *to get my way*
     Identity type: confrontational and fear inducing

(6.a) *I pull out the big guns*
     Language feature: WEAPONS ARE PURPOSES and BIG IS BETTER metaphors which equates to a wider belief that BUSINESS IS WARFARE metaphor, all of which maps the notions of aggression, ruthlessness and effectiveness.

Pragmatic function: the mappings of aggressive, ruthless and effective nature, being apparently prized as identity traits of successful members of the business CoP, appear to be used as an attempt, by Jessica, to represent her positive (approval) face at an effective level for recognition as a business CoP member.

(6.b) *I* always tend *to get my way*
Language feature: LIFE IS A JOURNEY metaphor with DIRECTIONS ARE DECISIONS implied metaphor, here, too, in terms of the context of use.
Pragmatic function: the positive face enhancement strategy of herself that Jessica attempts to construct here is one which suggests that getting her way is seen as an admirable trait in business CoP.

(7)   Grianne: I think everyone thought 'oh she's just a make-up artist' [...] but I'm a make-up artist who wants *to think outside the box*
Identity type: uniqueness
Language feature: a classic THINKING IS CONTAINED, and being outside the container means one's THINKING IS UNCONTAINED where THINKING is metaphoric for success, or metonymically associated with it.
Pragmatic function: Grianne's representation of self, with the self-oriented positive (approval) face enhancement suggests she considers that unconstrained thinking is an asset and a positive trait for successful businesspeople and hence successful members in terms of their identities of business CoP.

(8)   Richard: I've got a unique concept and a business plan that's really *cutting edge* [...] he'd be crazy to pass by Richard Woods
Identity type: uniqueness
Language feature: SLICING IS PROGRESS where the incisiveness and the SHARP IS GOOD and INCISION IS SUCCESSFUL MOVE metaphors implied by this suggest easier and more effective ways to success than current tried and tested, but old and tired routes regularly employed.
Pragmatic function: as with so many others in this collection of clichéd metaphors, the INNOVATION-IS-GOOD belief appears to be inherent in many apprentices' perspectives (e.g. see 9 below) on the identity of core and successful members of a business CoP. In this case, then, Richard is assuming/building self-enhancement of his own positive (approval) face wants and needs to represent himself as a stand-out member of the CoP.

(9)   Karthik: *I don't walk the path that others walk* [...] *my way is a separate superhighway*
Identity type: uniqueness

(9.a) *I don't walk the path that others walk*
Language feature: the LIFE IS A JOURNEY metaphor with the mappings of a successful traveller who finds their own 'path', implying a ROUTE IS AN EFFECTIVE STRATEGY metaphor.
Pragmatic function: in terms of representation of self in terms of an attempt at enhancing own positive face (approval wants), Karthik is apparently challenging the concept of doing things only as others do. In this way it is a representation of aspects of self, claimed, that appear to be prized in business CoPs – innovative and alternate routes to success being valued.

(9.b) *my way is a separate superhighway*
Language feature: the LIFE IS A JOURNEY extended / QUICK IS SUCCESSFUL PROGRESS metaphor which maps the notions of quick and efficient ways of travelling/succeeding and an ability to 'take' a lot of people with you given the ability of superhighways to carry a lot of traffic. The TRAFFIC IS PEOPLE metaphor, and the extension of the LIFE IS A JOURNEY metaphor with the concept of a superhighway suggests mass movement of people which equates to making a lot of people successful through the original and innovative route Karthik chooses to take.
Pragmatic function: The mappings in 9a and 9b, when coupled with the pragmatic function in 9a seem to suggest that Karthik considers innovation and the concept of less well-travelled routes to success as being prized concepts and traits in the identities of successful members of a business CoP.

(10)   Dan: If you *cross me* [...] then *it's like hitting a brick wall* [...] you're never going to get past
Identity type: tough and controlling

(10.a) if you *cross me*
Language feature: this is a LIFE IS A JOURNEY metaphor, where to 'cross' is to move into the path of directions risking hindering that progress
Pragmatic function: The 'if you cross me' comment seems to be like the formation of a speech act of a conditional threat. Those who threaten successfully are those who assume power and control is in operation and they are at the centre of that power and control. As such, this, again as we see with all others, appears to be the speaker, in this case, Dan,

(10.b) *it's like hitting a brick wall*
Language feature: ACTION IS MOVEMENT and SUCCESS IS AN OPEN PATH and COLLIDING WITH OBSTACLES IS FAILURE and DAN IS AN OBSTACLE.

Pragmatic function: this cliché metaphor operates as a threat to an assumed, hypothetical 'other' (as in 10.a) as the notions of self (Dan's self, that is) that are being constructed here are those of ruthlessness and being unyieldingly tough in the face of adversity. Again, these appear to be assumed traits of core members of a business CoP, and this appears to be Dan's attempt to enhance his positive (approval) face and hence his identity in the eyes of the presumed members of said CoP.

(10.c) you're never going to get past

Language feature: SUCCESS IS AN OPEN PATH. FAILURE IS STATIONARY. Pragmatic function: the pragmatic function includes the construction of Dan's positive face, or at least the attempt at the construction of his face, in such a way as to represent his identity and credentials for membership of the CoP of business.

(11)   Paul$_2$: I've got no problems stepping up and being a project manager on any of the tasks [...] the way to *fend off* your strongest rivals is to not let them see you coming [...] I'm just going to sit there and *pull the strings* and *do what I need to do* to *get through to the end*

Identity type: tough and controlling

(11.a) the way to *fend off* your strongest rivals

Language feature: This is a BUSINESS IS WARFARE metaphor, with 'fend off' (as an etymological sibling of 'defend') connoted, and maps notions of strength, capability and being unassailable despite intense attempts.

Pragmatic function: The face strategy Paul uses to construct his own positive face (desire/want for approval) is one where he sees metaphorical strength, capability, and stoic unassailability as central traits to identity and membership as a member of a business CoP.

(11.b) *pull the strings*

Language feature: BUSINESS IS A PUPPET SHOW metaphor, with Paul putting himself in the metaphorical role: PAUL IS A PUPPETEER, with notions and understandings of Paul as the controller and director.

Pragmatic function: Paul's making quite the assumption for a contestant in an essentially extended interview process where he is relatively less powerful than those deciding on his level of success in the process. In any case, he is attempting to identify himself as a leader – again, a positive trait in a business CoP, and hence an attempt to offer his own positive face as one to be enhanced and valued within said CoP.

(11.c) *do what I need to do* to *get through to the end*
Language feature: LIFE IS A JOURNEY and SUCCESS IS DESTINATION with the additional metaphor of ACTIONS ARE SUCCESSES.
Pragmatic function: the face enhancement strategy Paul engages in here is identical to those immediately prior, and can therefore be seen to be a pragmatic repetition with elegant variation for the purposes of foregrounding for reinforcement effect.

(12)   Kayode: When it comes to business [...] I don't *just grab the bull by the horns* [...] I put it in a headlock and squeeze every opportunity that comes out of him
Language feature: PROBLEM IS A POWERFUL ANIMAL metaphor, with the horns being metonymical to the 'head' and the HEAD IS THE SOURCE OF THE PROBLEM metaphor implied (via a flout of Grice's (1975) maxim(s) of manner and possibly quality) by this. This maps the understanding from the various SOURCE domains to Kayode himself (as the TARGET domain) that Kayode considers himself fierce, fearless, bold, decisive and effective in tackling problems bigger and stronger than himself.
Pragmatic function: this would all operate to create, or at least offer the notion that Kayode is enhancing his positive face (his desire or want for approval) by those at the centre of his tacitly assumed, generic business CoP.

(13)   Alex: *money makes the world go round* [...] and to me [...] it is my world [...] I'm like a cash machine [...] if *you push the right buttons* [...] I will give you money
Identity type: ambitious

(13.a) *money makes the world go round* [...] and to me [...] it is my world
Language feature: MONEY IS A POWERFUL FORCE with the power we, as members of monetised societies give to this social construct being seen to be immense, and of a scale equal to a gravitational force of nature within the field of the universe's physical mechanics for the movement of planetary bodies.
Pragmatic function: quite a weak face-oriented strategy which, at this point in the utterance, can really only be said to show that Alex is demonstrating core and fundamental understandings of the concepts of value to members of a business CoP. This operates merely to (pre-)show that Alex has the same positive face wants (pursuit of money as a measure of success) as members of any business CoP.

(13.b) I'm like a cash machine [...] if *you push the right buttons* [...] I
will give you money
Language feature: PERSON IS A MACHINE and KNOWLEDGE IS REWARD
which seem to map the concept that a skilled and lucky interactant
can 'win' the attention and support of Alex.
Pragmatic function: This is a self-positive face enhancement,
where Alex is attempting to communicate the sense that he can
be generous under the right conditions and when interacting with,
or rewarding, the skilled and talented. Whether we share these
assumptions as viewers of *The Apprentice*, whether already members of a business CoP, or not, is immaterial to the way in which
Alex has constructed his identity here.

(14) Daniel: money is the *be all and end all* [...] some people say
money can't make you happy [...] but I'd rather cry in a sports
car than cry in a banger
Identity type: ambitious

(14.a) money is the *be all and end all*
Language feature: MONEY IS EVERYTHING metaphor, with mappings
identifying with the idea that money is the route to, genesis of, and
pathway to everything of value in Daniel's reality paradigm.
Pragmatic function: this sees Daniel construct his own positive and
negative face wants in a highly partial way. His wants are specific
to the face wants of the idealised identity of a successful member
of any business CoP, as apparent by his use of this metaphor

(14.b) some people say *money can't make you happy*
Language feature: MONEY INVOKES EMOTION metaphor
Pragmatic function: both 14b and 14c seem to work in identical
ways and we explore the negative face wants; and positive face
construction that Daniel engages in, in 14c.

(14.c) but I'd rather cry in a sports car than cry in a banger
Language function: metonymic reference to sports cars (costing a
lot of money to purchase and run) and 'bangers' (being very old,
unreliable and, crucially here, cheap second-hand cars), this seems
to be an intertextual allusion to the clichéd idiom 'money can't
buy you happiness' (more explicitly referenced in example 14c).
Pragmatic function: this seems an interesting attempt to construct
his own face as needing fewer attentions to negative (unhindered;
free from imposition) face wants of self. We might conclude that
for people to be happy they need to be free from the impositions
on their negative face which might cause them to feel or experience being hindered. Further, this is, as discussed, an attempt by

Daniel as one of the contestants on *The Apprentice* to proffer his own positive face as being that of the identity of a core member of a business CoP in that being successful (and by metonymic extension based on our schematic assumptions of business success) and being rich is more important than being happy, which echoes Daniel's comments in 14a.

(15)   April: I'm *there* […] I'm *where it needs to be* […] *I'm suited I'm booted* […] come on
         Identity type: ready for business

(15.a) I'm *there* […] I'm *where it needs to be.*
         Language feature: this is a SUCCESS IS A LOCATION metaphor with the mappings that April is attempting to demonstrate that she is already in a position of success.
         Pragmatic function: as previously, this is the speaker's attempt to construct their own positive (approval) face in a way which is presumably in keeping with their own understandings, and their assumed understandings of the idealised identity of an effective member of a business CoP.

(15.b) *I'm suited, I'm booted*
         Language feature: metonymic and intertextual references to the uniform of business, the business suit complete with smart and formal footwear and although the concept of 'boots' doesn't gel with the schematically expected uniform of business (at least in the Western world), the word 'boot(ed)' rhymes with 'suit(ed)' to create an intensifying-foregrounded effect through assonance.
         Pragmatic function: maxims of relation and manner: ready and capable of operating effectively within the CoPs that regularly require such a wardrobe; self-oriented positive face enhancement, attempting to demonstrate own effectiveness within generic business CoP.

References

Aaker, D., Stayman, D. and Hagerty, M. (1986). Warmth in advertising: Measurement, impact and sequence effects. *Journal of Consumer Research*, 12(4), 364–381.

Abrams, D. (1999). Social identity, social cognition, and the self: The flexibility and stability of self-categorization. In D. Abrams and M. A. Hogg, eds., *Social Identity and Social Cognition*. Oxford: Blackwell, pp. 197–229.

Akbari, M. (2015). Different impacts of advertising appeals on advertising attitude for high and low involvement products. *Global Business Review*, 16(3), 478–493. https://doi.org/10.1177/0972150915569936.

Albers-Miller, N. D. and Stafford, M. R. (1999). An international analysis of emotional and rational appeals in services vs. goods advertising. *Journal of Consumer Marketing*, 16(1), 42–57.

Almgren, S. and Olsson, T. (2015). 'Let's get them involved'... to some extent: Analyzing online news participation. *Social Media + Society*, 1(2). https://doi.org/10.1177/2056305115621934.

American Marketing Association (2021). Advertising. www.ama.org/topics/advertising/ [Last accessed March 2021].

Anderson-Gough, F., Grey, C. and Robson, K. (1998). 'Work hard, play hard': An analysis of organizational cliché in two accountancy practices. *Organization*, 5(4), 565–592.

Aragbuwa, A. (2020). Dialogic contractions in online news discourse on violence against women in Nigeria. *Journal of Gender Studies*, 29(2), 130–145. https://doi.org/10.1080/09589236.2019.1584553

Archer, D., Wilson, A. and Rayson, P. (2002). Introduction to the USAS category system. http://ucrel.lancs.ac.uk/usas/usas_guide.pdf [Last accessed 10 March 2021].

Aristotle (2006). *Art of Rhetoric*. Reprint of 1926 edition. Cambridge, MA: Harvard University Press.

Augoustinos, M. and Walker, I. (1995). *Social Cognition: An Integrated Introduction*. London: Sage.

Austin, J. L. (1962). *How to Do Things with Words*. 2nd edn. J. O. Urmson and M. Sbisá, eds., Cambridge, MA: Harvard University Press.

Baider, F. (2013). Cultural stereotypes and linguistic clichés: Usefulness in intercultural competency. *International Journal for Cross-Disciplinary Subjects in Education (IJCDSE)*, 4(2), 1166–1171. https://doi.org/10.20533/ijcdse.2042.6364.2013.0164.

Baker, K. (2015). At the end of the day, it's a game of two halves: Survey reveals the top punditry cliches that make us cringe while watching football. *Mail Online*. www.dailymail.co.uk/news/article-3228791/Survey-reveals-punditry-cliches-make-hate-football.html [Last accessed February 2017].

Barthes, R. (1977). *Image, Music, Text*. A. Lavers, trans. London: Fontana Press.

Bartlett, F. C. S. (1932). *Remembering: A Study in Experimental and Social Psychology*. Cambridge: Cambridge University Press.

BBC (2008). 20 of your most hated clichés. *BBC News*. http://news.bbc.co.uk/1/hi/7733264.stm [Last accessed February 2017].

Benczes, R. (2009). What motivates the production and use of metaphorical and metonymical compounds? In M. Brdar, M. Omazić and V. Pavičić Takač, eds., *Cognitive Approaches to English. Fundamental, Methodological Interdisciplinary and Applied Aspects*. Newcastle upon Tyne: Cambridge Scholars Publishing, pp. 49–67.

Biber, D. (2009). A corpus-driven approach to formulaic language in English multi-word patterns in speech and writing. *International Journal of Corpus Linguistics*, 14(3), 275–311. https://doi.org/10.1075/ijcl.14.3.08bib.

Boers, F. (2014). Idioms and phraseology. In J. Taylor and J. Littlemore, eds., *The Bloomsbury Companion to Cognitive Linguistics*. London: Bloomsbury, pp. 185–201.

Boers, F. and Stengers, H. (2008). Adding sound to the picture: Motivating the lexical composition of metaphorical idioms in English, Dutch and Spanish. In M. S. Zanotto, L. Cameron and M. C. Cavalcanti, eds., *Confronting Metaphor in Use: An Applied Linguistic Approach*. Amsterdam: John Benjamins, pp. 63–78.

Boorstin, D. (1987). *The Image: a Guide to Pseudo-Events in America*. New York: Atheneum.

Bousfield, D. (2007a). Impoliteness, preference organization and conductivity. *Multilingua*, 26(1/2), 1–33.

Bousfield, D. (2007b). Beginnings, middles and ends: Towards a biopsy of the dynamics of impoliteness. *Journal of Pragmatics*, 39(12), 2185–2216.

Bousfield, D. (2008). *Impoliteness in Interaction*. Vol. 167. Amsterdam: John Benjamins.

Bousfield, D. (2013). Face in conflict. *Journal of Language Aggression and Conflict*, 1(1), 37–57.

Bousfield, D. (2018). Face(t)s of self in interaction. *Journal of Politeness Research*, 14(2), 87–305.

Bousfield, D. and McIntyre, D. (2018). Creative linguistic impoliteness as aggression in Stanley Kubrick's Full Metal Jacket. *Journal of Literary Semantics*, 47(1), 43–65.

Boyce, L. (2015). Revealed: Ten most common mistakes job hunters make on CVs and overused clichés that can put employers off. *This is Money*. www.thisismoney.co.uk/money/news/article-3236760/Ten- common-mistakes-job-hunters-make-CVs-overused-clich-s-employers- off.html [Last accessed February 2017].

Bronwen, M. and Ringham, F. (1999). *Dictionary of Semiotics*. London: Bloomsbury.

Brown, P. and Levinson, S. (1987). *Politeness: Some Universals in Language Use*. Cambridge: Cambridge University Press.

Bruns, A. (2008). *Blogs, Wikipedia, Second Life, and Beyond: From Production to Produsage*. New York: Peter Lang.

Buckledee, S. (2018). *The Language of Brexit*. London: Bloomsbury.

Bullo, S. (2014). *Evaluation in Advertising Reception: A Socio-Cognitive and Linguistic Perspective*. Basingstoke: Palgrave Macmillan.

Bullo, S. (2018). Exploring disempowerment in women's accounts of endometriosis experiences. *Discourse and Communication*, 11(6), 1–18.

Bullo, S. (2019). Clichés as evaluative resources: A socio-cognitive study. *Text and Talk*, 39(6), 289–313.

Cambridge University Press (2017). Cambridge international dictionary of idioms. http://itools.com/tool/cambridge-international-dictionary-of-idioms. [Last accessed April 2021].

Channell, J. (2000). Corpus analysis of evaluative lexis. In S. Hunston and G. Thompson, eds., *Evaluation in Text: Authorial Stance and the Construction of Discourse*. Oxford: Oxford University Press, pp. 38–56.

Chilton, P. (2004). *Analysing Political Discourse: Theory and Practice*. London: Routledge.

Chomsky, N. (1964). *Current Issues in Linguistic Theory*. The Hague: Mouton.

Chomsky, N. (2004). *The Generative Enterprise Revisited: Discussions with Riny Huybregts, Henk van Riemsdijk, Naoki Fukui and Mihoko Zushi*. New York: Mouton de Gruyter.

Chouliaraki, L. and Fairclough, N. (1999). *Discourse in Late Modernity: Rethinking Critical Discourse Analysis*. Edinburgh: Edinburgh University Press.

Christensen, L. T. and Askegaard, S. (2001). Corporate identity and corporate image revisited: A semiotic perspective. *European Journal of Marketing,* 35(3–4), 292–315.

Chumbley, J. I. and Balota, D. A. A. (1984). Word's meaning affects the decision in lexical decision. *Memory and Cognition* 12: 590–606. https://doi.org/10.3758/BF03213348.

Church, K. W. and Hanks, P. (1990). Word association norms, mutual information, and lexicography. *Computational Linguistics*, 16, 222–229.

van Cranenburgh, A. (2018). Cliche expressions in literary and genre novels. In *Proceedings of Workshop on Computational Linguistics for Cultural Heritage, Social Sciences, Humanities and Literature*. Santa Fe, New Mexico, USA, 25 August, pp. 34–43 https://pure.rug.nl/ws/portalfiles/portal/72810336/W18_4504.pdf.

Culpeper, J. (1996). Towards an anatomy of impoliteness. *Journal of Pragmatics*, 25(3), 349–367.

Culpeper, J. (2005). Impoliteness and entertainment in the television quiz show: *The Weakest Link. Journal of Politeness Research*, 1(1), 35–72.

Culpeper, J. (2009). Impoliteness: Using and understanding the language of offence. *ESRC project* website: http://www.lancs.ac.uk/fass/projects/impoliteness/.

Culpeper, J. (2010). Conventionalised impoliteness formulae. *Journal of Pragmatics*, 42(12), 3232–3245.

Culpeper, J. (2011). *Impoliteness: Using Language to Cause Offence*. Cambridge: Cambridge University Press.

Dann, G. M. S. (2001). The self-admitted use of cliché, in the language of tourism. *Tourism Culture and Communication*, 3(1), 11–14.

Dervin, F. (2015). Discourses of Othering. In K. Tracy, T. Sandel and C. Ilie, eds., *The International Encyclopedia of Language of Social Interaction*. London: Wiley-Blackwell, pp. 1–9.

van Dijk, T. A. (1977a). Semantic macro-structures and knowledge frames in discourse comprehension. In M. A. Just and P. A. Carpenter, eds., *Cognitive Processes in Comprehension*. Hillsdale, NJ: Lawrence Erlbaum, pp. 3–32.

van Dijk, T. A. (1992). Discourse and the denial of racism. *Discourse & Society*, 3(1), 87–118.

van Dijk, T. A. (1997b). The study of discourse. In T. A. van Dijk, ed., *Discourse as Structure and Process. Discourse Studies: A Multidisciplinary Introduction*. Vol 1. London: Sage, pp. 13–14.

van Dijk, T. A. (1997c). What is political discourse analysis? In J. Blommaert and C. Bulcean, eds., *Political Linguistics*. Amsterdam: John Benjamins, pp. 11–52.

van Dijk, T. A. (2000). On the analysis of parliamentary debates on immigration. In M. Reisigl and R. Wodak, eds., *The Semiotics of Racism: Approaches to Critical Discourse Analysis*. Vienna: Passagen Verlag, pp. 851–903.

van Dijk, T. A. (2001). Multidisciplinary CDA. In R. Wodak, and M. Meyer, eds., *Methods of Critical Discourse Analysis*. London: Sage, pp. 95–121.

van Dijk, T. A. (2007). Editor's introduction: The study of discourse – an introduction. In T. A. van Dijk, ed., *Discourse Studies, Vol. 1*, London: Sage, pp. xix–xlii.

van Dijk, T. A. (2009). Critical discourse studies: A sociocognitive approach. In R. Wodak and M. Meyer, eds., *Methods of Critical Discourse Analysis*, 2nd ed. London: Sage, pp. 62–86.

Down, S. and Warren, L. (2008). Constructing narratives of enterprise: Clichés and entrepreneurial self-identity. *International Journal of Entrepreneurial Behaviour and Research*, 14(1). 4–23.

Dubrofsky, R. E. (2011). Surveillance on reality television and Facebook: From authenticity to flowing data. *Communication Theory*, 21(2), 111–129.

Dunmire, P. (2012). Political discourse analysis: Exploring the language of politics and the politics of language. *Language and Linguistics Compass*, 6(11), 735–751.

Eckert, P. (2006). Communities of practice. In K. Brown, ed., *Encyclopedia of Language and Linguistics*. 2nd edn. Elsevier, Amsterdam, pp. 683–685. http://dx.doi.org/10.1016/B0-08-044854-2/01276-1.

Eckert, P. and McConnell-Ginet, S. (1992). Communities of practice: Where language, gender, and power all live. In K. Hall, M. Bucholtz and B. Moonwoman, eds., *Locating Power. Proceedings of the Second Berkeley Women and Language Conference*. Berkeley: Women and Language Group, pp. 89–89.

Eco, U. (1979). *The Role of the Reader: Explorations in the Semiotics of Texts*. Bloomington: Indiana University Press.

Economou, D. (2012). Standing out on critical issues: Evaluation in large verbal-visual displays in Australian broadsheets. In W. L. Bowcher, ed., *Multimodal Texts from Around the World*. Palgrave Macmillan, London, pp. 246–269.

Ekström, M., Patrona, M. and Thornborrow, J. (2018). Right-wing populism and the dynamics of style: A discourse-analytic perspective on mediated political performances. *Palgrave Communications*, 83(4). https://doi.org/10.1057/s41599-018-0132-6

Eyben, R. (2019). 'The moustache makes him more of a man': Waiters' masculinity mtruggles, 1890–1910, *History Workshop Journal*, 87: 188–210. https://doi.org/10.1093/hwj/dbz008.

Fairclough, N. (1992). *Discourse and Social Change*. London: Polity Press.

Fairclough, N. (2003). *Analysing Discourse Textual Analysis for Social Research*. London: Routledge.

Fairclough, N. and Wodak, R. (1997). Critical discourse analysis. In T. A. van Dijk, ed., *Introduction to Discourse Studies*. London: Sage, pp. 258–284.

Filley, A. (1975). *Interpersonal Conflict Resolution*. Glenview, IL: Scott Foresman.

Firth, R. (1957). *Man and Culture: An Evaluation of the Work of Bronislaw Malinowski*. London: Routledge and Kegan Paul.

Fountain, N. (2012). *Clichés: Avoid them Like the Plague*. London: Michael O'Mara.

Fowler, R. (1956). Linguistic theory and the study of literature. In R. Fowler, ed., *Essays on Style and Language: Linguistic and Critical Approaches to Literary Style*. London: Routledge, pp. 1–28.

Fowler, H. (1965). *A Dictionary of Modern English Usage*. 2nd edn. Oxford: Oxford University Press.

Garcés-Conejos Blitvich, P. and Sifianou, M. (2017). Im/politeness and identity. In J. Culpeper, M. Haugh and D. Kádár, eds., *Handbook of Linguistic (Im) Politeness*. Basingstoke: Palgrave MacMillan, pp. 227–256.

Gibbs, R. W. (1993). Process and product in making sense of tropes. In A. Ortony, ed., *Metaphor and Thought*, 2nd edn. New York: Cambridge University Press, pp. 252–277.

Gibbs, R. W. (2014). Embodied metaphor. In J. Littlemore and J. Taylor, eds., *The Bloomsbury Companion to Cognitive Linguistics*. London: Bloomsbury, pp. 167–184.

Giddens, A. (1991). *Modernity and Self-Identity: Self and Society in the Late Modern Age*. Stanford, CA: Stanford University Press.

Goffman, E. (1959). *The Presentation of Self in Everyday Life*. New York: Double Day.

Goffman, E., ed. (1967). *Interaction Ritual: Essays on Face-to-face Behavior*. Garden City, NY: Anchor Books.

Granger, S. and Paquot, M. (2008). Disentangling the phraseological web. In S. Granger and F. Meunier, eds., *Phraseology: An Interdisciplinary Perspective*. Amsterdam: John Benjamins, pp. 27–49.

Grant, L. and Bauer, L. (2004). Criteria for re-defining idioms: Are we barking up the wrong tree? *Applied Linguistics*, 25(1), 38–61.

Grant, D., Hardy, C., Oswick, C. and Putnam, L. (2004). Introduction: Organizational discourse: Exploring the field. In D. Grant, C. Hardy, C. Oswick & L. Putnam, eds., *The SAGE Handbook of Organizational Discourse*. London: SAGE, pp. 1–37.

Grice, H. P. (1975). Logic and conversation. In P. Cole and J. L. Morgan, eds., *Syntax and Semantics 3: Speech Acts*. New York: Academic Press, pp. 41–58.

Grimshaw, A. D. (ed.) (1990). *Conflict Talk. Sociolinguistic Investigations of Arguments in Conversations*. Cambridge: Cambridge University Press.

Gumperz, J. J. and Wilson, R. (1971). Convergence and creolization: A case from the Indo-Aryan/Dravidian border in India. In D. Hymes, ed., *Pidginization and Creolization of Languages*. Cambridge: Cambridge University Press, pp. 151–168.

Hall, S. (1980). Encoding/decoding. In Centre for Contemporary Cultural Studies, ed., *Culture, Media, Language: Working Papers in Cultural Studies*. London: Hutchinson, pp. 128–138.

Halliday, M. A. K. (1978). *Language As Social Semiotic: The Social Interpretation of Language and Meaning*. London: Hodder Education.

Halliday, M. A. K. (1994). *An Introduction to Functional Grammar*. London: Edward Arnold.

Halliday, M. A. K. (2014). Language as social semiotic. In J. Angermuller, D. Maingueneau and R. Wodak, eds., *The Discourse Studies Reader*. Amsterdam: John Benjamins, pp. 263–272.

Halliday, M. and Matthiessen, C. (2004). *An Introduction to Functional Grammar*, 3rd edn. London: Arnold.

Hamawand, Z. (2015). *Semantics: A Cognitive Account of Linguistic Meaning*. Sheffield: Equinox.

Hanks, P. (1996). *Collins English Dictionary*. 2nd edn. Glasgow: William Collins.

Hargraves, O. (2014). *It's Been Said Before*. Oxford: Oxford University Press.

Holmes, J. (1984). Modifying illocutionary force. *Journal of Pragmatics*, 8(3), 345–365.

Holt, D. (2004). *How Brand Become Icons: The Principles of Cultural Branding*. Boston, MA: Harvard Business Review Press.

Hunston, S. and Thompson, G. (eds.). (2003). *Evaluation in Text: Authorial Stance and the Construction of Discourse*. Oxford: Oxford University Press.

Hymes, D. (1968). The ethnography of speaking. *Readings in the Sociology of Language*, 2, 99–138.

Ilie, C. (2000). Cliché-based metadiscursive argumentation in the Houses of Parliament. *International Journal of Applied Linguistics*, 10(1), 65–84.

Jackendoff, R. (1995). The boundaries of the lexicon. In M. Everaert, E. J. van der Linden, A. Schenk, R. Schreuder and R. Schreuder, eds., *Idioms: Structural and Psychological Perspectives*. Hillsdale, NJ: Erlbaum, pp. 133–165.

Jenkins, R. (1996). *Social Identity*. London: Routledge.

Johnson, M. (1992). Philosophical implications of cognitive semantics. *Cognitive Linguistics*, 3(4), 345–366.

Jones, R. H., Chik, A. and Hafner, C., eds., (2015). *Discourse and Digital Practices: Doing Discourse Analysis in the Digital Age*. London: Routledge, pp. 1–17.

Joseph, J. E. (2013). Identity work and face work across linguistic and cultural boundaries. *Journal of Politeness Research*, 9(1), 35–54.

Kádár, D. (2017). Politeness in pragmatics. *Oxford Research Encyclopedia of Linguistics*. https://oxfordre.com/linguistics/view/10.1093/acrefore/9780199384655.001.0001/acrefore-9780199384655-e-218. [Last accessed May 2021].

Kapferer, J. N. (1997). *Strategic Brand Management: New Approaches to Creating and Evaluating Brand Equity*. London: Kogan.

Kapferer, J. N. (2002). Corporate brand and organizational identity. In B. Moingeon and G. Soenen, eds., *Corporate and Organizational Identities: Integrating Strategy, Marketing, Communication and Organisational Perspectives*. London: Routledge, pp. 175–193.

Khosravi Nik, M. (2017). Social media critical discourse studies (SM-CDS). In J. Flowerdew and J. Richardson, eds., *Handbook of Critical Discourse Analysis*. London: Routledge, pp. 582–596.

Kienpointner, M. (1992). How to classify arguments. In F. H. van Eemeren, R. Grootendorst, J. A. Blair and C. A. Willard, eds., *Argumentation Illuminated*. Amsterdam University Press: Amsterdam, pp. 178–188.

Kienpointner, M. (2011). 'Rhetoric'. In J. Ostman and J. Verschueren, eds., *Pragmatics in Practice*. Amsterdam: Benjamins, pp. 264–277.

Kirkpatrick, B. (1996). Cliches: Neither defence nor a condemnation. *English Today*, 12(3), pp. 16–25.

Kjeldsen, J. (2016). Studying rhetorical audiences: A call for qualitative reception studies in argumentation and rhetoric. *Informal Logic*, 26(2), 136–158

Koller, V. (2008a). Corporate brands as socio-cognitive representations. In G. Kristiansen and R. Dirven, eds., *Cognitive Sociolinguistics: Language Variation, Cultural Models, Social Systems*. Berlin: de Gruyter, pp. 389–418.

Koller, V. (2008b). 'The world in one city': Semiotic and cognitive aspects of city branding. *Journal of Language and Politics*, 7(3), 431–450. https://doi.org/10.1075/jlp.7.3.05kol.

Koller, V. ed. (2019). *Discourses of Brexit*. London: Routledge.

Kotler, P. (2003). *Marketing Management*. 11th edn. Hoboken, NJ: Prentice Hall.

Kövecses, Z. (2002). *Metaphor: A Practical Introduction*. New York: Oxford University Press.

Kress, G. R. and van Leeuwen, T. (2006). *Reading Images: The Grammar of Visual Design*. 2nd edn. London: Routledge.

Kuiper, K. and Scott Allan, W. (1996). *An Introduction to English Language*. London: Macmillan.

Kupferberg, I. and Green, D. (2005). *Troubled Talk: Metaphorical Negotiation in Problem Discourse*. Berlin: Mouton de Gruyter.

Labov, W. (1972). *Language in the Inner City: Studies in the Black English Vernacular*, No. 3. Philadelphia: University of Pennsylvania Press.

Lachenicht, L. G. (1980). Aggravating language: A study of abusive and insulting language. *Research on Language & Social Interaction*, 13(4), 607–687.

Lakoff, G. (1993). The contemporary theory of metaphor. In A. Ortony, ed., *Metaphor and Thought*. Cambridge: Cambridge University Press, pp. 202–251.

Lakoff, G. (1996). Sorry, I'm not myself today: The metaphor system for conceptualising the self. In G. Fauconnier and E. Sweetser, eds., *Spaces, Worlds, and Grammar*. Chicago: University of Chicago Press, pp. 91–123.

Lakoff, G. and Johnson, M. (1980). *Metaphors We Live By*. Chicago: University of Chicago Press.

Lalić-Krstin, G. and Silaški, N. (2018). From Brexit to Bregret: An account of some Brexit-induced neologisms in English. *English Today*, 34(2), 3–8.

Van Lancker-Sidtis, D. and Rallon, G. (2004). Tracking the incidence of formulaic expressions in everyday speech: Methods for classification and verification. *Language & Communication*, 24(3), 207–240.

Langacker, R. W. (1999). 10 The contextual basis of cognitive semantics. *Language and Conceptualization*, 1, 229–252.

Larner, S. (2019). Formulaic sequences as a potential marker of deception: A Preliminary investigation. In T. Docan-Morgan, ed., *The Palgrave Handbook of Deceptive Communication*. Basingstoke: Palgrave Macmillan, pp. 327–346.

Lave, J. and Wenger, E. (1991). *Situated Learning: Legitimate Peripheral Participation*. Cambridge: Cambridge University Press.

Le Sage, L. (1941). The cliché basis for some of the metaphors of Jean Giraudoux. *Modern Language Notes*, 56(6), 435–439.

Leary, M. R. and Kowalski, R. M. (1990). Impression management: A literature review and two component model. *Psychological Bulletin*, 107, 34–47.

Leech, G. (1983). *Principles of Pragmatics*. London: Longman.

van Leeuwen, T. (1996). The representation of social actors. In C. Caldas-Coulthard and R. M. Coulthard, eds., *Texts and Practices: Readings in Critical Discourse Analysis*. London: Routledge, pp. 32–71.

Lerner, L. D. (1956). Cliché and commonplace. *Essays in Criticism*, 6(3), 249–265.

Liu, F. (2018). Lexical metaphor as affiliative bond in newspaper editorials: A systemic functional linguistics perspective. *Functional Linguistics*, 5(2), 1–14. https://doi.org/10.1186/s405540–180–054-z.

Lorenzo-Dus, N. (2009). 'You're barking mad, I'm out': Impoliteness and broadcast talk. *Journal of Politeness Research*, 5, 159–187.

Malinowski, B. (1923). The problem of meaning in primitive languages. In C. K. Ogden and I. A. Richards, eds., *The Meaning of Meaning. A Study of the Influence of Language upon Thought and of the Science of Symbolism*. Supplement I. 4th edn. revised 1936. London: Kegan Paul, Trench, Trubner, pp. 296–336.

Makkai, A. (1972). *Idiom Structure in English*. Berlin: De Gruyter Mouton.

Markus, H. R. and Nurius, S. (1986). Possible selves. *American Psychologist*, 41, 954–969.

Martín, P. (1985). Genre and discourse community. *ES Review. Spanish Journal of English Studies*, 25, 153–166.

Martin, J. R. (2004). Sense and sensibility: Texturing evaluation. In J. Foley, ed., *Language, Education and Discourse: Functional Approaches*. New York: Continuum, pp. 270–304.

Martin, B. and Ringham, F. (1999). *Dictionary of Semiotics*. London: Bloomsbury.

Martin, J. R. and White, P. R. R. (2005). *The Language of Evaluation: Appraisal in English*. Basingstoke: Palgrave Macmillan.

Matthiessen, C. M. (2012). Systemic Functional Linguistics as appliable linguistics: Social accountability and critical approaches. *DELTA: Documentação de Estudos em Lingüística Teórica e Aplicada*, 28(SPE), 435–471.

Mazzone, M. (2011). Schemata and associative processes in pragmatics. *Journal of Pragmatics*, 43(8), 2148–2159.

McQuail, D. (1997). *Audience Analysis*. London: Sage

Miller, J. and Weinert, R. (1998). *Spontaneous Spoken Language: Syntax and Discourse*. Oxford: Clarendon.

Monroe, J. (1990). Idiom and cliché in TS Eliot and John Ashbery. *Contemporary Literature*, 31(1), 17–36.

Moon, R. E. (1998). *Fixed Expressions and Idioms in English: A Corpus Based Approach*. Oxford: Clarendon Press.

Moore, R. E. (2003). From genericide to viral marketing: On 'brand'. *Language and Communication*, 23(3–4), pp. 3313–3357.

Moriarty, S. E. (1991). *Creative Advertising Theory and Practice*. 2nd edn. Englewood Cliffs, NJ: Prentice-Hall.

Moscovici, S. (1981). On social representations. *Social Cognition: Perspectives on Everyday Understanding*, 8(12), 181–209.

Moscovici, S. (2000). *Social Representations: Explorations in Social Psychology*. Cambridge: Polity Press.

Moscovici, S. and Duveen, G. (2000). *Social Representations: Explorations in Social Psychology*. Cambridge: Polity.

Mumby, D. and Clair, R. (1997). Organisational discourse. In T. A. Van Dijk, ed., *Discourse as Structure and Process: Discourse Studies A Multidisciplinary Introduction*. Vol. 2. London: Sage, pp. 181–205.

Mussolf, A (2017). Truths, lies and figurative scenarios: Metaphors at the heart of Brexit. *Journal of Language and Politics*, 16(5), 6416–6457.

Nattinger, J. R. and DeCarrico, J. S. (1992). *Lexical Phrases and Language Teaching*. Oxford: Oxford University Press.

Nunberg, G., Sag, I. A. and Wasow, T. (1994). Idioms. *Language*, 70(3), 491–538.

Olmos, P. (2018). The social nature of argumentative practices: The philosophy of argument and audience reception. *Informal Logic*, 38(1), 1511–1583.

O'Keeffe, A., McCarthy, M., and Carter, R. (2007). *From Corpus to Classroom: Language Use and Language Teaching*. Cambridge: Cambridge University Press.

Ostermann, A. C. (2015). Community of practice. In K. Tracy, T. Sandel and C. Ilie, eds., *The International Encyclopedia of Language of Social Interaction*. London: Wiley-Blackwell, pp. 177–186.

Oteiza, T. and Pinuer, P. (2013). Valorative prosody and the symbolic construction of time in recent national historical discourses. *Discourse Studies*, 15(1), 43–64.

Oswick, C. A. and Grant, D., eds. (1996). *Organisation Development: Metaphorical Explorations*. London: Pitman Publishing.

Oswick, C., Keenoy, T. and Grant, D. (2002). Metaphor and analogical reasoning in organization theory: Beyond orthodoxy. *Academy of Management Review*, 27(2), 294–303.

Oswick, C., Putnam, L. L. and Keenoy, T. (2004). Tropes, discourse and organising. *The Sage Handbook of Organisational Discourse*. London: Sage, pp. 105–127.

Paquot, M. and Granger, S. (2012). Formulaic language in learner corpora. *Annual Review of Applied Linguistics*, 32, 130–149.

Partridge, E. (1978). *A Dictionary of Clichés*. 5th edn. London: Routledge.

Peterson, K. (2017). Clichés and other stressful components of writing. *Grassroots Writing Journal*, 8(1), 51–62.

Phillips, N. and Hardy, C. (2002). *Discourse Analysis: Investigating Processes of Social Construction*. London: Sage.

Pragglejaz Group (2007). MIP: A method for identifying metaphorically used words in discourse. *Metaphor and Symbol*, 22(1). 1–39.

Punch Magazine (1900). *An Evening from among the thousand evenings which may be spent with 'Punch'*. London: Bradbury, Agnew & Company.

Putnam, L. L. and Cooren, F. (2004). Alternative perspectives on the role of text and agency in constituting organizations. *Organization*, 11(3), 323–333.

Putnam, L. L. and Fairhurst, G. T. (2001). Discourse analysis in organizations: Issues and concerns. *The New Handbook of Organizational Communication: Advances in Theory, Research, and Methods*, London: Sage, pp. 78–136.

Rank, H. (1984). A few good words for clichés. *English Journal*, 73(5), 45–47.

Reisigl, M. and Wodak, R. (2009). The discourse-historical approach. In R. Wodak and M. Meyer, eds., *Methods for Critical Discourse Analysis*. 2nd edn. London: Sage, pp. 87–121.

Reyes, A. (2011). Strategies of legitimization in political discourse: From words to actions. *Discourse & Society*, 22(6), 781–807.

Ricks, C. (1980) Clichés. In L. Michaels and C. Ricks, eds., *The State of the Language*. Berkeley: University of California Press, 54–63.

Rogers, J. (1991). *Dictionary of Clichés*. New York: Ballantine Books.

Rubinelli, S. (2009). *Ars Topica: The Classical Technique of Constructing Arguments from Aristotle to Cicero*. Berlin: Springer.

Santamaría-García, C. (2014). Evaluative discourse and politeness in university students' communication through social networking sites. *Evaluation in Context*. Amsterdam: John Benjamins, pp. 2423–2487.

Scannell, P. (ed.) (1991). *Broadcast Talk*. Vol. 5. London: Sage.

Schmitt, N. and Carter, R. (2004). Formulaic sequences in action. In N. Schmitt, ed., *Formulaic Sequences: Acquisition, Processing and Use*. Amsterdam: John Benjamins Publishing Company, pp. 1–22.

Schultz, J. (2015). Cliché as reification: Nurturing criticality in the undergraduate creative writing classroom. *The International Journal for the Practice and Theory of Creative Writing*, 12(1), 79–90.

Scollon, R. and Scollon, S. W. (2001). *Intercultural Communication: A Discourse Approach*. Oxford: Blackwell.

Scollon, R. and Scollon, S. W. (2001). *Intercultural Communication: A Discourse Approach*. Oxford: Blackwell.

Searle, J. R. (1975). Indirect speech acts. In P. Cole and J. L. Morgan, eds., *Syntax and Semantics, 3: Speech Acts*. New York: Academic Press, pp. 59–82.

Semino, E. (2008). *Metaphor in Discourse*. Cambridge: Cambridge University Press.

Serafini, F. and Clausen, J. (2012). Typography as semiotic resource. *Journal of Visual Literacy*, 31(2), 11–6

Shapin, S. (2001). Proverbial economies: How an understanding of some linguistic and social features of common sense can throw light on more prestigious bodies of knowledge, science for example. *Social Studies of Science*, 31(5), 731–769.

Sharma, E., Saha, K., Kiranmai Ernala, S., Ghoshal, S. and de Choudhury, M. (2017). Analyzing ideological discourse on social media: A case study of the abortion debate. In Proceedings of CSSSA's *Annual Conference on Computational Social Science*, Santa Fe, NM, USA, 19–22 October 2017. https://doi.org/10.1145/3145574.3145577.

Smith, L. (2015). Online dating: Top 20 most common clichés and what they really mean. *International Business Times*. www.ibtimes.co.uk/online-dating-top-20-most-common-cliches-what- they-really-mean-1499341 [Last accessed February 2017].

Spencer-Oatey, H. (2005). (Im)Politeness, face and perceptions of rapport: Unpacking their bases and interrelationships. *Journal of Politeness Research*, 1(1), 95–119.

Sperber, D. (1985). Anthropology and psychology: Towards an epidemiology of representations. *Royal Anthropological Institute of Great Britain and Ireland*, 20(1), 73–89.

Swales, J. and Rogers, P. (1995). Discourse and the projection of corporate culture: The Mission Statement. *Discourse & Society*, 6(2), 223–242.

Tajfel, H. (1978). The achievement of inter-group differentiation. In H. Tajfel, ed., *Differentiation Between Social Groups*. London: Academic Press, pp. 77–100.

Terkourafi, M. (2008). Toward a unified theory of politeness, impoliteness, and rudeness. In D. Bousfield and M. Locher, eds., *Impoliteness in Language*. Berlin: De Gruyter Mouton, pp. 45–76.

Thomas, J. (1984). Cross-cultural discourse as 'unequal encounter': Towards a pragmatic analysis. *Applied Linguistics*, 5(3), 226–235.

Thompson, G. (2004). *Introducing Functional Grammar*. London: Arnold.

Tindale, C. W. (2015). *The Philosophy of Argument and Audience Reception*. Cambridge: Cambridge University Press.

Toddington, R. (2015). *Impoliteness as a vehicle for humour in dramatic discourse*. Unpublished Doctoral Thesis. Preston: University of Central Lancashire.

Tracy, K. (1990). The many faces of facework. In H. Giles and P. Robinson, eds., *Handbook of Language and Social Psychology*. Chichester: Wiley, pp. 209–226.

Tretyakova, T. P. (2010). English communicative clichés as a lexicographer problem. In O. Karpova and F. Kartashkova, eds., *New Trends in Lexicography: Ways of Registrating and Describing Lexis*. Newcastle-upon-Tyne: Cambridge Scholars Publishing, 57–65.

Unger, J., Wodak, R. and Khosravinik, M. (2016). Critical discourse studies and social media data. In D. Silverman, ed., *Qualitative Research*, 4th edn. London: Sage, pp. 277–293.

Verma, S. (2009). Do all advertising appeals influence consumer purchase decision: An exploratory study. *Global Business Review*, 10, 33–43.

Walters, S. D. (1995). *Material Girls: Making Sense of Feminist Cultural Theory*. Berkeley: University of California Press.

Webb, R. (2013). *101 Clichés: B2B's Most Notorious Creative Faux Pas*. London: SteinIAS.

Webster, L. (2018). 'I wanna be a toy': Self-sexualisation in gender-variant Twitter users' biographies. *Journal of Language and Sexuality*, 7(2), 205–236. https://doi.org/10.1075/jls.17016.web.

Wegener, P. (1885/1991). *Untersuchungen über die Grundfragen des Sprachlebens (Newly edited)*. Amsterdam: Benjamins.

Weinert, R. (1995). The role of formulaic language in second language acquisition: A review. *Applied Linguistics*, 16(2), 180–205.

Wenger, E. (1998). Communities of practice: Learning as a social system. *Systems Thinker*, 9(5), 2–3.

White, P. R. R. (2003). Beyond modality and hedging: A dialogical view of the language of intersubjective stance. *Text*, 23(2), 259–284.

White, P. R. R. (2015). Appraisal theory. In K. Tracy, C. Ilie and T. Sandel, eds., *The International Encyclopedia of Language and Social Interaction*. Oxford: Wiley, pp. 1–7.

Wodak, R. (2015). *The Politics of Fear. What Right-Wing Populist Discourses Mean*. London: Sage.

Wodak, R. and Idema, R. (2004). Constructing boundaries without being seen: The case of Jörg Haider, Politician. *Revista Canaria de Estudios Ingleses*, 49, 157–178.

Wood, D. (2002). Formulaic language acquisition and production: Implications for teaching. *TESL Canada Journal*, 20(1), 1–15.

Wood, D. (2006). Uses and functions of formulaic sequences in second language speech: An exploration of the foundations of fluency. *Canadian Modern Language Review*, 63(1), 13–33.

Wood, D. (2020). Classifying and identifying formulaic language. In S. Webb, ed., *The Routledge Handbook of Vocabulary Studies*. London: Routledge, pp. 30–45.

Wray, A. (2002). *Formulaic Language and the Lexicon*. Cambridge: Cambridge University Press.

Wray, A. (2008). *Formulaic Language: Pushing the Boundaries*. Oxford: Oxford University Press.

Wray, A. (2009). Identifying formulaic language: Persistent challenges and new opportunities. *Formulaic Language*, 1, 27–51.

Wray, A. and Grace, G. W. (2007). The consequences of talking to strangers: Evolutionary corollaries of socio-cultural influences on linguistic form. *Lingua*, 117(3), 543–578.

Wray, A. and Perkins, M. R. (2000). The functions of formulaic language: An integrated model. *Language & Communication*, 20(1), 1–28.

Zijderveld, A. C. (1979). *On Clichés: The Supersedure of Meaning by Function in Modernity*. London: Routledge.

Index

CPSIA information can be obtained
at www.ICGtesting.com
Printed in the USA
BVHW091851021122
650988BV00004B/53

9 781108 458139